DUKE

We're Glad We Knew You

DUKE

We're Glad We Knew You

John Wayne's Friends and Colleagues
Remember His Remarkable Life

HERB FAGEN

A BIRCH LANE PRESS BOOK
Published by Carol Publishing Group

Carol Publishing Group Edition, 1997

A Birch Lane Press Book
Published by Carol Publishing Group
Brich Lane Press is a registered trademark of Carol Communications, Inc.

Editorial, sales and distribution, rights and permissions inquiries should be addressed to Carol Publishing Group, 120 Enterprise Avenue, Secaucus, N.J. 07094

In Canada: Canadian Manda Group, One Atlantic Avenue, Suite 105, Toronto, Ontario M6K 3E7

Carol Publishing Group books may be purchased in bulk at special discounts for sales promotions, fund-raising, or educational purposes. Special editions can be created to specifications. For details, contact Special Sales Department, Carol Publishing Group, 120 Enterprise Avenue, Secaucus, N.J. 07094

MANUFACTURED IN THE UNITED STATES OF AMERICA
10   9   8   7   6   5   4   3   2

LIBRARY OF CONGRESS CATALOGING-IN-PUBLICATION DATA

Fagen, Herb.
    Duke, we're glad we knew you : John Wayne's friends and colleagues remember his remarkable life / Herb Fagen ; foreword by Ronald Reagan.
        p.   cm.
    "A Birch Lane Press book."
    Includes bibliographical references.
    ISBN 1-55972-369-6 (hc)
    1. Wayne, John, 1907-1979. 2. Motion picture actors and actresses—United States—Biography. I. Title.
PN2287.W454F35   1996
791.43′028′092—dc20   96-31416
[B]   CIP

To The Memory of My Dad
MIKE FAGEN
An Extraordinary Man in Such an Ordinary Way

Contents

Acknowledgments   *ix*

Contributors   *xi*

Introduction   *xv*

The Unforgettable John Wayne . . . by Ronald Reagan   *xxi*

1.   Clyde Morrison and Son   3
2.   A Sister's Song   13
3.   Pappy   22
4.   *Stagecoach* and Stardom   34
5.   The War Years: Dietrich, DeMille, and Dmytryk   46
6.   The Hawks Connection   65
7.   The Producer: Boetticher and *The Bullfighter and the Lady*   86
8.   Hondo Lane and *The Quiet Man*   102
9.   From Ethan Edwards to Genghis Khan: A Study in Contrast   117
10.   *The Alamo:* A Noble Dream   127
11.   Pappy's Last Hurrah   141
12.   *McLintock!*, Maureen, and Majesty   152
13.   C for Courage: The Duke's Finest Hour   159
14.   Politics and the Sixties: Duke Under Siege   172
15.   *True Grit:* A Well-Deserved Oscar   179
16.   Maturity, Mirth, and Mentor   192
17.   The Waning of the Western   202
18.   Still Sexy at Sixty   217
19.   A Hero for All Seasons   226

Epilogue: The Unbroken Legacy   *233*

Bibliography and Notes   *236*

Index   *243*

Acknowledgments

My sincere thanks to the twenty-six people who made this book possible through extensive interviews and conversations and who gave so freely of their time: Lee Aaker, John Agar, Peri Alcaide, Luster Bayless, Budd Boetticher, Harry Carey Jr., Tom Corrigan, Robert Donner, Edward Faulkner, Leo Gordon, Ben Johnson, Burt Kennedy, Jeannette Mazurki Lindner, Pierce Lyden, Michelle Mazurki, Andrew McLaglen, Bill McKinney, Christopher Mitchum, John Mitchum, Nancy Morrison Marshall, Walter Reed, Dean Smith, Robert Totten, Ron Talsky, Marie Windsor, and Yvonne Wood.

A special thanks to *Reader's Digest* for permission to include "The Unforgettable John Wayne," by Ronald Reagan, and to Irv Kupcinet of the *Chicago Sun Times* and Cary O'Dell of the Chicago Museum of Broadcast Communication for permission to use Mr. Kupcinet's 1970 interview with John Wayne.

Thanks to the following for allowing the use of their personal photographs: Luster Bayless, Jeanette Mazurki Lindner, Harry Carey Jr., Dean Smith, Walter Reed, Peri Alcaide, and Edward Faulkner.

To friends Paul 'Kelo' Henderson, star of the TV series *26 Men,* and his wife Gail, who somehow always managed to point me in the right Western direction; Will Hutchins, star of TV's *Sugarfoot,* for hours of great movie and cowboy talk; and to Gunn Mosqueda, for his help in securing segments of the Ben Johnson interview which appears in the text of this book: my deepest appreciation.

To my mom Gert Fagen and sister Ruth Phillips. There is nothing like a good family. To my agent Jake Elwell of Wieser & Wieser, and to Kevin McDonough, my editor at Birch Lane Press, my deep thanks.

And on a sad note: to Ron Talsky, my good friend Robert Totten, and Oscar winner Ben Johnson, who died this past year. They gave so much and left us far too soon. "Lest we forget!"

— Herb Fagen, 1996

Contributors

Lee Aaker Appeared with John Wayne as Geraldine Page's young son in the 1953 Western *Hondo*. He is best remembered as Rusty in the popular *Rin Tin Tin* television series. See chapter eight.

John Agar Handsome leading man of the late nineteen forties and early fifties and one-time husband of Shirley Temple. Appeared with Wayne in *Fort Apache, She Wore a Yellow Ribbon,* and *Sands of Iwo Jima,* which earned Duke his first Oscar nomination. As a character actor in the late sixties and early seventies, Agar appeared in three more Wayne films: *The Undefeated, Big Jake,* and *Chisum.* See chapters six and nine.

Peri Alcaide Hollywood's top foreign movie correspondent (Turkey) in the nineteen fifties and nineteen sixties. Interviewed Wayne and director Howard Hawks on the set of *Hatari* in 1962. Married to actor Chris Alcaide. See chapter twelve.

Luster Bayless Wayne's personal costumer and close friend the last fifteen years of Duke's life. Owner of United/American Costume Company in North Hollywood, he designed, among other things, the eye patch Wayne wore for his Oscar-winning role in *True Grit.* He also is a good friend of Michael Wayne, Duke's oldest son and president of Batjac Productions. See chapter fifteen.

Budd Boetticher Distinguished American director and international icon. Wayne produced two of Boetticher's finest films, *The Bullfighter and the Lady* and *Seven Men From Now.* See chapter seven.

Harry Carey Jr. One of the industry's most durable character actors and veteran of more than one hundred films.

Contributors

Appeared with Wayne in ten films, more than any actor alive today, including some of Duke's best: *Red River, She Wore A Yellow Ribbon, Rio Grande,* and *The Searchers.* A member of John Ford's famed stock company, his dad (legendary actor Harry Carey) was Wayne's hero. See chapters four, five, six, nine, and Epilogue.

Tom Corrigan Son of actor Ray "Crash" Corrigan, who played opposite Wayne in the popular *Three Mesquiteer* film series during the late nineteen thirties. Episodes were filmed at Corriganville, Ray Corrigan's ranch. See chapter three.

Robert Donner Appeared with Wayne in a number of his later films including *Rio Lobo, Chisum, The Undefeated,* and *Rio Bravo.* Still a working actor, Donner also appeared with Robin Williams in the hit TV series *Mork and Mindy* and was a regular on *The Waltons.* See chapter thirteen.

Edward Faulkner Appeared in six films with Wayne between 1962 and 1970, including *McLintock, The Green Berets, The Undefeated,* and *Chisum.* A former air force pilot, he is currently on the board of directors for the Palm Springs Film Festival. See chapter twelve.

Leo Gordon Veteran actor who appeared as Geraldine Page's husband in *Hondo* and as "Pilgrim" who gets slugged by Wayne in *McLintock* in one of Duke's most unforgettable scenes. See chapters eight and twelve.

Ben Johnson Oscar-winning actor and world rodeo champion. One of John Ford's most appealing discoveries before becoming a film favorite himself. Appeared in six Wayne films, including *The Train Robbers* and *Chisum,* two of the best films from Duke's later career. See chapter six.

Burt Kennedy Award-winning writer and director. Directed Wayne in two films: *War Wagon* with Kirk Douglas and *The Train Robbers* with Ann-Margret. Wrote and directed *Welcome to Hard Times* and wrote *Seven Men From Now,* which Wayne produced. See chapter thirteen.

Contributors

Jeannette Mazurki Lindner One-time wife of actor Mike Mazurki and top Hollywood columnist and lecturer. Interviewed Wayne on the set of *Dakota* in 1945. See chapters two and five.

Pierce Lyden Best of the B Western Badmen for more than thirty years. Worked with Wayne in *Red River.* See chapter six.

Michelle Mazurki Daughter of Mike and Jeanette Mazurki. Appeared with her father and Wayne in *Donovan's Reef,* John Ford's final picture. She is a talent agent today. See chapter eleven.

Andrew McLaglen Outstanding director and son of the late Oscar-winning actor Victor McLaglen. Worked as production assistant to John Ford on *The Quiet Man.* Directed Wayne in more films than anyone except Ford, Robert Bradbury, and Henry Hathaway, including *McLintock, The Undefeated, Chisum,* and *Cahill, United States Marshal.* See chapter five.

Bill McKinney Veteran character actor. Appeared with Wayne in *The Shootist.* Also appeared in Westerns *The Outlaw Josie Wales* and *Junior Bonner* and scores of other films such as *Deliverance, Bronco Billy,* and *Pink Cadillac.* See chapter eighteen.

Christopher Mitchum Appeared with Wayne in *Rio Lobo, Chisum,* and *Big Jake.* Also involved in a controversial TV appearance with Wayne on the *Tonight Show* with Johnny Carson. Son of actor Robert Mitchum, Chris Mitchum was chosen one of the three top young actors in 1970. See chapter seventeen.

John Mitchum. Character actor, composer, poet, and writer. Brother of Robert Mitchum. Wrote lyrics for "America, Why I Love Her," which Wayne recorded for RCA. Appeared in a number of films with Wayne, but is best remembered as Clint Eastwood's partner in *Dirty Harry* and *The Enforcer.* See chapter sixteen.

Contributors

Nancy Morrison Marshall Wayne's stepsister. Duke's father, Clyde Morrison, married Nancy's mother in 1930 when Nancy was eight years old. See chapter two.

Walter Reed Veteran character actor, closely associated with John Ford. Appeared with Wayne in *The Horse Soldiers* and worked in many of the films Duke produced. One of Wayne's card-playing buddies and drinking pals. See chapter seven.

Dean Smith Olympic Gold Medalist in the hundred-yard dash in the 1952 Helsinki games. Remains one of the industry's leading stuntmen. Worked with Wayne as actor and stuntman in *The Alamo, McLintock, Rio Lobo,* and more. Recently elected to Texas sports Hall of Fame with baseball player Nolan Ryan and football's Mean Joe Greene. See chapter ten.

Robert Totten Award-winning director of television versions of *The Red Pony* and *Huckleberry Finn* and the television miniseries *The Sacketts.* A regular director and writer of TV's *Gunsmoke* for more than ten years. See chapter eight.

Ron Talsky Wayne's wardrobe man for *The Alamo, How The West Was Won,* and *The Man Who Shot Liberty Valance.* Worked on two Academy Award telecasts, including the 1979 show on which Duke made his final appearance four months before his death. See chapters eleven and nineteen.

Marie Windsor Actress who worked with Wayne for over three decades on such films as *The Fighting Kentuckian, Trouble Along the Way,* and *Cahill, United States Marshal.* See chapter eighteen.

Yvonne Wood Costume designer for some of the leading stars in Hollywood from the nineteen thirties through the nineteen sixties. Designed the male costumes for Wayne's ill-fated film *The Conqueror.* See chapter nine.

Introduction

In a special television program on ABC in 1989 Barbara Walters commented on her trail-blazing but difficult rise through the ranks of the male-dominated TV industry. She mentioned that she got hundreds of letters from women wishing her well but just one from a supportive man. The note read simply: "Don't let the bastards get you down! Stick with it!" It was signed "John Wayne."

An unlikely shot in the arm from an American film icon, better known for his conservative politics, flag-waving, and manly screen persona? Hardly! If Walters was surprised at first by her newfound ally, those who knew John Wayne were not. Because fair play, honor, and decency were always the fabric of which "Duke" Wayne was made.

John Wayne's career spanned six decades. He was featured in some 160 films, many of which rank with the best ever shown. A number of his performances border on the legendary. He was the top box-office draw in 1950, 1951, 1954, and 1971. John Wayne stayed among the top ten box-office stars from 1949 through 1973, with the exception of 1958.

His last public appearance came in April 1979. Obviously ill and shockingly gaunt, he introduced the Best Picture award at the Oscar ceremony, receiving a long, standing ovation that moved him greatly. In turn, Duke reminded his audience that both he and Oscar first came to Hollywood in 1928. "We're both a little weather-beaten," he said, "but we're still here and plan to be around for a whole lot longer."

It was not to be. On June 11, 1979, John Wayne lost his battle with cancer, leaving seven children and sixteen grandchildren. While the book finally closed on a human life, the unique legacy of the man and what he represented to so many for so long remains very much alive today.

John Wayne once said people should not go to the movies unless they believe in heroes. And to millions of fans everywhere Wayne was more than just a hero, he was heroism personified.

Introduction

"He was bigger than life, he sure was," says Andrew V. McLaglen, son of Oscar-winning actor Victor McLaglen and a fine director who worked with Wayne on five films, including *McLintock, The Undefeated,* and *Chisum.* "Two people I never thought would die were Duke Wayne and my father.

"When you think of all the movie stars, what movie star gets mentioned more in the course of a week, in posthumous terms that is, than John Wayne? Unfortunately, now that we are getting a little older, there are not as many of us around who have worked with Wayne."

McLaglen's message is well taken. But while the old guard is clearly dwindling in number, many others who knew Wayne well, personally and professionally, are still with us.

How fortunate that over the past two years I have been able to meet and interview many of these people: actors, directors, stuntmen, writers, who worked with Wayne professionally and knew him personally. And how lucky, too, that they and others have agreed to share their recollections and remembrances of a man they all agree was indeed "bigger than life."

Duke, We're Glad We Knew You makes no pretense of being a definitive or inclusive biography of John Wayne. Over the years many books of varying degrees of merit have sought to do that. Rather, what we present here is a story of an American legend as seen through the eyes of his friends, family, and colleagues.

This book offers a unique assortment of stories and remembrances about a larger-than-life film hero, set against the backdrop of an evolving film industry and an ever-changing America. People such as Oscar winner Ben Johnson, Harry Carey Jr., Budd Boetticher, John Agar, Burt Kennedy, Christopher Mitchum, Andrew McLaglen, Nancy Morrison Marshall (Duke's stepsister), and many others share their memories of a man who inspired the respect and admiration of all who knew him.

They tell the story of a good man who was not perfect, a strong man who could be soft and vulnerable, a thorough professional, and a straight shooter who said what he felt and did what he said. He was a man who personified dignity and grace, courage and strength—a man simply called "the Duke."

Wayne was the consummate American screen star. A small-

Introduction

time boy from the Midwest heartland who somehow managed to ride the trail of life from B Western cowboy to movie immortal with such magnificence that he became an American institution.

"If you ever worked with him, the first time he came on the set you would say, 'Here comes a movie star,' " says Harry Carey Jr., a veteran of more than one hundred films and an integral member of John Ford's stock company, whose actor father was Wayne's private hero and mentor. "A whole quiet came on the set, because he was the most impressive looking man I have ever seen. He was handsome and rugged and a huge guy. He had an aura that was just movie star."

Wayne's accolades have come from unlikely sources as well. In 1979, more than 400 Iranians packed into a small cinema house to see Wayne in Ford's 1939 classic, *Stagecoach*, as part of the Fajir International Film Festival. "He's the best," a 1990 issue of *Variety* quoted Khalil Hansonjour, one of the young Iranians, as saying at the time. "There is no one like him."

"When John Wayne spoke, there was no mistaking his intentions; he had sexual authority so strong that even a child could perceive it," wrote author John Didion in the *Saturday Evening Post* in 1965.

And a good actor? "My God, yes!," says Harry Carey Jr. "In *The Searchers, The Shootist,* and *Three Godfathers,* he was a superb actor. A lot of people don't give him the credit he deserves."

Writing in the *New Republic* shortly after Wayne's death, Andrew Sarris, hardly a conservative partisan, noted that, "Like William Faulkner's hero in *Knight's Gambit,* he improved with age, and learned before our eyes how to feel and how to project a deep and abiding love. . . . It took me a long time to appreciate him as an actor, and now I hope to make amends by explaining his subtler virtues to the stubbornly unbelieving."

And Wayne was not unappreciated by more classically trained performers. Shortly before Duke's death the great Shakespearean actor Ralph Richardson remarked in an interview that the "Duke projected the kind of mystery one associated with great acting." Sarris also cites how Jean-Luc Goddard once observed that, as much as he despised the reactionary politics of John Wayne, he could never help but be moved when watching *The Searchers* by the

Introduction

emotion of the awesomely avuncular gesture in which Wayne gathers Natalie Wood in his arms.

Actor Will Hutchins, best remembered for the TV series *Sugarfoot* and an astute and serious student of film, has told the author: "If anyone tells me John Wayne wasn't a very good actor, I just tell them they should watch one of his movies at home some time. When he reads a line of dialogue, try saying it right after him. Then see if you can say it half as good as he did. Remember, too, that John Ford is considered by many to be the greatest American director and Ford never messed around with mediocrity."

Professionalism, loyalty, sentiment, patriotism, honesty, integrity, family, these are the things we hear most often about John Wayne. And there were flaws. He loved to gamble, had a huge temper, and was a hard drinker as were many of his crowd. He was easily hurt and admitted to Barbara Walters that he was a lot softer with women and a lot tougher with men, especially himself, than he should have been. But if there were failings, they were human failings, never failings of character.

On June 11, 1979, John Wayne died. He left a professional and personal legacy unmatched in American cinema. He won an Oscar for *True Grit* in 1969 and earned an Oscar nomination for *Sands of Iwo Jima* in 1949. It can also be argued that he was deserving of Oscar consideration in five other films: *She Wore a Yellow Ribbon, Red River, The Quiet Man, The Searchers,* and *The Shootist,* his final film.

Today, John Wayne's birthplace, a four-room cottage on South Second Street in Winterset, Iowa, has become a shrine visited by more than thirty-four thousand people through the first eight months of 1995. Decked with American flags and filled with movie memorabilia such as the eye patch he wore in *True Grit,* it has become a good barometer of the nation's mood and John Wayne's standing in America. With the fall of Communism and with the sixties values under attack from many quarters, John Wayne's view—discredited for years by the cultural elite—have become mainstream once again.

So strong is the legacy of John Wayne that a Harris Poll conducted in November 1995—more than seventeen years after his death—placed Wayne ahead of both Clint Eastwood and Tom Hanks as America's favorite movie star. In fact, his stature is so

Introduction

far-reaching both President Bill Clinton and Speaker of the House Newt Gingrich say he was the dominant pop culture figure of their youth.

Is John Wayne a hero? Just ask the people who knew him. They'll no doubt say yes. What's more they just might say, "Duke, we're glad we knew you. You made our lives so much richer."

Shortly after John Wayne's death, Paul Conrad, the Pulitzer Prize–winning cartoonist and artist for the *Los Angeles Times*, paid what was perhaps the greatest tribute to the life and times of John Wayne. Conrad featured a drawing of Mount Rushmore. The huge carved heads of presidents Washington, Jefferson, Lincoln, and Theodore Roosevelt which adorn the national monument had some company that day: None other than John Wayne.

The Unforgettable John Wayne

by Ronald Reagan

We called him Duke, and he was every bit the giant off the screen that he was on. Everything about him—his stature, his style, his convictions—conveyed enduring strength, and no one who observed his struggle in those final days could doubt that strength was real. Yet there was more. To my wife, Nancy, "Duke Wayne was the most gentle, tender person I ever knew."

In 1960, as president of the Screen Actors' Guild, I was deeply embroiled in a bitter labor dispute between the Guild and the motion-picture industry. When we called a strike, the film industry unleashed a series of stinging personal attacks against me— criticism my wife was finding difficult to take.

At 7:30 one morning the phone rang and Nancy heard Duke's booming voice. "I've been reading what those damn columnists are saying about Ron. He can take care of himself, but I've been worrying about how all this is affecting you." Virtually every morning until the strike was settled weeks later, he phoned her. When a mass meeting was called to discuss settlement terms, he left a dinner party so that he could escort Nancy and sit at her side. It was, she said, like being next to a force bigger than life.

Countless others were also touched by his strength. Although it would take the critics 40 years to recognize what he was, the moviegoing public knew all along. In this country and around the world, he was the most popular box-office star of all time. For an incredible 25 years he was rated at or around the top in box-office appeal. His films grossed $700 million—a record no performer in Hollywood has come close to matching. Yet John Wayne was more than an actor; he was a force around which films were made. As Elizabeth Taylor Warner stated last May when testifying in favor of the special gold medal Congress struck for him: "He gave the whole world the image of what an American should be."

He was born Marion Michael Morrison in Winterset, Iowa. When Marion was six, the family moved to California. There he picked up the nickname Duke—after his Airedale. He rose at 4 A.M. to deliver newspapers, and after school and football practice, he made deliveries for local stores. He was an A student, president of the Latin Society, head of his senior class and an all-state guard on a championship football team.

Duke had hoped to attend the U.S. Naval Academy and was named as an alternate selection to Annapolis, but the first choice took the appointment. Instead, he accepted a full scholarship to play football at the University of Southern California. There coach Howard Jones, who often found summer jobs in the movie industry for his players, got Duke work in the summer of 1926 as an assistant prop man on the set of a movie directed by John Ford.

One day, Ford, a notorious taskmaster with a rough-and-ready sense of humor, spotted the tall U.S.C. guard on his set and asked Duke to bend over and demonstrate his football stance. With a deft kick, Ford knocked Duke's arms from beneath his body and the young athlete fell on his face. Picking himself up, Duke said in a voice which even then commanded attention, "Let's try that once again." This time Duke sent Ford flying. Ford erupted in laughter, and the two began a personal and professional friendship which would last a lifetime.

From his job in the props, Duke worked his way into roles on the screen. During the Depression he played in grade-B westerns until John Ford finally convinced United Artists to give him the role of the Ringo Kid in his classic film *Stagecoach*. John Wayne was on the road to stardom. He quickly established his versatility in a variety of major roles: a young seaman in Eugene O'Neill's *The Long Voyage Home*, a tragic captain in *Reap the Wild Wind*, a rodeo rider in the comedy *A Lady Takes a Chance*.

When war broke out, Duke tried to enlist but was rejected because of an old football injury to his shoulder, his age (34), and his status as a married father of four. He flew to Washington to plead that he be allowed to join the Navy but was turned down. So he poured himself into the war effort by making inspirational war films—among them *The Flying Seabees, Back to Bataan,* and *They Were Expendable.* To those back home and to others around the world he became a symbol of the determined fighting man.

Duke could not be kept from the front lines. In 1944 he spent three months touring forward positions in the Pacific theater. Appropriately, it was a wartime film, *Sands of Iwo Jima,* which turned him into a superstar. Years after the war, when Emperor Hirohito of Japan visited the United States, he sought out John Wayne, paying tribute to the one who represented our nation's success in combat.

As one of the true innovators of the film industry, Duke tossed aside the model of the white-suited cowboy/good guy, creating instead a tougher, deeper-dimensioned western hero. He discovered Monument Valley, the film setting in Arizona-Utah desert where a host of movie classics were filmed. He perfected the choreographic techniques and stunt-man tricks which brought realism to screen fighting. At the same time he decried pornography, and blood and gore in films. "That's not sex and violence," he would say. "It's filth and bad taste."

In the 1940s, Duke was one of the few stars with the courage to expose the determined bid by a band of communists to take control of the film industry. Through a series of violent strikes and systematic blacklisting, these people were at times dangerously close to reaching their goal. With theatrical employees' union leader Roy Brewer, playright Morrie Ryskind and others, he formed the Motion Picture Alliance for the Preservation of American Ideals to challenge this insidious campaign. Subsequently Congressional investigations in 1947 clearly proved both the communist plot and the importance of what Duke and his friends did.

In that period, during my first term as president of the Actors' Guild, I was confronted with an attempt by many of these same leftists to assume leadership of the union. At a mass meeting I watched rather helplessly as they filibustered, waiting for our majority to leave so they could gain control. Somewhere in the crowd I heard a call for adjournment, and I seized on this as means to end the attempted takeover. But the other side demanded I identify the one who moved for adjournment.

I looked over the audience, realizing that there were few willing to be publicly identified as opponents of the far left. Then I saw Duke and said, "Why I believe John Wayne made the motion." I heard this strong voice reply, "I sure as hell did!" The meeting—and the radicals' campaign—was over.

Later, when such personalities as actor Larry Parks came forward to admit their Communist Party background, there were those who wanted to see them punished. Not Duke. "It takes courage to admit you're wrong," he said, and publicly battled attempts to ostracize those who had come clean.

Duke also had the last word over those who warned that his battle against communism in Hollywood would ruin his career. Many times he would proudly boast, "I was 32nd in the box-office polls when I accepted the presidency of the Alliance. When I left office eight years later, somehow the folks who buy tickets had made me number one."

Duke went to Vietnam in the early days of the war. He scorned VIP treatment, insisting that he visit the troops in the field. Once he even made his helicopter land in the midst of a battle. When he returned, he vowed to make a film about the heroism of Special Forces soldiers.

The public jammed theaters to see the resulting film, *The Green Berets*. The critics, however, delivered some of the harshest reviews ever given a motion picture. The *New Yorker* bitterly condemned the man who made the film. *The New York Times* called it "unspeakable . . . rotten . . . stupid." Yet Duke was undaunted. "That little clique back there in the East has taken great personal satisfaction reviewing my politics instead of my pictures," he often said. "But one day those doctrinaire liberals will wake up to find the pendulum has swung the other way."

I never once saw Duke display hatred toward those who scorned him. Oh, he could use some pretty salty language, but he would not tolerate pettiness and hate. He was human all right: he drank enough whiskey to float a PT boat, though he never drank on the job. His work habits were legendary in Hollywood—he was virtually the first to arrive on the set and the last to leave.

The Unforgettable John Wayne

His torturous schedule, plus the great personal pleasure he derived from hunting and deep-sea fishing or drinking and card-playing with his friends may have cost him a couple of marriages; but you had only to see his seven children and 21 grandchildren to realize that Duke found time to be a good father. He often said, "I have tried to live my life so that my family would love me and my friends respect me. The others can do whatever the hell they please."

To him a handshake was a binding contract. When he was in the hospital for the last time and sold his yacht, *The Wild Goose,* for an amount far below its market value, he learned the engines needed minor repairs. He ordered those engines overhauled at a cost to him of $40,000 because he had told the new owner the boat was in good shape.

Duke's generosity and loyalty stood out in a city rarely known for either. When a friend needed work, that person went on his payroll. When a friend needed help, Duke's wallet was open. He was also loyal to his fans. One writer tells of the night he and Duke were in Dallas for the premier of *Chisum.* Returning late to the hotel, Duke found a message from a woman who said her daughter lay critically ill in a local hospital. The woman wrote: "It would mean so much to her if you could pay her just a brief visit." At three o'clock in the morning he took off for the hospital where he visited the astonished child—and every other patient on the hospital floor who happened to be awake.

I saw his loyalty in action many times. I remember when Duke and Jimmy Stewart were on their way to my second inauguration as a governor of California they encountered a crowd of demonstrators under the banner of the Vietcong flag. Jimmy had just lost a son in Vietnam. Duke excused himself for a moment and walked into the crowd. In a moment there was no Vietcong flag.

Like any good John Wayne film, Duke's career had a gratifying ending. In the 1970s a new era of critics began to recognize the unique quality of his acting. The turning point had been the film *True Grit.* When the Academy gave him an Oscar for the best actor of 1969, many said it was based on the accomplishments of his entire career. Others said it was Hollywood's way of admitting that it had been wrong to deny him Academy Awards for a host of previous films. There is truth, I think, to both these views.

Yet who can forget the climax of the film? The grizzled old marshal confronts the four outlaws and calls out: "I mean to kill you or see you hanged at Judge Parker's convenience. Which will it be?"

"Bold talk for a one-eyed fat man," their leader sneers.

Then Duke cries, "Fill your hand, you sonofabitch!" and, reins in his teeth, charges at them firing with both guns. Four villains did not live to menace another day.

"Foolishness?" wrote Chicago *Sun Times* columnist Mike Royko, describing the thrill the scene gave him. "Maybe. But I hope we never become so programmed that nobody has the damn-the-risk spirit."

Fifteen years ago when Duke lost a lung in his first bout with cancer, studio press agents tried to conceal the nature of the illness. When Duke discovered this, he went before the public, and showed us that a man can fight this dread disease. He went on to raise millions of dollars for private cancer research. Typically, he snorted: "We've got too much at stake to give government a monopoly in the fight against cancer."

Earlier this year, when doctors told Duke there was no hope, he urged them to use his body for experimental medical research, to further search for a cure. He refused painkillers so that he could be alert as he spent his last days with his children. When he died on June 11, a Tokyo newspaper ran the headline, "Mr. America passes on."

"There's right and there's wrong. Duke said in *The Alamo*. "You gotta do one or the other. You do the one and you're living. You do the other, you may be walking around, but in reality you're dead."

Duke Wayne symbolized just this, the force of the American will to do what is right in the world. He could have left no greater legacy.

DUKE
We're Glad We Knew You

1. Clyde Morrison and Son

Was John Wayne a great actor? Perhaps not in the
sense that Spencer Tracy was. But was John Wayne
convincing in what he did? There's no question of that.
People believed that this was the real John Wayne,
that he wasn't acting at all. Perhaps this is the greatest
compliment anybody could pay him.

> — Leonard Maltin, *Young
> Duke*, A&E *Biography*
> series, 1995

When John Wayne was born on May 7, 1907, his Winterset,
Iowa birthplace typified the great American heartland. Situated
between two rivers, against a backdrop of rolling hills, the town
of Winterset was the seat of Madison County.

Patriotism ran high in Iowa. The Civil War had taken a toll of
its young men nearly a half century earlier. Approximately seven
hundred of the town's nine hundred men between the ages of
eighteen and thirty-five had joined the Union army. One hundred
and four never came home. One hundred and six more were
either severely wounded or spent time as Confederate prisoners
of war.

Independence Day was the biggest day of the year in Madison
County, with parades every Fourth of July. In the early 1900s,
hundreds of men were still marching in parades, telling all within
hearing where and when they fought the rebellious southern
states.

In 1876, an imposing courthouse was constructed from milky-
white limestone to honor America's centennial. Large Victorian
homes adorned the green landscape. The voting population of
Madison County was almost entirely Republican and Protestant.
The Democratic party was generally associated with disunion and
disloyalty. Most of the area's small Catholic population lived in Lee
Township in the county's northeast corner.

Clyde Leonard Morrison was just three years old in 1887, when his parents moved to Iowa from Monmouth, Illinois. After leaving Indianola High School in 1898, Clyde Morrison enrolled in the Middle Academy, a preparatory school of Simpson College. Good looking and unusually bright, Clyde played football at Iowa State University in Ames before returning to Simpson College to enroll in the local conservatory of music.

Football and music were Clyde Morrison's main passions, but reality soon set in and Clyde decided that a job as a pharmacist would eventually allow him to make a better living. He left Simpson College, and in 1903 entered the Highland Park College of Pharmacy (later part of Drake University) in Des Moines where he graduated two years later. He passed his licensing examination in 1905 and received his credentials as a registered pharmacist.

During his last summer at college, Clyde met nineteen-year-old Mary Alberta Brown, a small young woman with red hair and green eyes who worked as a telephone operator in Des Moines. They attended the same Methodist Church. Outspoken and opinionated, she smoked cigarettes in public long before it was acceptable for a woman to do so. She was brought up in a comfortable middle-class urban world and favored college boys because she found them more interesting and she yearned to marry well.

Known as "Molly" to her friends, Mary Brown fell in love with Clyde Morrison. He was handsome, kind, and well-educated. When Clyde was offered a job at a pharmacy in Waterloo, Iowa, Clyde and Molly decided to bypass a church wedding. Instead, they eloped to Knoxville in Marion County, where on September 29, 1905, they were married by justice of the peace I. H. Garritson.

Clyde and Molly Morrison made their first home in Waterloo, Iowa, where Clyde was about to take a job at a pharmacy. But both yearned to be closer to their parents. When they heard that the M. E. Smith Drug Store in Winterset was looking for a registered pharmacist, Clyde and Molly Morrison rented a small frame house on South Second Street. Winterset was an ideal location, just thirty-five miles from Molly's family in Des Moines, and only twenty miles from Clyde's folks in Indianola.

They were young, did not know each other very well, and were terribly mismatched. Molly had assumed because Clyde was

Clyde Morrison and Son

a college boy with a profession that he would be a good provider. But the years would prove her wrong.

In late 1906 Molly became pregnant. She received good prenatal care from Dr. Jessie Smith, one of Iowa's few female physicians. On May 25, 1907, Molly went into labor. The delivery process was a long, torturous ordeal, and in Molly's mind, the birth of her thirteen-pound son almost killed her. Mary and the baby survived. They named him Marion Robert Morrison. His middle name was later changed to Michael in 1912 when his brother was born.

Clyde and Molly's marriage was not a happy one and only became worse. They had been married fewer than four years and had already lived in three separate homes. "Mom was just not a happy woman," Duke told one of his friends many years later. "No matter what I did or Dad did, it was never enough." By 1912 when their second son, Robert, was born, Clyde and Molly were broke and living off the generosity of Molly's folks.

As Clyde's business endeavors continued to fail, Molly turned increasingly sour on her husband, and her tolerance for her oldest son waned as well. She had never forgotten his difficult delivery. Moreover, young Marion Morrison was clearly "Daddy's boy." From the start, father and son were inseparable. When Marion was upset, Clyde, not Molly, would comfort him. Clyde enjoyed having his son around, and Molly grew jealous of their relationship.

Wherever they lived, it was common to see Clyde and his son playing football together. Clyde had been a talented athlete at Simpson College and an all-state tackle on the football team. At a shade taller than 5'8" and weighing 185 pounds, his body was firm and muscular. He taught young Marion almost every physical aspect of the game: to throw, run, kick, block, and tackle. Later, when the family moved to Glendale, Clyde had his son running pass patterns on the beaches of Southern California, often throwing the ball into the rushing surf just before the waves crashed into him.

By 1912, Clyde had already developed heart trouble. The problem was compounded by a nasty cough and shortness of breath. A three-pack-a-day cigarette smoker, Clyde was advised by a physician that the dry desert climate of Southern California might help. In 1909, Clyde's father had purchased a home in Los Angeles and began to dabble in real estate. He urged Clyde to consider farming, and suggested that Lancaster County, just outside of the Los Angeles Basin, would be a good place for Clyde and his family to start over. Certainly, the climate was dry enough. By 1913 Clyde's father had located some desert property available for homesteading. Clyde left Molly and the boys in Iowa and joined his father in California, where they worked the land and met the minimum requirements for establishing title. In 1914, he sent for Molly and the boys. The family settled in a three-room frame house Clyde built near the town of Lancaster in the Mojave Desert. It was not to Molly's liking. "When I got off the train in Lancaster, I couldn't believe my eyes. Clyde had chosen a no-man's land," she told Mary St. John, (Wayne's secretary) years later.

Clyde tried his hand at farming, but it was difficult. He worked long hours, seven days a week. But he was basically a city boy, a professional man who had little talent for agriculture. An abundance of jackrabbits and rattlesnakes made the work even more arduous. Clyde would take Marion on rattlesnake hunts, the memories of which long haunted the young lad. "Shooting those snakes gave me some sleepless nights," Wayne later confessed. "Visions of thousands of slithering snakes coming after me. I used to wake up in a cold sweat in the middle of the night, but my dad or my family never knew. I kept my fears to myself."

It was a disastrous first year in the desert for the Morrisons. The heat was oppressive, and their crop failed. Their labor had come to naught, and what was left of the Morrison marriage crumbled even further.

In September 1914 Clyde and Molly enrolled young Marion in Lancaster Grammar School as a second-grader. He soon earned the nickname "Skinny" because of the mare he rode to classes every day. The animal had a metabolic disorder which gave its exposed rib cage a swayback look. In fact, the animal was so skinny some of the local women accused the Morrisons of mistreating it.

Faced with unbearable heat and increasing poverty, the arguments between Clyde and Molly became more frequent and more intense. Each night as Molly would scream at her husband, eight-

Clyde Morrison and Son

year-old Marion would lie in bed and cover his ears with a pillow, wondering why his mother hated his dad. By 1916 Molly had enough. She issued an ultimatum to Clyde. He could either move across the San Gabriel Mountains and get a job, or he could get a lawyer because she would file for divorce. Clyde agreed to make the move. They left the Mojave, and settled in Glendale, California, not far from Hollywood.

They arrived in Glendale in the fall of 1916. It was a rebirth of sorts for the family—at least for a while. Nestled between the Verdugo foothills to the north and the Hollywood Hills to the south, Glendale was located at the eastern end of the San Fernando Valley. Clyde, Molly, and the two boys moved into a house at 421 Isabel, and Clyde landed a good job as a druggist at the Glendale pharmacy where he sold everything from medicine to ice cream.

Clyde gained a new, well-needed respectability. People started calling him "Doc." The family joined the First Methodist Church, and Clyde became a member of the Unity Chapter of the Royal Arch Masons.

The move to Glendale was a blessing for nine-year-old Marion too. He managed to shake his first name, which he had never liked. The other kids would say it was a girl's name, and the taunts led to fist fights. He also hated the nickname Skinny, which he felt was weak and unattractive. He hated hearing his mother screech it out whenever she was mad at him. Soon he insisted his friends just call him Morrison.

In 1918 eleven-year-old Marion Morrison acquired the nickname that would accompany him throughout his life. The family had a pet dog, a huge Airdale they named "Duke." Each day the dog would dutifully follow young Marion to school. As boy and dog passed the nearby fire station, the local firemen would say, "Here comes big Duke and little Duke." Before long "Little Duke," became "Duke" and the name stuck.

Glendale also gave Duke his first real taste of the movies. His mother would constantly mimic actors and actresses. By the time Duke was ten, he had made an old box to look like a camera and formed a "movie company" for the neighborhood kids.

Glendale was near the hub of the movie industry. On his way to school, Duke would watch takes on *The Perils of Pauline*. He

7

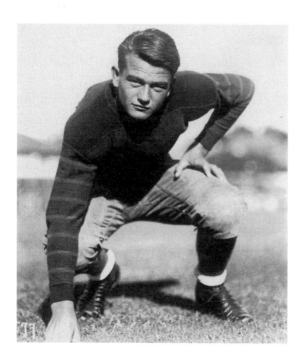

Duke Morrison, football star.

watched intensely to see how scenes were done, how they would dig ditches between the train tracks so actress Pearl White could roll in between the tracks into a ditch when the train passed over.

And Glendale had no shortage of movie palaces: the Glendale Theater, first built on West Fourth Street in 1910 and rebuilt on South Grand in 1920, and Jensen's Palace Grand Theater, built on South Brand in 1914. The movies were special to young Duke Morrison: "My folks always let me go to the movies every Saturday. In those days it was the most inexpensive entertainment in the country; movies cost about ten cents and the Saturday afternoon show was a nickel."

During the summer months Duke would spend hours watching filmmakers at work. They would even let him act as gofer at times, and he loved it. During World War I, many film stars came to Glendale to give patriotic speeches urging Americans to buy war bonds. Duke and the other kids would go to a vacant lot to "play movies," where he emulated the likes of Douglas Fairbanks, Tom Mix, and Rudolph Valentino.

Clyde Morrison and Son

While in junior and senior high, Duke escaped to the movies four or five times a week. One of his early heroes was the daring Fairbanks. "I admired his dueling, stunts, fearlessness and impish grin," Duke told an interviewer in 1969. Duke also became a voracious reader, spending hours in the library devouring such adventure novels as *Ivanhoe, Robinson Crusoe,* and *The Last of the Mohicans.*

Biographies were also among his favorites, particularly the stories of heroic men like George Washington, John Paul Jones, Abraham Lincoln, Kit Carson, Buffalo Bill Cody, and George Rogers Clark. "I became a confirmed reader when I was growing up in Glendale," he told a reporter in 1972. "I've loved reading all my life." In fact, Duke would win an award at Glendale High School for doing a Shakespearean oration.

By the time Duke Morrison entered Glendale Union High in 1921, he was six feet tall with piercing blue eyes. "I don't think it's possible to realize from watching his movies how absolutely stunningly handsome he was then," one of his female classmates recalled years later. "His looks alone would stop traffic. He was the handsomest young man that ever walked on two legs." Yet during those years he was rather bashful with the girls. Although many would have loved to date him, he rarely dated in high school.

Football, scholastics, personality, and good looks helped make Duke Morrison one of the most popular students at Glendale Union. "Duke could not abide bullies even back then," according to one of Duke's classmates, Archie Neel. "Everybody liked him. He always took care of the underdog. He either stopped fights or took over for the little guy." Norm Nelson, who played football with Duke at Glendale, paints a similar picture. "He was a great guy. I thought a lot of him. . . . He was very friendly. . . . I never knew him to be mean or nasty to people."

Clearly, football was Duke's great passion. One of his early heroes was Harold "Red" Grange, the famed "Galloping Ghost" from the University of Illinois. In the years before the advent of professional football when college football reigned supreme, Grange's enormous popularity even led to a role in movie serials.

By the time he was a junior in 1923, Duke had filled out to 155 pounds and attracted regional attention as a left guard for Glendale Union High, which barely lost the state prep championship to

9

Long Beach High that year by a score of 15 to 8. He went head-to-head against an opponent who was reputedly the best prep guard in Southern California, and according to one of the local sportswriters, "[Duke] made that jackrabbit look like a fuzzy bunny."

In his senior year, Duke shot up to 6'4" and 175 pounds. Glendale won the state championship in 1924, and Duke Morrison was suddenly attractive to college recruiters. Clyde originally wanted his son to secure an appointment to one of the military academies. Duke opted for Annapolis, but the appointment was turned down.

He was only modestly disappointed, and a few months before high school graduation in 1925, the University of Southern California offered him a football scholarship. With the scholarship money, Duke could play football for USC and prepare himself for a career in law.

Under the leadership of coaches Elmer C. Henderson and the legendary Howard Jones, the Trojans were on their way to becoming a national football powerhouse. Jones's freshman team at USC went undefeated in seven games and outscored opponents 261 to 20. Duke had enough playing time to win a freshman letter and to catch the eye of Jones, who was already making plans for the 1926 season. One of Duke's teammates at USC was a rugged lineman with big ears and thick lips by the name of Wardell Bond. John Wayne and Ward Bond would appear together in 19 motion pictures and remain close friends until Bond's death in 1960. Ward Bond became one of the great character actors in the movie business and an important member of John Ford's stock company before gaining TV stardom as the wagonmaster on *Wagon Train*.

One day Coach Jones told his team that Fox Studios was looking for someone who could double for Francis X. Bushman running a pass in for a touchdown in a movie called *The Brown of Harvard*. John Wayne volunteered and rather casually made his film debut.

As a student, Duke took the standard pre-law curriculum. He won academic honors, became leader of the freshman debate team, and pledged Sigma Chi, the most popular fraternity on campus. But at the end of the football season something far more significant happened. One of his teammates fixed him up with a girl named Polly Ann Belzer, a student at the Romana Convent, an exclusive Catholic boarding school in Alhambra. Interestingly, Polly Ann's younger sister Gretchen would soon be better known to movie audiences as Loretta Young.

Duke's friendship with Polly in turn led to another blind date with one of Polly's friends, Carmen Saenz. When Duke escorted Carmen home, he met Carmen's younger sister Josephine. He was as instantly attracted to Josie as she was to him. Soon they started seeing each other on a regular basis.

The Saenz family were Hispanic bluebloods, and Duke never felt totally comfortable in their presence. Nevertheless, Duke and Josie were madly in love and after dating a number of years, they were married on June 24, 1933. The wedding took place in the gardens of Loretta Young's mother and stepfather's Bel Air estate. Duke's best man and all eight ushers were his Sigma Chi fraternity brothers. What is interesting is the fact that Duke's USC football career received more attention in the society page wedding announcements than his fledgling film career.

Producer-writer Lindsley Parsons, who wrote and directed many of Duke's early Westerns, recalled those romantic interludes between Duke and Josie.

"John and all the rest of us used to go to the Rendezvous Ballroom in Balboa every night. Josephine and her sister Carmen were the most beautiful girls in Balboa that summer, or for that matter, any summer we went down there. You had to have tickets for every dance so we would look around, and if we could scrounge any off the floor, we would split it and get two dances out of it."

Duke may have been falling in love, but the years had taken a toll on his mother and father. On May 1, 1926, Clyde and Molly Morrison separated after twenty years of unhappy marriage. Molly took Bobby and moved in with her folks in Los Angeles. Clyde moved to Beverly Hills, renting a room in an electrical supply company where he had found a job. Molly filed the necessary papers for divorce in 1929. The following year Clyde Morrison finally found the happiness he deserved. Mutual friends introduced him to Florence Buck, a twenty-nine year-old divorcée working at Webb's Department Store in Glendale.

Several weeks after Clyde's divorce became final in February. 1930, Clyde Morrison and Florence Buck were married. After kissing his new wife at the wedding ceremony, Clyde turned to Florence's eight-year-old daughter Nancy, embraced her, and whispered, "I will always love you as my one and only daughter." Florence and Nancy Buck left Glendale and moved to Beverly Hills with Clyde. Clyde Morrison now had a second family.

2. A Sister's Song

I won't be wronged. I won't be insulted and
I won't be laid a hand on. I don't do these things to
other people and I require the same from them.
> — John Wayne, as John
> Bernard Books in *The
> Shootist*

Nineteen thirty, the year of his father's second marriage, was
also the year twenty-two-year-old Duke Morrison got his first big
screen break. In 1930, he was cast as the lead in Raoul Walsh's epic
Western *The Big Trail*. That same year Marion Morrison from Winterset, Iowa, officially became John Wayne.

Nancy Morrison Marshall, Duke's stepsister, lives in McAlester,
Oklahoma. She fondly recalls meeting Clyde Morrison and her
soon-to-be-famous stepbrother for the first time.

Nancy Morrison Marshall

"My mother was Clyde's second wife. They were married when I
was eight years old and Duke was about twenty-two and had just
started in pictures. When he left college to start in movies, he and
his friend Ward Bond were more or less struggling actors. Those
were the years I was living in Beverly Hills. My dad—Duke's dad
Clyde—owned a drugstore there. We saw Duke all the time. Dad
died in 1937 at age fifty-two. I moved away after I married, and
Duke and I corresponded while my mother was alive. During that
time, Duke wrote lovely letters to my mother. He was wonderful
to my mother, just wonderful.

"Although Clyde and my mother were married a relatively
short time, they were supremely happy. It was a very happy

household. Daddy [Clyde] had such a strong sense of loyalty and integrity. When my stepdad died, he was president of the Lyons Club in Beverly Hills. They had a huge membership and he had just been reelected. He was such a moral man. He told me he would never bawl me out for anything unless he found out I had lied to him or that I was not being honest. He insisted on that. He lived by that rule, and I know Duke picked that up, too. I know Duke was loyal. He carried a lot of movie people when they couldn't do it themselves. He got those values from his father.

"When he made *The Big Trail*, they had a premier in Grauman's Chinese Theater. My mother and stepdad attended the premier. They were all dressed up and were just so thrilled. I was also at Duke's wedding when he married Josephine. It was at Loretta Young's house. Later he would come to dinner with Josie and his two children, Michael and Toni. I think Ward [Bond] came a couple of times, too.

"Clyde did not live to see Duke become such a big star. He did not want to see Duke leave college. The movie business seemed too risky, too uncertain for Clyde. But he was still very proud of Duke. It's too bad he didn't live to see him make *Stagecoach* and some of the others. It's a shame because Duke did so well.

"His father died very suddenly. Clyde drove me to school that morning. He didn't feel very good and went home to lie down. And that was it. It was all over. Duke, Josephine, and my mother came to get me in school at noon. Duke was absolutely crushed, so very crushed, because they had been so close. Duke was heartbroken, sobbing in the car as I was. He hugged me and we cried some more. It's very nice when fathers and sons have that kind of relationship. My son had that same relationship with his father before my husband became ill.

"I recall the first time I met him [Duke]. He was in a hospital bed after having his appendix out. His feet stuck out at the bottom of the bed and he had long hair. He was getting ready for a movie. This was the late nineteen twenties and you didn't see anybody with long hair back then. After the operation he came to our house to recuperate. He stayed there a week to ten days, then he went back to make whatever picture he was making.

14

A Sister's Song

"I was an only child, and I was happy to just have two brothers. That meant more to me than what they did or how important they were. Duke adored his younger brother Bob, and watching the two of them together was the sweetest thing. So even though we were very close, I was so happy to have somebody in my life other than just my mother and my dad.

"Clyde Morrison was a wonderful man, a wonderful, wonderful man. Duke and he had the closest relationship. Not too long ago, I heard Bob Dorian on AMC [American Movie Classics] say Duke was close with his mother, but not so close with his father. It was just the opposite. I never saw them when they didn't embrace. And I saw him kiss his dad many times. And his father was the most honest of men. He taught me so many values. I know nothing about Duke's mother because Clyde never talked about her. I never heard him say anything ugly about anybody, in fact. I never heard him talk about his first marriage.

"Duke was very handsome. He had the same forehead, my stepfather's eyes and forehead. They were exactly alike. Daddy was only 5'10", but all through the eyes they looked exactly alike. At one time I had this Sigma Chi book from college, and it showed him in his football uniform. When we were moving from Texas back to California, it disappeared. This has always been a sad regret for me.

"Duke was just the way you see him. There was no pretense. I didn't see any ego. He learned a lot and was so professional. He remained the same person. Everyone I have talked with concurs. I remember one time we were all eating at a drive-in, and people just kept asking and asking him for autographs. I said, 'Doesn't that upset you?' He said, 'No, it will upset me when they stop asking.' I used to go out to eat a lot in Beverly Hills and saw so many stars sitting around. Many would say, 'No, I don't sign while I'm eating.' Some said it nicely, and some didn't. Duke was always very nice about it. So was Chuck Connors.

"I only saw Duke two times after I moved away from California. Once in Waco, Texas, and another time when we went back to California on a visit. I couldn't get out to California when he died, and he couldn't get out here when my mother died because he was outside the country making a picture.

15

Duke, We're Glad We Knew You

"A lot of people out here know now that I am John Wayne's stepsister. I didn't tell many at first. But everybody who comes into this house to repair anything sees his pictures. They say, 'Were you a fan, too?' When I tell them Duke was my stepbrother, it goes all over town. This is a small town and people are quite impressed. It's amazing how popular he became and how popular he still is.

"Looking back, all of this is so amazing to me. What a lucky girl I was. Those days in Beverly Hills I ran around with Gloria Swanson's daughter. I went up to her home on the hills. All the people I'd see on the street—I'd see Boris Karloff buying nails in the dime store. I was ten years old and worked at the [drugstore] counter to help daddy out because these were hard times. Clark Gable and Carole Lombard, Robert Taylor and Barbara Stanwyck would come into the drugstore on Sunday morning, buy papers, and eat breakfast at the counter. You tell people that now and their mouths just fall open, and I think 'My God, was I lucky!'

"One of Duke's pictures I thoroughly enjoyed was *Hatari*, because it was out of his realm. But my favorite John Wayne picture is *The Quiet Man*. Ward was in that one, too. They were friends for so long. He was the priest in [*The Quiet Man*]. And I can see him now [in the film] lifting that skirt of his or whatever and running through town because he knew Duke and Victor McLaglen were going to fight. While I have never met Maureen O'Hara, I know she and Duke had the most professional respect for each other. She had this fiery temperament with her red hair. It was just a delightful picture. I just loved it!"

When Nancy Morrison graduated from Glendale High School, John Wayne had already made *Stagecoach* and become a major movie star. One of her friends and classmates was Jeannette Briggs, who would later marry Mike Mazurki, an actor who worked with Wayne in a number of films. Born in Chicago where her father was a famous trial attorney, she would go on to a successful career as a Hollywood journalist, working as movie and TV editor for Copley News Service.

Today Jeannette Mazurki Lindner lives in Escondido, California. During her career as a journalist she interviewed such stars as Gary Cooper, Spencer Tracy, Clark Gable, Cary Grant, Rita Hayworth, and of course, John Wayne. She has vivid recollections of Wayne and of those years she calls "Hollywood's Golden Era."

Jeannette Mazurki Lindner

"Nancy Morrison and I graduated from Glendale High where Duke also went to high school. We had a large class, so we were the first to graduate on the football field. It was kind of a big deal for us. We graduated on June 14, and word got around that Duke was coming to the graduation. He had made *Stagecoach,* and had become what I guess you'd call a big superstar. In fact, we were sitting in the bleachers on the football field, looking to see if we could spot our parents or whomever else we invited. It was our graduation and we were supposed to be the stars. But we were all looking for John Wayne, especially the girls.

"Anyway, he was there and he gave Nancy her graduation present. He gave her an emerald ring. Emeralds weren't exactly cheap back in 1939 and she was just flabbergasted. She was showing it to all of us around her locker when we were putting on our caps and gowns. That beautiful emerald still stands out in my mind. It was also my first recollection of John Wayne. In those early years he was so handsome. The drinking took its toll on his looks in later years, but he was just so handsome back then. Boy was he gorgeous! But when you are just eighteen, he seemed a little old for us high school girls. My reaction was [my heart going] 'pitter-patter, here's a movie star.'

"I went to Glendale College and received an associate of arts degree. My last year there I started working in the copy department of the local papers. There was no way they could keep copy boys because they were all going off to war. I was doing a campus chatter column for the college. They asked me to find a copy boy for the local paper. I came back the next day and said I found one—me. There were no women in the city room those days. That's how I got started. When the motion picture editor left for the war, I became motion picture editor. The first woman ever. I interviewed Mazurki in 1943 and married him in 1945. That's

The muscular young man

when I got to interview John Wayne on the set. He was making the picture *Dakota* with Mike. I got hold of Nancy and she set up the interview with her brother.

"It was night shooting at Republic (we used to call it Repulsive). They were shooting the burning of the wheat field. That was when Duke was romancing Chata, his second wife. We didn't know she was there at the time. He wanted to give his full attention to his sister. Mike was there, too, and we were taking pictures. We were supposed to eat dinner together. But since they were filming the burning of the wheat fields, they set up the tables outside.

"We conducted our business, and then [Duke] said he was awfully sorry but he had something else to do. Chata was very much in the background. We didn't see her. I think Mike knew. We were pleased. I got my story and everybody was happy.

"Nancy said to Duke, 'I want to thank you for taking care of mother's operation. That was really good of you, fine of you to do that.' Duke was embarrassed. That's the way he was. He was very generous, but he didn't want anybody to know it. He didn't know how to handle it. He could play the same kind of thing very well in the movies, too.

"I think Mike made four pictures with Duke, including *Blood Alley* for William Wellman, and *Donovan's Reef* for John Ford. When you worked on a picture with Duke, he always gave his principals an inscribed coffee mug, with a big gold handle and a ship going up. So Mike had this beautiful gold cup with the inscription 'Mike, from Duke.' He was very proud of that. The last fifteen years or so Duke never gave autographs per se. He gave out little business cards which said 'John Wayne.' On the other side, his autograph was printed. He carried these because his autograph was so much in demand. [Wayne's secretary,] Mary St. John would keep them and give them to him so he could hand them out. I've got two in my possession. I also have a copy of the script for *The High and the Mighty*. The script had no notes, or maybe Duke didn't make any. It was his name and address: Bayshore, Balboa.

"Duke and Mike loved to drink and play cards, although Mike was no boozer. His body was too important to him. Many of the guys like Ward Bond and Grant Withers were what I'd call functioning alcoholics. They'd be in places like Monument Valley for months, and what else could you do? Drink and play cards. Duke and Mike were the same height. Mazurki always made him look good, especially in the fight scenes. There was no jealousy. They were just good buddies.

"I do remember one card game in particular, the one that I got drunk with Esperanza [Chata]. Two women getting a little pie-eyed. The men were in the poker room playing cards. Duke told Mike to bring his wife along. He figured I would be company for Chata. The card-playing bunch was in the back. She didn't speak much English, and I recall she was quite pretty. I was twenty-five and a new bride then. I didn't have any children, and it was still the honeymoon stage for me. She had some tequila. We talked, but you really had to listen because her English wasn't very good. So we got plastered.

"But when she'd get half looped, she'd get so jealous she'd start throwing tantrums. She was a real alcoholic, as was her mother. Later on she drank herself to an early death, which was quite sad. But I had no reason to dislike her. She was very hospitable. Wayne had this thing for Latin women. You give me a lineup of women, and I could tell you the ones he would pick. Dark, exotic Latin-type women appealed to him.

"Maybe it was because they were so different from his mother. His mother was an Irish woman and was always fighting with his dad. Duke would run away from home, and I don't think he particularly liked his mother. But he loved his father dearly, and his mother was so mean to his dad. She knew how to pull the strings, and his father would give in. She ruled the roost. But after they separated and divorced, Clyde had a good marriage with Nancy's mother.

"Duke was basically a shy man when it came to women. Hedda Hopper really liked Duke. He was a far-right Republican like she was, but he was ill at ease even around her. I felt he was ill at ease around me. He was quoted many times as saying he didn't understand women. He couldn't have a confrontation with a woman. Again, I'm going back to his mother and his father. The way she treated his father and how Clyde would give in. Often what happens in the next generation is that you do the same thing, no matter how much you hate it.

"Yet Duke had a basic respect for women. While he was married, he was mainly a one-woman guy, which was really rare in Hollywood. He was not a womanizer. It was one woman at a time. Duke was not a player. And everybody knew it and respected it. He did have an affair with Marlene Dietrich. She was an aggressive woman and usually got what she wanted. He knew it and there was no problem.

"Then there was the relationship between Duke and Gail Russell. They made *Angel and the Badman* together for Republic in 1947. But this was different. He had genuine feelings for her. But Gail was a boozer, a defenseless woman, and she hung on to Duke. Well, then he was helping someone. Here was the whole pattern. She needed him. They did have a love affair. After the picture it was over. You go on to another picture. This was Hollywood. But he was very fond of her.

"Again I think he was basically a shy man. He was 6'4" and when he walked out in center stage, he naturally commanded attention. But his whole manner of speech tells you he was a modest man.

"I thought his son Patrick was going to be a big star. Duke always spent time with the boys. But he didn't quite know what to do with his girls. Duke was working hard and was always away. But he did somehow manage the boys. That tells you something.

"He once recited something about 'The Twilight Years.' It certainly says a lot about Duke and his feelings. I believe it went like this:

" 'If this is twilight, then hell give me more. I'm fifty-three years old and 6'4". I've had three wives, five children, and three grandchildren. I love good whiskey. I still don't understand women. And I don't think there is any man who does.' "

3. Pappy

Wayne has never underestimated one of the greatest axioms of a good Western—A good silent man with a horse is better than two hours of talk.

— David Sutton, the *Saturday Evening Post* (Spring, 1972)

On February 15, 1939 *Stagecoach* had opened to rave reviews and the thirty-two-year-old Wayne had become an overnight sensation. But as all who are familiar with Wayne's career know, there was nothing overnight about his success, nor did he follow the usual path to stardom in Hollywood. Most actors graduate from bit parts to leads and stay there. Not so for Duke. His initial thrust to stardom melted with *The Big Trail* in 1930, and he was forced to find his early niche as a B Western actor. By the time he was cast as the Ringo Kid in *Stagecoach,* he had already appeared in some sixty-four pictures, most of them routine at best.

But he probably wouldn't have had a career at all had it not been for a surly director who had a boundless impact on Wayne's film career. Duke called him "Coach." Those close to the four-time Oscar winner referred to him as "Pappy." To the world at large, he was John Ford. Acerbic, mean, vindictive, brilliant, loyal, regimented, is how others have described John Ford. Though his Oscar-winning films were not Westerns, no one before or since has filmed Westerns with more efficiency and care.

He was emotional, not cool and detached like most Western directors. Employing a rare blend of poetry, beauty, and excitement, Ford's films have celebrated the Western way of life and mourned its passing. He depicts the West as it should have been, rather than as it was. When fact collided with legend, he always insisted, he would go with the legend.

In his 1979 book, *Pappy: The Life of John Ford,* Ford's grandson Dan relates the first meeting between Ford and Wayne. Duke was

Pappy

John Wayne with
Marguerite Churchill in
The Big Trail (1929)

an undergraduate at USC when Ford saw him working as a third assistant prop man at Fox Studios. Coach Howard Jones had arranged for Duke to get a summer job at Fox, where he worked as a swing-gang laborer, striking sets and moving from one location to another. One day he was told to report to the set of *Mother Machree,* the story of an Irish housekeeper who sacrificed everything so her son would have a better life. According to Dan Ford's account:

> John Ford noticed Duke on the set. He went up to him and
> said, "You one of Howard Jones's boys?"
>   "Yeh," said Morrison.
>   "What position do you play?"
>   "Guard."
>   "Guard, huh?"
>   "Yeah."
>   "I used to be a fullback. You think you can take me out?"
> Morrison looked at the director. "Yeah, I know I could."

Ford and Duke then crouched down, knuckles on the stage floor, and started slamming into each other. But at age thirty-two, Ford hadn't broken a tackle since 1914, while twenty-one-year-old Duke Morrison at 6'4" and 200 pounds, was in prime physical condition.

The crusty director couldn't budge the USC guard. Going back to the stage Ford challenged Duke to try and stop him. He began running at Duke, then tried to break free. But Duke Morrison had him, not cleanly, but he had him. Then just as Ford was breaking free, Duke kicked the director squarely in the chest and sent him sprawling.

"There was dead silence on the set," Dan Ford continues. "All eyes were on Morrison, whose brief career in pictures was surely at an end. But John [Ford] simply got up, dusted himself off, and said, 'Come on, let's get back to work. That's enough of this bullshit.'"

It was this encounter which first got Duke to think seriously about the picture business. By his own accounts, he was greatly impressed by Ford. "I watched how he handled people, how he got his actors to communicate without the spoken word," he said. "I began to appreciate what a great artist he really was." Ford, in turn, appreciated that Duke was more than just another prop man and that he was truly trying to get an education.

Another factor weighed heavily on Duke's mind. Most aspiring law students at USC had connections, fathers or uncles who had law firms. Duke had no such connections. This meant that if he went into law, he would spend years writing back room briefs before his law career could get off the ground.

"This really started playing on me," he later said. "And the more I thought about the picture business, the more attractive it became. I had no thoughts about becoming an actor—I wanted to be a director like Jack Ford. He was my mentor, my ideal, and I made up my mind I wanted to be like him."

The relationship between Ford and Wayne would twist and turn throughout the years. Together they worked on thirty-one film projects. Duke's personal feelings toward Ford remained a bit ambivalent. Professionally, though, there was never any doubt. Not only did Ford give him his start in the picture business, but many of Wayne's finest roles were also under Ford's direction. He was always humble in Ford's presence even after he became a big star. No other director could command this kind of reverence from Duke Wayne, not even Howard Hawks or Henry Hathaway, both of whom he respected greatly.

The subject of Ford always was a touchy one for Duke. Ford could be hard on Duke, even humiliating at times. But Wayne's sense of loyalty to his irascible mentor prevailed. Ford might have been a tyrannical father figure of sorts, but he was a beloved one as well.

"I worked on and off for years in menial jobs for him, as a prop boy, stuntman, and bit player," said Wayne. "I developed a hero worship which still exists. But when I got stuck in three-and-a-half-day Westerns, Ford passed me by without speaking. This went on for three years; he just wouldn't look at me. *Stagecoach* made me a star and I'll be grateful to him forever. But I don't think he had any kind of respect for me as an actor until I made *Red River* for Howard Hawks ten years later. Even then, I was never quite sure."

It was Ford who recommended Duke Morrison to Raoul Walsh for *The Big Trail*. Walsh was one of Fox's most highly regarded directors. Specializing in action pictures, in 1929 he directed *In Old Arizona*, Hollywood's first outdoor talkie. *The Big Trail* would be a big-budget project, an epic story of a wagon train's struggle along the overland trail between Missouri and Oregon. Like other early sound directors, Walsh searched for talent with stage experience. He chose Marguerite Churchill, whose Broadway roots matched her incandescent beauty, as the female lead. The best secondary roles went to proven stage actors Ian Keith, Tyrone Power Sr., Tully Marshall, and El Brendel.

Finding a male lead was more difficult. Many silent film stars lacked the proper voice for talkies. Walsh wanted Tom Mix, but Mix was working on another film. Gary Cooper was making *The Virginian* for Samuel Goldwyn. Cooper also commanded around $17,000 per picture. Because Walsh knew that in *The Big Trail* dialogue took a backseat to action and scenery, he agreed to go with an untested Duke Morrison. At least Duke was available.

Duke went into training, and Walsh prescribed lessons for his new leading man. Duke learned to be a cowboy from cowboys turned stuntmen. Steve Clemente, a weapons expert, taught him

25

to throw a knife. Jack Padgin, a Montana cowboy and one of Fox's leading stuntmen, taught him to draw a gun, mount a horse, and ride with the natural grace which distinguished Duke's career. Others taught him to rope, to shoot, and to act.

Making the film, however, was hardly a pleasant experience. In a 1971 interview with *Playboy*, Duke recalled some of the difficulties:

"One of the times I felt like a fool was when I was making my first important film, *The Big Trail*. I was three weeks flat on my back with 'Montezuma's Revenge' or the 'Aztec two-step,' or whatever you want. Anyway that was the worst case I ever had in my life. I'd been sick for so long, that they finally said. 'Jeez, Duke, if you can't get up now, we've got to get someone else to take your place.'

"So with a loss of eighteen pounds I returned to work. My first scene was carrying in an actor named Tully Marshall, who was known to booze it up quite a bit. He had a big jug in his hand in this scene, and I set him down and we have a drink with another guy. They passed the jug to me first, and I dug back into it; it was straight rotgut whiskey. I'd been puking and crapping blood for a week and now I just poured that raw stuff right down my throat. After the scene, you can bet I called him every kind of an old bastard."

Duke was to play an authentic American hero named Breck Coleman, who would lead a wagon train from St. Louis along the Oregon Trail. But the studio felt that the name Duke Morrison did not sound American enough. Director Raoul Walsh was a Revolutionary War buff, and a great admirer of General "Mad Anthony" Wayne. Because the general had been a tough nonconformist, Walsh suggested the name to production boss Winfield Sheehan. However, Sheehan felt the name Anthony sounded too Italian, and he thought Tony sounded like a girl's name. When someone on the set suggested the name "John," Sheehan said fine. Why not? "John" was all-American, as well as the first name of Duke's sponsor John Ford. So Duke Morrison became John Wayne.

The name had a nice honest sound to it, and contrary to Hollywood legend, Duke's work in his first major role was certainly adequate. He went on personal appearances to promote the film. Wayne had good looks and audiences felt he had star potential. Yet

Pappy

The man about town

the film failed miserably at the box office. As a purported epic, the film was shot in wide-screen 55mm format and released at a time when cinema owners were recovering from the cost of converting to sound. They were unwilling to invest in the type of production equipment needed to show *The Big Trail* in "Fox Grandeur," as the wide-screen process was called.

The film may have flopped, but it did land Duke his first magazine profile in the December 1930 issue of *Photoplay*. As the handsome trail boss, Wayne showed enough natural affinity for the screen that his employers gave him a second chance in a film called *Girls Demand Excitement*, giving him second billing to Virginia Cherrill. He made one more film for Fox, playing an architect in *Three Girls Lost* opposite Loretta Young, before departing for Columbia Pictures in 1931.

Wayne made three films for Columbia in 1931: *Men Like That* with Laura LaPlante, *Range Feud* with Buck Jones, and *Maker of Men* with Jack Holt, in which he again portrayed a college football player. Producer Leon Schlesinger then signed Wayne to do a series of quickie Westerns for Warner Brothers. While doing one-day bit parts at Warners, he was also getting top billing in low-budget Saturday matinee serials.

As his star-studded fortunes slid down the Hollywood scale, Duke ruefully accepted an offer from Mascot Picture Corporation to do serials. Mascot—later to become the nucleus of Republic Pictures—promoted him as a star. He did three twelve-chapter serials for Mascot in 1932 and 1933, each produced by Nat Levine: *Shadow of the Eagle, Hurricane Express,* and *The Three Musketeers.* All were fast-paced, low budget, and had plenty of action. Duke may have been on Hollywood's "Poverty Row," but it was also the Great Depression. As Will Rogers once reminded Duke when he was feeling low, "You're working, ain't you?"

In the fall of 1935, Mascot and Monogram Pictures merged to form Republic Pictures under the stewardship of business tycoon Herbert J. Yates. It was Trem Carr, production head at Monogram, who decided John Wayne had a good face for Westerns. Under the banner Lone Star/Monogram, Duke made at least eight pictures a year for the next ten years. All fast-paced, rugged little action dramas, they proved a valuable training ground for the Duke.

It was a time for learning and he was steadily growing into his craft. When he entered the arena of B Westerns, Duke had lots of competition. Buck Jones, Tim McCoy, and Ken Maynard had been around since the silent days. But he had something the others lacked—genuine sex appeal.

Film writer Lindsley Parsons worked with Wayne during this period and recalled his early days at Monogram:

> His [Duke's] problem was that he didn't feel he was an actor. We'd be out on location and he'd do a dialogue sequence and he'd just cuss himself out terribly. He would go behind a rock and talk about how lousy he was. I think I kept the dialogue simple and easy to speak. I didn't try to write long speeches for him. I think that is one of the reasons we became very good friends. In fact, I treasured a picture he gave me for a long time that someone stole. It said I was his favorite author.

28

Pappy

John Wayne found his niche in B Westerns. His principle director at Monogram/Lone Star was Robert Bradbury, father of cowboy star Bob Steele. It was Bradbury who directed Wayne as "Singin' Sandy Saunders," the first singing cowboy. Of course, Duke couldn't sing, but then he didn't really sing in the film. Bradbury's other son was back in the brush singing while Duke as Singin' Sandy was trying to be the West's most notorious gunman since Billy the Kid.

Cecilia Parker, Singin' Sandy's leading lady, felt from the start that Duke had star potential. "It was laughable to imagine him breaking into song. I liked him. He was a real nice young man. He had just gotten married. You can tell when somebody has it and somebody doesn't. He had a certain aura about him. You knew he was going to go. He was a natural."

Despite repeated attempts, Singin' Sandy Saunders never caught on. Another young performer would soon become Hollywood's first successful singing cowboy. His name was Gene Autry. He tells an interesting story:

> I was under contract with Mascot and John Wayne was under contract to Monogram. And when they merged, that is, when Republic Pictures came in, John Wayne and I made the first two pictures for Republic. He made *Westward Ho,* and I made *Tumbleweed.* It was a step up for Wayne. The picture cost almost twice as much as the Lone Star pictures. It was shot at a beautiful location with more horses, cattle, and cowboys. It garnered top booking at theaters which didn't generally play that kind of picture. Audiences in some cases were seeing John Wayne for the first time. And they liked him. He began to show a growing maturity in front of the camera.

Another person who became instrumental in Duke's future success was Enos Canutt, a daring stuntman from Yakima, Washington. The movie world remembers him as Yakima Canutt who played the heavy in many of Duke's Saturday matinee movies. Yakima Canutt would also double for Duke if a particular stunt was too tough. Acknowledged as the best rodeo rider and stuntman in the business, Yakima taught Wayne all his tricks. Together they sweated out the technique of the barroom brawl and the right way to draw and shoot a gun. Canutt even taught Duke how to fall from a running horse without getting hurt.

In 1936 Republic began the best Western series ever produced, *The Three Mesquiteers.* Duke moved into the role of Stony Brooke that had been vacated by Bob Livingston. He joined a cast which included Ray "Crash" Corrigan as Tucson Smith and Max Terhune as Lullaby Jones. Their hallmark was nonstop action, with the stuntwork arranged and performed by Yak Canutt, who was also a second unit director. The series covered an unusually wide variety of settings with plots involving everyone from early pioneers to Nazi spies.

The Cooriganville Ranch where the series was filmed was purchased in 1935 by Crash Corrigan. Corrigan had worked with Clark Gable on *Mutiny on the Bounty,* and the two hunted together at the ranch site. Corrigan thought it would be a good movie location, and as picture companies began to use it, they started building sets. Columbia built a big lake. By 1950 Corriganville was a major movie ranch with as many as seven picture companies filming there at a time.

Tom Corrigan, Crash's son, has been owner of Corrigan's Restaurant in Thousand Oaks, California, since 1982. The restaurant is decorated in Western style and the walls arc lined with pictures of Corriganville and the many cowboy stars who worked there. Corrigan is proud of his heritage and recalls meeting John Wayne as a young boy.

Tom Corrigan

"I only met Duke Wayne once. That was when they were filming *Fort Apache* in 1947. It was filmed at Corriganville, and the fort was actually built there. John Ford built many of his movie sets at our ranch. I was little and my mom took me to the movie set one night to meet John Wayne. She told me I was meeting someone who used to film with my dad.

30

Pappy

"My dad made eight pictures with Wayne, and a portion of all eight were filmed at our ranch. These were all for Republic Pictures. When Wayne came into the *Mesquiteer* series, Republic wanted to bolster Wayne's career, because he was with Lone Star Productions before that. He wasn't yet a big-name star, but when he went to Republic, he became one. So they put him in the *Mesquiteer* series, which was the hottest series they had running at the time in B Westerns. They were high production B Westerns and a lot of them were directed by Sol Siegel who later became head of MGM. He spent more money in those than many other low-budget productions.

"Right before Wayne came into the series, my dad was rated Hollywood's number-one box office cowboy. He gave way to Gene Autry when Autry recorded his first gold record. Wayne, I believe, came into the series in late 1937, or perhaps in 1938. I recall my dad remarked that Wayne had taken some of his thunder away. He never disliked Wayne for that, but Wayne did manage to become as big a star or better than my dad.

"Wayne replaced Bob Livingston, who played the part of Stony Brooke. Republic was having a lot of trouble with Livingston. He was a little temperamental. Wayne was just coming into his own with Republic and they had high hopes of him being a big star. And they were right. He fit right in. He did as good a job or better than Livingston. At least he filled his boots. So Wayne was right in there as the lead.

"My dad kind of got into it with Republic studios at the time, so he left Republic and went over to Monogram where he continued to make more Westerns.

"From time to time, my dad would talk about Wayne. His remarks were that Wayne was a different type of actor than he was. He would look at Wayne and say he had 'hero charisma.' My dad called himself more of an athletic kind of actor. He had that Tarzan physique, while Wayne was more of a hero type actor. He was the type of man who'd walk into a room and he didn't have to say anything. Everybody knew he was there. He had tremendous presence. When my dad got a little older he said he probably was a little jealous of Wayne, and he probably should have stayed at Republic.

31

With Gwen Gaze in *I Cover the War* (1937)

"I think they remained friends because Wayne came on out again some ten years later and did a lot of filming for *Fort Apache*. My dad said Wayne adapted very well to horses. Wayne learned a lot from [Stuntman] Yakima Canutt, so did my dad.

"Wayne definitely had his own style. He didn't want to wear fancy guns, while my dad had that two-gun silver holster. Wayne liked to be a little plainer. He had his own way of shaping his hat. My dad said he liked to wear solid color shirts. He kind of designed his own clothes, the type he felt would look good on him. He had good taste, too. He had his own style and maintained it through all of his pictures.

"My dad saw Wayne's stardom coming. They were filming *Stagecoach* when they did the last *Mesquiteer* picture. Wayne came off the *Stagecoach* set and filmed the last *Mesquiteer* episode. That was 1939. My dad always maintained no one gave Wayne anything. He earned everything he got. [He said] 'I was a little jealous of him in my younger days, but the guy's a great man and I think we respected each other. But when he came into the series, I started losing ground.'

"I've loved Duke's movies since I [was] a boy. *The Searchers* has always been one of my favorites. He played a tremendous role, almost like he was playing himself. I always felt he should have received an Oscar for *Red River*. It was a difficult role for him to play.

"When he did *True Grit* everyone said he got an Academy Award because of his contribution to the industry. Bull! He earned that one. The more I see it the more I see what he did. It was tremendous the way he pulled off that part of Rooster. When you see it more than once you really can appreciate it.

"Yesterday I went to town and showed some films at a school. It seems this new generation is really curious about the Westerns. I was very well-received to the point that I was overwhelmed. I couldn't believe these kids would have so much interest. I showed them a John Wayne/Crash Corrigan Western called *Pals of the Saddle* and they just loved the thing. It says a lot about the staying power of John Wayne."

4. "Stagecoach" and Stardom

> I never used a mechanical horse in my life. To do
> closeups on *Stagecoach* with six lines in your hand, I
> suggested the use of elastic like that used in arm
> exercises on the opposite end of the reins to give them
> a look of natural movement.
>
>

> — John Wayne, in a letter to
> Dr. Cory Sen Vas, the Curtis
> Publishing Company. The
> *Saturday Evening Post*
> (July/August, 1979)
>

As almost every movie buff probably knows, *Stagecoach* made a
star out of John Wayne. But Duke's rise to stardom did not come
easily. John Ford made sure of that. As Dan Ford says in the biography of his grandfather, Ford went out on a limb for Duke. "Now
he was going to extract his pound of flesh." But beyond the sadistic pleasure Ford took in humiliating Duke, there was a proverbial
method to his madness. Dan writes:

> As a newcomer, and as an actor with no formal training,
> Wayne already felt insecure playing with such seasoned
> professionals as Thomas Mitchell, Claire Trevor and George
> Bancroft. [Ford] made it even worse by bullying him in
> front of the entire company calling him a 'dumb bastard,'
> a "big oaf," and the like. He even criticized the way Wayne
> moved: "Can't you walk, for Chrissake, instead of skipping
> like a goddamn fairy?"

The Ringo Kid was the key character in *Stagecoach,* as well as
the romantic lead. Ford had given the part to an upstart actor
everybody knew was his personal friend and drinking buddy.

He knew the veterans resented Wayne. By humiliating and harassing him, Ford got the rest of the company to pull for the kid, and before long they were doing everything they could to help him.

Ford could be cruel. But he was a master of psychology, so he also knew when to be kind. He realized Wayne was reaching deep inside himself and giving his finest performance to date. His best qualities—charisma, physical grace, vulnerability—were shining through. In fact, Ford was so pleased with Wayne's performance that when the Monument Valley sequences were completed and the company returned to Hollywood, he reshot Wayne's entrance. In the new scene, he had Duke fire a Winchester to attract the stage driver's attention, then twirl it like a pistol as the camera trucked in for a close-up. This shot is usually remembered as the moment Wayne's career took off.

The timing was just right. In spite of his popularity as a B Western cowboy star, Duke's career seemed to be going nowhere. His contract with Republic demanded that he grind out a B Western every eight days. His popularity with the kids in Saturday matinee seats was not shared by the high-brow Hollywood establishment. Agents and casting directors thought he looked good, rode good, and moved good, but couldn't act.

There were personal problems as well. His ten-year marriage to Josie was coming apart. The daughter of a doctor and part-time Panamanian diplomat, Josie was a prominent member of Los Angeles society. Duke was uncomfortable among her society friends, who seemed to regard him as little more than another low-grade actor. He maintained a respectable façade for the sake of his four children. But the last thing he wanted to do after fourteen hours of arduous filming was to dress up, stay sober, and hobnob with boring people. He was retreating from his marriage and spending more and more free time aboard John Ford's yacht, the *Araner*.

Popular lore dictates that Ford gave Duke a script to read for an upcoming project called *Stagecoach*, then asked him to suggest an actor for the role of the Ringo Kid. Duke obliged by suggesting Lloyd Nolan for the role. Supposedly, when Ford responded by saying something like "what the hell is the matter with you doing it," Duke was totally flabbergasted. But according to Dan Ford's account, Duke was not nearly as astonished as some folks think.

In the summer of 1938 John [Ford] invited Wayne to spend a weekend at Catalina. As the *Araner* powered past the San Pedro breakwater, John handed [Wayne] a copy of the *Stagecoach* script and told him to read it. That night the two men sat up playing cards. Finally [Ford] said:

"I've got Claire Trevor, George Bancroft, John Carradine, and Tommy Mitchell, but I need your help on something. You know a lot of these young actors. Do you know anybody who could play the Ringo Kid?"

Wayne grimaced. He knew he was being set up.

"Why don't you get Lloyd Nolan," he answered. John didn't acknowledge Wayne's sarcastic reply.

"Jesus Christ," he said, "I wish to hell I could find some young actor in this town who can ride a horse *and* act. Goddammit, Duke, you must know somebody. But then you've been out at Republic. You're not likely to see a lot of talent out there."

The next day as they sailed back across the channel, Ford continued his roundabout recruiting. He fully intended to offer Wayne the part, yet still wanted to see him squirm a little. According to Dan Ford, "The hand of the giver always did have a vicious backhand."

Finally on Sunday evening, as the *Araner* was docking at San Pedro, Ford broke the news to Wayne: "Duke, I want you to play the Ringo Kid!" Wayne smiled and answered, "Yeah, Coach, I know!"

It wasn't a shot in the dark. Ford knew exactly what he wanted. For years Ford believed Duke had the tools—that with the proper growth, maturity, and development, he had what it took to be a first-rate actor. He sensed a charm, a charisma, and a vulnerability with which audiences could identify. In spite of his 6'4" frame, Duke "could move like a dancer." The bad habits and rough edges were there and Ford was a tough taskmaster. But slowly things fell into place. Much of what Wayne learned was the result of on-the-job training. Ford was wielding a heavy whip, and Duke was learning the trade big time. Claire Trevor was a seasoned pro and worked with Wayne for hours to prepare for their scenes together. He may have been learning how to be an actor, but Ford knew it was in him all along.

By using the *Grand Hotel* formula of placing a group of unrelated characters together in common settings and dangerous situations, by engaging some of Hollywood's best character actors, and by employing the magnificent setting of Monument Valley and Yakima Canutt's marvelous stuntwork, John Ford had lifted the Western to new heights.

Canutt credited Wayne with bringing him to the attention of John Ford. "I was working a lot with John Wayne, and when he got hired for *Stagecoach,* he put in a good word with Mr. Ford. When I first went to see him, Ford said, 'Well Enos, how are you?' Hardly anyone in Hollywood knew my name was Enos. I said, 'I see Wayne's given you the inside dope on me.' 'That's right,' said Ford. 'In fact, he's said so much about you that you are going to have trouble living up to it all.'

"I knew Ford liked to shoot fast and didn't want any delays, so I planned the chase as closely as possible," Canutt said. "We had the saddle and the horses to do first, so the night before I hired a farmer to dig up twenty acres of the lake bed with his tractor. That way we'd have soft ground to land on and get the job done safer and faster."

Ford also knew just how to dub a scene. The sound of thundering horse hooves, with no whoops or war cries, added greatly to the feeling of speed. The Oscar-winning score by Richard Hageman, Frank Harling, John Leipold, and Leo Shuken, consisting of traditional American folk songs with full orchestration, perfectly defined the sense of time and place.

John Ford had a hit and he knew it. The year 1939 gave us such film classics as *Gone With the Wind, Goodbye, Mr. Chips, Mr. Smith Goes to Washington, The Wizard of Oz, Ninotchka, Wuthering Heights,* and *Of Mice and Men.* Many consider it the best year for film in American cinema history. Yet *Stagecoach* was nominated for seven Academy Awards including Best Picture. Thomas Mitchell garnered

I Cover the War (1937)

a Best Supporting Actor Oscar as Doc Boone, a physician too fond of liquor. Ford's direction was honored by the New York Film Critics, and Ford was nominated for an Academy Award as Best Director, losing to Victor Fleming, who directed *Gone With the Wind*.

After more than ten years in the trenches and a long tenure in movieland's Poverty Row, Duke had become an A picture movie star. Wayne later recalled that when the film was previewed at the Village Theater in the Westwood section of Los Angeles, the audience went wild with excitement during the chase scene. "The audience yelled and screamed and stood up and cheered. They loved it."

So did the critics. *Varity* called *Stagecoach* "a display of photographic grandeur." *Newsweek* labeled it "a rare screen masterpiece," and the *Nation* dubbed it "the best Western in years."

Stagecoach was a true watershed for John Wayne—more so because no major studio wanted to take a chance with the film, especially with its untried, untested star. Finally Walter Wanger, an independent producer, agreed to sponsor it. But even the most enthusiastic participants never expected the magnitude of the film nor the lasting popularity of its new star.

There is a touch of irony, too. When Thomas Mitchell took home the Best Supporting Actor Oscar, he defeated longtime Western great Harry Carey, who was nominated for his role as the kindly vice president in *Mr. Smith Goes to Washington.*

Carey was Wayne's screen hero and would appear with Duke in such films as *The Shepherd of the Hills, Angel and the Badman,* and *Red River,* Carey's final film before his death in 1947. While Duke looked up to Carey, Harry Carey Jr., nicknamed "Dobe," spent much of his childhood in the early nineteen thirties watching John Wayne movies.

Carey Jr. has been one of the industry's more durable character actors for nearly fifty years. He appeared with Wayne in ten films, more than anyone in the movie business today.

A veteran of more than one hundred films and scores of TV shows, Carey Jr. and his wife Marilyn (daughter of the late character actor Paul Fix) live in Durango, Colorado. In 1987 he appeared with Bette Davis and Lillian Gish in *The Whales of August.* More recently, he was seen as the sheriff gunned down in the streets of *Tombstone,* the 1994 film starring Kurt Russell and Val Kilmer.

Harry Carey Jr.

"My first real awareness of Duke was when I was a kid. I loved John Wayne movies. This was in the thirties before he became a legendary star, a big star. The theater we used to go to was in the San Fernando Valley, about fifteen miles east of our ranch in Saugus, California. It was the closest movie theater around, and each time there was a John Wayne movie at the Rennie Theater I'd beg my mom to take me. I particularly liked John Wayne and Bob Steele.

"So my mother, Ollie, who was also quite a wonderful actress, would take me. There would be a double bill, a John Wayne movie and something else. I loved these movies. Duke had a quality about him even back then which was fascinating to me. These were the years when he was doing these Westerns for Mascot, Monogram, Republic, and some other little companies.

"The thing which most amazed me about Duke and what I admired in him the most, was that he totally remade himself. Not only was he a warm, friendly guy, but Duke actually took something somewhat clumsy and awkward and turned it into an incredible screen personality which just swept the world.

"He told me himself in 1968, when we were working on *The Undefeated,* that he couldn't stand to look at himself in those old Westerns. We were sitting off alone and he was speaking of many of those pre-*Stagecoach* Westerns. He couldn't stand watching himself, he said, and he told me he had to get a role model. Then he said 'The guy I admired most on the screen was Harry Carey. I decided I'd copy Harry.' So he had mannerisms and that sort of broken speech pattern like my dad. He copied my dad and told me so himself. I think he said the same thing once on the *Merv Griffin Show.* Some books say William S. Hart was his hero. That's not true. My father was Duke's hero.

"The day my father died, John Ford, Duke Wayne, and I were at his bedside. After he passed away and after the shock which was reverberating around the house, Ford came up to my mother and said he wanted to make *Three Godfathers* with Duke, Pedro Armendariz, and with me playing The Kid. He dedicated the film to my father.

"I loved Duke and he loved me. The thing is, I don't think he ever forgave me for being the son of Harry Carey. Harry Carey was his absolute hero. I watched some films of my dad the other night. As an older man myself now, I can see him in total objectivity. I don't wonder why he was Duke's hero. He had that strong screen personality and he was a strong actor who could carry a picture. But what Duke liked about my dad were his mannerisms, and the way he always added something to his roles. No wonder my father was a great influence on Duke in developing his technique. There's another factor in Duke's development as well. My wife Marilyn was the daughter of Paul Fix, the great character actor. Paul was also a great influence on Duke Wayne. He helped Duke with that unique walk of his.

"Stagecoach" and Stardom

"Duke also helped me with my career. He got me my part in *Red River*. That's a fact. Originally, there was another kid who was supposed to play my part. The actor Howard Hawks had under contract was told to practice his riding. Well, when the day came where he was supposed to work on his scene he said he was sick and couldn't work. Hawks told him it was OK, and he would just shoot another scene that day. That same night Hawks went to Tucson and found the kid drinking and having a good time. Hawks immediately fired him and supposedly said he didn't know who he could get to play the part of Dan Lattimore. Then Duke said, 'I don't know if he can act or not, but the guy who looks just right for the part is Dobe Carey.' So that's how I got into *Red River*. It was the only film I did with my father.

"In those early films Duke helped me through a whole lot. Ford made it very rough on me in *Three Godfathers*. He rode me something awful and I wanted to quit more than a few times. Duke was a great help. He told me I'd just have to take it, that Ford did the same thing to him in *Stagecoach*. He said to listen carefully to him, because sometimes you couldn't understand what Ford was saying. He'd have that handkerchief in his mouth.

"When Ford was directing, Duke was like a pussycat around the set. I'll tell you something else, too. Duke could have been a hell of a director. He was humble with Ford, but in those other films we did in Durango, Mexico, later in his career, he was a hard guy to talk to on the set. That was because he really did know so much. The only thing stopping him from being a great director was his temper. But he really knew what he was talking about. He knew the film game and he knew the film business. But he had no tact. So he wasn't as full of camaraderie on the set in these later years.

"The first time I saw Duke in person was in 1939. World War II was just starting and my father was the grand marshal of the Saugus Rodeo on the old Gibson Ranch. I knew John Wayne was supposed to be there. I was eighteen years old, and I was back there in the stable area with Monte Montana and some other guys behind the stadium.

"All of a sudden this big Cadillac convertible pulls up and Wayne gets out. I don't know if *Stagecoach* was out yet, but he had

41

finished it. I recall John Ford was there, so was Ward Bond and some other people. Wayne and this other fellow got out of that big convertible and you could tell they were both drunk. They had been to a big party and had never gone to bed (he told me that later). I remember the beer which was around in those days. It was a local beer called Brown Derby. That's what they were selling at the rodeo and John Wayne started drinking that Brown Derby beer.

"So by the time he rode in the parade around the arena he was really soused. This story and others like it seem to indicate that the guy had a terrible problem. But that isn't the way it really was. I never saw him in that kind of shape when he was working or had to work the next day. Anyhow, it was a tremendous thrill for me to see him. There he was. That great big guy, and he looked like he did in the movies. That's the first time I ever saw John Wayne in person.

"Duke was good-natured when he was drinking, but he was also very physical. He'd want you to do something that was totally bizarre, and if you'd say no, he would get you around the neck and haul you all over the room. But always in a playful way. There was a time in Catalina right after we finished *Three Godfathers* when John Ford invited all of us over to his boat. So there were John Wayne and Chata and Marilyn and myself. I was twenty-seven and Marilyn was twenty-three. Pedro Armendariz and his wife, Carmen, were there, too.

"Back then the Isthmus of Catalina was a great spot for all the movie stars, especially those with boats. Humphrey Bogart and Errol Flynn and the others who owned boats would wind up at the Isthmus. It's a bay on Catalina Island where there was a fine restaurant and a Hawaiian orchestra.

"Now this is 1948 and we are all sitting at the bar. Marilyn and I are just kids. I'm sitting next to Chata, and Duke is on the other side next to Marilyn. Well, I was so busy talking to Chata about something like stopping hiccups, and I look around and Marilyn is gone. Now Duke never dances. I never saw him dance in my life. I turn around, the orchestra is playing, and Duke is dancing with Marilyn. But he's got her upside down. Her head is down at his feet and she doesn't know what to do. So I went up and said, 'Duke, you're going to make her sick, turn her right side up!'

"Again, I never thought Wayne was an alcoholic. I never believed that. He only drank when he wanted to have a good time. But he did have blackouts when he didn't remember what he did. The next day I told him. He said, 'Bullshit, I wouldn't do that. I've known her since she was a little girl. I'd never do something like that.' I said, 'Well you did!' So just to be on the safe side, when we got back to our home in the Valley, Wayne had sent her a great big bunch of flowers. But that was the way he was. He was very playful and mischievous when he drank.

"There was another story which goes back to World War II. Wayne bought this big hog ranch near Fallbrook [California] for a tax write-off or something. I was off in the navy then, so I got the story from Paul Fix. Paul, Duke, and Ward Bond went to the Duke's ranch. Paul didn't drink much, but Duke and Ward drank like crazy. They'd get drunk at the ranch, which wasn't very far from San Diego. Duke says, 'We're all out of liquor and we're going to San Diego.' Paul didn't want to go and Ward was already in bed. So he goes into where Ward is sleeping and says, 'Come on, we're going to San Diego, goddammit.' Ward is laying there on his back with his skivvies on.

"So there is Ward on his back with his very hairy chest. He told Duke he wanted to go back to sleep. So Duke took out his lighter and lit his chest. It was all in fun, but sometimes the fun kind of ran over. Anyhow they wound up going to San Diego and they tore up a whole hotel and stuff. They got the Marine Corps and the navy. They could raise a lot of hell.

"Duke was a good guy and fun to be with. But I'll tell you this. Thirty-one years ago I quit drinking and that almost broke his heart. I was getting in trouble with booze, and finally to keep my family together and to try to get more organization and productivity, I knew I had to stop. I had a lot of help and I did—no beer, no wine, nothing! This was in 1963, but from that point he couldn't accept it. Duke really did not like to lose his drinking buddies. He found out about that and it really pissed him off.

"I mentioned this to his daughter Melissa on our trip to Cannes [France] recently when we were invited there to help honor the films of John Ford at the 1995 Cannes Film Festival. She said, 'Well, he lost his drinking buddy and he didn't like to do that.' If

I really told him some of the things I was doing, maybe he would have changed his mind. But as you see, Duke could get into trouble with booze, too. He was pretty cold to me at Ward Bond's funeral, and until 1968 I never saw him again.

"Yet he was a warm wonderful guy. You never saw him turn down an autograph. The public loved him and he always said they were his bread and butter, and he loved them back.

"I'll tell you something else about him. If you ever saw him work, the first time he came on the set you would say, 'Here comes a movie star!' A whole quiet came on the set, because he was the most impressive looking man I have ever known. He was handsome and rugged and a huge guy. He had an aura that was just movie star. In those early films with Ford, he was a wonderful guy to have on the set with you. Like I said, he was a warm and wonderful guy. That was as long as you didn't get into a political discussion with him.

"But let me tell you this. Duke was no extremist. He was a Republican. He was a conservative, and he was very, very patriotic. His love for his country was real. He didn't go into service [during World War II] because he had four kids and was thirty-four years old. But he was right on the line there. His love for his country was immense. The only man I think who loved his country more was John Ford, and Ford, remember, was military. He was an admiral in the naval reserve and he filmed [the Oscar-winning documentary] *The Battle of Midway*.

"Duke was very set in his conservative beliefs. Even though I often did not agree with them, somehow I have always found political conservatives like Duke to be much warmer and friendlier on the whole than the super serious political left of the movie business. I'm not sure why, but that's the way it seems to be.

"I really believe there were some political implications in explaining why he never received more Oscar nominations. I've never been as conservative as Duke—I guess I get [my politics] from my dad. But I'm firmly convinced in my own mind that his politics and the fact that he was outspoken hurt him because most of the people who made movies back then were liberals. The thing that is strange is that when Duke met those guys he was extremely nice to them. Duke respected anybody who had definite opinions, so when he worked with those guys or met them socially he was extremely pleasant. But they thought of him as the enemy. I think that really affected the voting because most people who vote on the Academy Awards are political liberals.

"And a good actor? My God, yes! In *The Shootist, The Searchers, Three Godfathers,* he was a superb actor. A lot of people don't give him the credit he deserves. Of course I was very pleased when Duke won the Oscar in 1969 for *True Grit.* But the first thing I thought was that he should have gotten a couple before that for *The Searchers* and for *Sands of Iwo Jima.* But he was also marvelous in *She Wore a Yellow Ribbon.* He became one hell of an actor and I don't think he's ever gotten enough credit for it. You look at his eyes and the way he plays scenes, there's so much honesty in him and reality in the way he plays scenes."

5. The War Years: Dietrich, DeMille, and Dmytryk

A man's character and personality is made up by the
incidents in his life. Mine has been made up of one
thing in *reel* life, and possibly every dramatic
experience that a human being could have in *real* life.
Somewhere in between lies John Wayne. I seldom lie.

> — John Wayne, in an
> interview with David
> Sutton. The *Saturday Evening
> Post* (March 1976)

In the part of the Ringo Kid, Duke displayed a natural combination of toughness and innocence, best conveyed in one of his most enduring lines, "There are just some things a man can't run away from." Soon every studio in Hollywood was asking for him. At first, Republic Pictures, the studio which had him under contract, considered his popularity a passing fad and went on casting him in low-budget Westerns. But he was lent to other studios for larger jobs and made future commitments left and right. Eventually Republic got the message and began putting more time and money into Wayne pictures. The result was two of the biggest box office smashes in the studio's history: *Wake of the Red Witch* and *Sands of Iwo Jima*.

Yet it would be wrong to dismiss all of his low-budget Republic Westerns. *Dark Command* (1940) with Claire Trevor, Walter Pidgeon, Gabby Hayes, and a young Roy Rogers in one of his earliest roles, is a dynamic shoot-em-up venture with an excellent score by Victor Young. It also reunited Duke with director Raoul Walsh for the first time since *The Big Trail* ten years earlier. With a budget of $70,000, *Dark Command* was Republic's most expensive film at the time.

The War Years: Dietrich, DeMille, and Dmytryk

RKO jumped on the Wayne bandwagon in 1939 with *Allegheny Uprising*. Released the same year as John Ford's *Drums Along The Mohawk,* this often forgotten film deals with the similar subject of pre–Revolutionary War America. And with *Stagecoach* such a big hit, RKO decided to capitalize on the film's success by romantically pairing Wayne and Trevor once again. Led by Duke, American settlers find themselves threatened by the British on one end and Indians on the other as they attempt to settle the wild frontier. "I only played one cautious part in my life, in *Allegheny Uprising,*" Duke would tell an interviewer many years later.

Costarring George Sanders, Brian Donlevy, and Chill Wills, it played to good reviews. The *Hollywood Spectator* called *Allegheny Uprising* "clean, wholesome, without a rough spot in it." *Variety* praised the careful research in settings and costumes "heretofore neglected in the screen compilation of historical fiction."

RKO hit the target again in 1944 with *Tall in the Saddle.* The free-spirited Duke drifts into town only to find himself embroiled in a confrontation between greedy landowners and honest but helpless settlers. Wayne is also caught in a romantic triangle, having to choose between cool eastern blond Audrey Long and fiery frontier gal Ella Raines.

In 1941 Paramount cast Wayne in his first color production, *The Shepherd of the Hills.* The film was directed by Henry Hathaway, who would go on to direct Duke in five more films—including his Oscar-winning role in *True Grit*—and starred his hero Harry Carey. As young Matt, Wayne is a hot-tempered mountaineer who vows to kill the man he holds responsible for destroying his mother's life—his own father. Matt learns his father (Carey) is the stranger called "the shepherd of the hills" by the mountain people because of his many kindnesses to them. The two finally come to grips with each other, and Carey helps clear the way for Duke to live happily with his mountain sweetheart Sammy, played by Betty Field.

According to Harry Carey Jr., it was while filming *The Shepherd of the Hills,* that his mother, Ollie, gave Duke a piece of advice he would need all his professional life.

Harry Carey Jr.

"When they were making the film, Duke and my mom were sitting on the set and my dad was sitting off by himself. Duke came up to my mom and they started talking. He began [belaboring] the fact that he wanted to play more variety on the screen and that he felt that he was falling into a niche. He felt he was the same in every picture and that was bothering him.

"My mom said, 'Now wait a minute. You are a big good-looking outdoor guy. You are more or less in the mold of Harry.' She pointed at my father who was sitting a little over by the way, and she said, 'Would you like to see him change on the screen?' And Duke went, 'Well, hell no! Not in any way!' She said, 'Well, that's the way you are!' "

Yet a role Duke treasured all his life found him out of the saddle and a long way from the open range. In 1940, John Ford cast Wayne as Ole Olson in United Artists Argosy production, *The Long Voyage Home*. Produced by Walter Wanger and superbly photographed by Gregg Toland, *The Long Voyage Home* was based on four one-act plays by Eugene O'Neill that screenwriter Dudley Nichols wove into a single screenplay.

As he did with *Stagecoach,* Ford surrounded Duke with some of the best character actors in the business, including such Ford regulars as Thomas Mitchell, Ward Bond, Barry Fitzgerald, Arthur Shields, and John Qualen. Wayne played a lumbering seaman who longed to return to his home and family in Sweden.

It was a difficult reach for Duke. His character was not a man of action. Wayne's Olson may have been physically strong, but his kindness and gentle demeanor conveyed his real strength. Danish actress Osa Massen agreed to help Duke with his Swedish accent. She worked steadily with him in preparation for a major sequence where Duke would have a prolonged conversation with a bar girl played by Mildred Natwick. Wayne was concerned he'd appear silly or laughable. Perhaps he did to some. But he handled the role very well and did himself no disservice. In later years *The Long Voyage Home* became a staple for film students, something of which Wayne was particularly proud.

The War Years: Dietrich, DeMille, and Dmytryk

Duke in *The Long Voyage Home* with Thomas Mitchell (right). It was nominated for six Academy Awards, including Best Picture.

Duke has often said *The Long Voyage Home* was a turning point in his career. In the first place it was not a Western. Second, it helped him gain the confidence he needed to take on more challenging roles. *The Long Voyage Home* picked up six Academy Award nominations, including Best Picture, Best Screenplay, and Best Cinematography. It was playwright Eugene O'Neill's favorite among the films made of his work. Nineteen forty was a banner year for John Ford as well. He won his second Oscar as Best Director for his skillful work on John Steinbeck's *The Grapes of Wrath*.

After *The Long Voyage Home*, Wayne was cast opposite Marlene Dietrich in Universal's *Seven Sinners* (1940), the first of three films with Dietrich for Universal. In 1942 Wayne and Dietrich teamed with Randolph Scott and Harry Carey in *The Spoilers*. It was Wayne, Dietrich, and Scott again in 1942 in *Pittsburgh* in which "Pitt" Markham (Wayne) and Cash Evans (Scott) battle each other in business and for the affections of the beguiling Josie Winters (Dietrich).

As Ole Olson in *The Long Voyage Home*

Cecil B. De Mille seized upon Duke's newfound stature by casting him as Capt. Jack Stuart in *Reap the Wild Wind*, his lavish 1942 costume piece. The film costars Ray Milland as Wayne's adversary, Steve Tolliver, and Paulette Goddard as the enchanting Loxi Claiborne. With a supporting cast that includes Robert Preston, Susan Hayward, and Raymond Massey, *Reap the Wild Wind* became one of Duke's biggest films. Upon its original release, Milland, who was enormously popular at the time, was billed over Wayne. In the 1954 release, Milland's box office popularity had decreased and Wayne was given top billing.

DeMille's productions were big-budget extravaganzas designed to provide entertainment on a grand scale. Budgeted at four million dollars, *Reap the Wild Wind* proved no exception. It was a raucous and exciting tale of the shipping and salvage business off the coast of Georgia during the early nineteenth century.

It also was the first major film in which Duke's character died, albeit in a heroic manner, as Captain Stuart was killed by a giant squid saving Tolliver's life. By adding an element of deceit and double-dealing to his role, Duke widened his emotional and intellectual growth as an actor. Bosley Crowther of the *New York Times* was impressed, calling *Reap the Wild Wind* "as jam-full a motion picture as has ever played two hours on the screen . . . definitely . . . DeMillestone."

By all accounts Duke and DeMille got along fine, eating lunch together regularly. The director also allowed Duke to select his own costume. For his part, Duke admired DeMille's moviemaking principles, especially the way he directed crowd scenes. "[He] could take a crowd and make them not look like a mob," Duke would later say. Yet he still felt DeMille's directing skills did not match those of Ford, Hawks, or Hathaway. *Reap the Wild Wind* was nominated for three Academy Awards: Best (color) Cinematography, losing to *The Black Swan;* Best (color) Art Direction, losing to *My Gal Sal;* and Best Special Effects, for which it won.

In the meantime, Wayne was still turning out films for Herb Yates and Republic Pictures, making ten films for Yates between 1940 and 1945, including the wartime features *Flying Tigers* with John Carroll and Anna Lee in 1942 and *The Fighting Seabees* with Susan Hayward and Dennis O'Keefe in 1944. But it was RKO which gave Duke his best-remembered wartime film, *Back to Bataan,* in 1945. Produced by Robert Fellows and directed by Edward Dmytryk. Duke was at his two-fisted best as Col. Joseph Madden.

An action-packed drama set in the Philippine Islands during the dark days of World War II, *Back to Bataan* is an exciting tale of courage and resistance against Japanese forces who occupied the Islands. With the help of Captain Andrés Bonifacio (played by Anthony Quinn), Madden organizes guerrilla resistance among fugitive Americans and Filipino citizens. In time, Madden and Bonifacio cut the ground from under the Japanese defenses, and pave the way for Douglas MacArthur's triumphant return to the Philippines.

Wayne was teamed up with Marlene Dietrich and Randolph Scott in *Pittsburgh.*

It is no secret Wayne and Dmytryk were at political logger-heads throughout the filming of *Back to Bataan.* The film was enhanced by some excellent battle scenes, but his battles with Dmytryk were Duke's first confrontations with Communists in the film industry. Dmytryk and young Canadian screenwriter Ben Barzman were later named as members of the American Communist Party.

What particularly irked Wayne was the way Dmytryk and his aides treated the film's technical advisor, Col. George S. Clarke. The army assigned Clarke to the project so he could give advice on the tactics and nature of the guerrilla war in the Philippines. Clarke, one of the last Americans to leave the Philippines in 1942, was a serious and conservative career soldier. When Wayne was

Wayne and Ella Raines in *Tall in the Saddle*

not around, Dmytryk took potshots at the patriotic and church-going Clarke by ridiculing his religious beliefs and singing the Communist anthem "Internationale."

No American community was more torn apart by the forces of history than Hollywood, which housed a proportionally large number of Communists.

Duke and Dmytryk lined up on opposite sides after the war. In 1949 Duke succeeded Robert Taylor as president of the Motion Picture Alliance for the Preservation of American Ideals. Two years earlier, in 1947, Edward Dmytryk was subpoenaed by HUAC (The House Un-American Activities Committee) along with Dalton Trumbo and Ring Lardner Jr. They were part of the Hollywood Ten, the famous band of writers, producers, and directors who refused to tell the Un-American Activities Committee whether they were or were not members of the Communist party. They would spend time in jail for contempt of Congress. The HUAC hearings paved the way for the more devastating and shameful McCarthy hearings which dominated much of American life in the early and mid 1950s.

In 1989 Ben Barzman, who wrote the screenplay for *Back to Bataan* and became one of the first screenwriters to be blacklisted, wrote a retrospective in *Los Angeles* magazine called "The Duke and Me." Among other things, he recalls a moment of levity between him and Duke. It was their last meeting after completing *Back to Bataan:*

> Bob Fellows had invited us all to a New Year's Eve Party at his place. The Duke was there with his beautiful wife Chata. I had never finally been sure of the Duke's feelings about me, but when we saw each other at that party, he threw his arms wide open and broke my back in a hug.
>
> "You remember you once asked me what I thought was the reason for my success," the Duke said. "And I told you I always wondered myself. I never kidded myself it was because I was a great actor."
>
> "Yeah, I remember," I said. "And you once said some woman stopped you for an autograph, and told you why she thought all the women were nuts about you. But you couldn't remember what she said."

In *Dakota* (1945) with Mike Mazurki (leaning on bar) and Vera Hruba Ralston

"I remember now," the Duke said, with that crooked smile he was famous for.

"She whispered to me, 'You have such wicked thighs!'"

Duke's final picture for Republic during the war years was *Dakota,* released on November 2, 1945. Duke played opposite Vera Hruba Ralston. Others in the cast were Walter Brennan, Ward Bond, and Mike Mazurki as "Bigtree" Collins. Studio chief Herb Yates wanted to use Duke to help advance the career of Ralston, one of the studio's new leading ladies and Yates's future wife.

Jeanette Mazurki Lindner recalls her days with husband Mike on the set of *Dakota,* and the intriguing tale of Republic boss Yates and the much younger, foreign-born Ralston. As she says, it was a situation which presented a problem of sorts for Duke as well.

Jeannette Mazurki Lindner

"[Vera] was a skating champion and 'Papa' Yates was a married man and had children. He saw her and imported her over here, like Darryl Zanuck did with Sonja Henie. He had seen Vera skating in the newsreels after Sonja had come over here. Yates fell madly in love with her. She was a nice person and everybody liked her. She just wasn't a very good actress.

"Vera was at least twenty years younger than Yates, and he wanted to make her into a big star. Each day Yates would be on the set every minute of every hour. It was an open thing. Everybody knew this but you didn't print those things back then. Wayne just hated to work with her. If there was a love scene, Yates was all over the place. Duke mentioned this to Mike on the side. Actually, none of the leading men wanted to work with Vera because of that.

"It was uncomfortable for Duke. Yates was a hard taskmaster. That's how he got that little old nothing studio. It was way down in the Valley on Ventura Boulevard. Yates was not well liked at all, and there was no real love lost between Duke and Herb Yates. Duke would just do his job. The less they had to do with each other the better."

Also on the set as one of the production assistants was twenty-five-year-old Andrew McLaglen. It was the start of a life-long association and friendship with John Wayne. The son of Oscar-winning actor Victor McLaglen, Andy McLaglen would soon emerge as one of the best directors of Westerns in the post–World War II era. An efficient director with a strong feel for sentiment and casting, McLaglen directed Wayne in five films, including *McLintock!, The Undefeated,* and *Chisum.*

Andrew V. McLaglen

"I met John Wayne with my father when I was about nineteen or twenty. I knew John Ford's two children, Patrick and Barbara, in my early twenties, so I was up at John Ford's home quite a bit. He [Wayne] had already left Josephine and was married or almost married to Chata.

"I was a young man then, but let me tell you he was bigger than life. He sure was. He was a real regular guy as well, a guy who knew the movie business totally. Anyone who doesn't think John Wayne was smart, just doesn't know what he is talking about. He had a college education, and I always considered him to be a very cerebral guy in a lot of ways. He was interested in world affairs and politics and vitally interested in his work. He knew the movie business backward and forward.

"Because of my association with Wayne during these years, I actually was a better friend of Duke than my father was, even though my father was with Duke in four pictures, Ford's Cavalry Trilogy, *[Fort Apache, She Wore a Yellow Ribbon, Rio Grande]*, and of course, *The Quiet Man*. But that was late in my dad's career. He had known Duke when Duke was an extra in a 1928 Ford film called *Hangman's House*, so my father actually knew him as far back as when Duke was playing football at USC.

"It was 1945 when I first started in the business as a production assistant at Republic. The very first movie I ever worked on was a picture called *Dakota* with John Wayne and Vera Ralston. From then on I saw a lot of Wayne. I was one of the assistant directors on *Sands of Iwo Jima*. That was in 1949.

"After that I was the production manager with Wayne on *Hondo,* and a first assistant to William Wellman on *Island in the Sky, The High and the Mighty,* and *Blood Alley*. So during that time I saw a lot of Wayne because I was sort of a permanent member of his company.

"After *Blood Alley,* Duke knew I wanted to be a director. So Duke's brother Bob and I got together in 1955 and found a script written by Burt Kennedy, who later became a director. In 1955, we did this picture and Duke guaranteed the loan from the bank. It

57

Wayne and Anthony Quinn in *Back to Bataan* (Collection of Michael B. Druxman)

wasn't a lot. The whole picture cost $100,000 and took ten days to shoot. It was an RKO release and starred Anita Ekberg who at the time was under contract to Wayne [at Batjac].

"So in the later nineteen fifties I got to know Wayne real well. It's hard to break into directing and he helped me. Then after that I was on my own. I did four other features including *The Abductors* with my dad. In the later fifties, I was under contract with CBS and did 116 episodes of *Have Gun, Will Travel*, 96 *Gunsmokes*, some 15 *Rawhides* with Clint [Eastwood], some *Perry Masons*. Just about everything CBS did I directed. So by 1960 I had five feature films and [about] 250 television shows under my belt. That was when Wayne decided he wanted me to do *McLintock!*. That was a big stepping stone into the big features.

"My wife and I and Pilar [Wayne's third wife] and Duke were very close. At one point Pilar was one of my wife's best friends.

The War Years: Dietrich, DeMille, and Dmytryk

Dakota (1945) with
Vera Hruba Ralston

Socially we were very close. Right up until he died, I considered myself a very close friend of Duke's.

"Duke was also a terrific guy to work with. As I said, he really was a bigger-than-life figure. Somehow you never thought John Wayne would die. In fact, two people I never thought would die were John Wayne and my father. My father was a giant of a movie star before he ever worked in those John Ford Westerns. So when he appeared with Duke in *Fort Apache, She Wore A Yellow Ribbon,* and *Rio Grande,* I was already twenty-seven years old and working in pictures myself.

Duke, We're Glad We Knew You

"Duke loved Mexico. We made *McLintock!* in Tucson [Arizona] and down on the border of Nogales [Mexico]. We made *Chisum* and *The Undefeated* in Mexico and Louisiana, and we did *Cahill* down in Durango [Mexico] in 1973. I have a feeling *McLintock!* may have been the best thing he did for me, but I thought he was awfully good in *Chisum.* I loved the byplay he did with Ben Johnson. Now that we're all getting a little older, there are just not that many of us around who have worked with Duke.

"He was a fellow who had the total courage of his convictions. I always admired him for that. I think he got dunked some because of his politics, especially in the nineteen sixties. They picked on *The Green Berets* in particular and said it was just a John Wayne propaganda movie. I think he did a good job on it. It was an entertaining movie. Wayne was not an extreme right-winger and certainly no fascist like some people implied. That's just a lot of crap. I couldn't impress that more on you. And he certainly wasn't any witch-hunter. Without mentioning names, a couple of his friends were far more extreme.

"He was a conservative Republican, but in some ways he was a moderate. He'd listen to all points of view. He'd be the first one to tell you that. But Duke Wayne was a patriot. He loved his country. He loved America. And he loved the American flag.

"He was a very emotional guy, too. A lot of people might not think so, but he was. He loved to play bridge and he loved chess. In the pictures I did with him, he'd always be playing chess over in the corner. Ed Faulkner was Duke's chess partner. Ed was a good actor and a good chess player, but I don't think he ever did beat Duke. And no one was more loyal to the people he had working for him. I mean the head of transportation or the chief driver. Make-up people. He was wonderfully loyal, but if you misused that loyalty, well, that wasn't a very good idea.

"I am often asked about Duke and John Ford. It's hard for me to really put my finger on Duke and John Ford. I know Ford was close to Duke, and Duke felt close to him. It was a good relationship. It's hard for me to say if it was a totally loving relationship. Duke certainly respected him as a director. As a human being, I don't know. Dobe [Harry Carey Jr.] told Duke he should go see Jack Ford, that he was really sick. Duke said, 'He's not sick, he's just depressed because he isn't working.' He felt that. I think just as soon he found out that he was medically sick, all that changed. This was at the end of Jack Ford's life.

"Listen, Ford was quite a guy. He was a great director. Wingate [Smith] and I were assistants on *The Quiet Man*. That was a great, fun movie for me. It was a lot of work. I was a young guy. I worked my tail off. Wingate was John Ford's brother-in-law. He was a little older and let me do most of the work. Ford was really nice to me, and I know Wayne really loved the picture.

"I think *The Quiet Man* was Duke's second picture with Maureen [O'Hara]. The first was *Rio Grande* in 1950. He did five pictures with Maureen. They had a special chemistry on the screen. I feel they loved working with one another. They worked great together. They were never romantically linked in their personal lives, but they sure could transmit [romance] on the screen. You can't get better chemistry than in *The Quiet Man*.

"Personally, I just loved the picture. It was one of Duke's finest performances. My father was the only one to get nominated for an Academy Award, and as much as I like that, I feel the other people got gypped. I think Wayne should have been nominated. I think Maureen should have been nominated, and I think Barry [Fitzgerald] should have won it. I could never figure that one out.

"Shortly after we made *McLintock!*, Duke had his lung taken out. So I worked with him four times after he recovered from the original cancer. I always thought he would never have to face that again. Then in 1978 he went back to Massachusetts General Hospital and had that valve put into his heart. I went back to visit him during his operation. Then I went to Germany to make a movie and stayed in Europe to make another movie. That's when he got sick. I couldn't believe it. He died in June 1979. It's unbelievable that it's that far back now."

It is ironic that what is arguably the best of Duke's wartime pictures and one of his best films overall was a box-office flop. The war was over before the release of *They Were Expendable* in December 1945. The boys were coming home, and audiences seemed just plain tired of combat films. In fact, the late Lindsay Anderson, the distinguished British film critic and director, felt *They Were Expend-*

Years after its 1945 release, British director Lindsay Anderson would call *They Were Expendable* "The most perfect picture ever made."

able was the most perfect picture ever made. He called it "one of the few great war films . . . a heroic poem." Similarly, James Agee in his book *Agee on Film* agrees: "Visually and in detail and in nearly everything he does with people, I think it is John Ford's finest movie."

Nominated for two Academy Awards, *They Were Expendable* is based on a story by William L. White with a screenplay by Lt. Com. Frank "Spig" Wead (whom Duke would play in the 1957 film *The Wings of Eagles*). The film highlights the significance of the PT boats in the Pacific Theater following the attack on Pearl Harbor.

Ford's casting was impeccable, and his direction of the action sequences shows an excellence seldom seen in films of this era. Filmed at various locations in Florida, it was based on the semi-fictional account of two real-life naval commanders, Lt. John Buckeley and Lt. J.G. Robert Kelly, whose names were changed to Brickley and Ryan, respectively. Actor Robert Montgomery, who commanded a PT boat during the War, was chosen to play Brickley, while John Wayne gave an excellent performance as Ryan. Impulsive and sometimes volatile, Ryan's romantic interlude with Sandy, the pretty army nurse played by Donna Reed, was one of the most believable and moving of John Wayne's career. And rarely has a song so aptly fit the flavor of a motion picture as the lovely "Marquita," which Herbert Stothart integrated into his inspiring musical score.

Yet *They Were Expendable* was not a pleasant experience for Duke. From the start, he felt uneasy working with Montgomery, an authentic war hero he greatly respected. And Ford, military to a fault, humiliated Duke at every turn. He rode Duke harder than at any time since *Stagecoach*.

Harry Carey Jr.

"It was a hard film for Duke to do because of the fact that Robert Montgomery was a commander in the navy when he made it. John Ford was a four-striper on leave, and Duke was not in the service. Ford was very mean to Duke. Horrible to him in fact. Finally, Montgomery really told Ford off.

"Ford had been caustic to Duke and was lording over him because Duke didn't serve in World War II. Duke had made a lot of war pictures, so when he had to salute somebody like he had done eight billion times, Ford said, 'Jesus, Christ, don't you know how to salute?' Wayne was just shattered. It just destroyed him. According to an interview Montgomery gave Lindsay Anderson, Montgomery walked over to Ford and put a hand on each arm of the chair and looked down and said, 'Don't you ever talk to him like that again, ever!' Ford started to weep. Actually Montgomery adored Ford, but that made him very angry."

Lindsay Anderson records the text of his interview with Robert Montgomery in his book *About John Ford*. According to Montgomery, John Ford blustered, "'I'm not going to apologize to that son of a bitch,' and came out with a lot of phony excuses. Then he ended up crying. But he made it up to Duke at the end by giving him that poem to recite at the funeral scenes, 'Under the Wide and Starry Sky,' which wasn't originally in the script, as a kind of recompense."

From 1940 through 1945, John Wayne made twenty-two films. In five, he traded in Western gear for military wear and combat gear, and became the anointed military hero of the movies. Many wondered how we could have won the war without John Wayne.

Duke's assignment in Hollywood was to keep morale. Even though only ten percent of his movies have war themes, Wayne came to epitomize combat bravery and heroism. The 1942 film *The Flying Tigers* was the story of American volunteers fighting the Japanese in China's defense before Pearl Harbor. It was nominated for three Academy Awards, grossed well at the box office, and provided a powerful tool for American morale.

Staying with the air corps, Wayne played a downed American pilot in *Reunion in France* with Joan Crawford. Then he moved to a lesser known war arena, the navy construction units, when he costarred with Susan Hayward in *The Fighting Seabees* in 1944. In 1945 he did his two best World War II films, *Back to Bataan* and *They Were Expendable.*

Duke had romanced the alluring Marlene Dietrich in three films, as well as such leading ladies as Paulette Goddard, Susan Hayward, Jean Arthur, Joan Blondell, and Joan Crawford. He had made a money-making sea epic *Reap the Wild Wind* in the grandest DeMille splendor, even managing to die as a fallen hero in the process. John Wayne may not yet have become the top box-office draw, but with the war years behind him he was rapidly approaching that position. In the early post-war era, between 1946 and 1953, John Wayne would perform some of his finest and best-remembered screen roles.

6. The Hawks Connection

> Other people . . . treasure memorable moments in their
> lives: the time one climbed the Parthenon at sunrise; the
> summer night one met a lovely girl in Central Park and
> achieved with her a sweet and natural relationship, as
> they say in the books. I too once met a girl in Central
> Park, but it's not much to remember. What I do
> remember is the time John Wayne killed three men
> with a carbine as he was falling to the dusty street in
> *Stagecoach,* and the time the kitten found Orson Welles
> in the doorway in *The Third Man.*
>
> — Walker Percy, *The Moviegoer,*
> 1961

Almost from the start, John Wayne's marriage to Josephine was plagued by problems. Josie's strict Catholicism contrasted with Duke's casual religious attitudes. She wasn't enthusiastic about Duke's hard-drinking buddies, and he was generally bored by her society friends. Together they had four children: Michael (1934), Antonia Maria [Toni] (1936), Patrick (1938), and Melinda (1940). Shortly after Melinda's birth, Duke and Josie separated. Duke wanted an immediate divorce, but Josie's religious beliefs made her hesitate. After six years she finally granted him a divorce. Duke quickly married Esperanza Baur (Chata), a Mexican actress he first met in Mexico City in 1941.

That same year, Duke also became an independent producer at Republic where two people entered his life who would be vital to his professional career.

In 1936, a former law student and law clerk named Mary St. John left Kansas City, Missouri, to vacation in California. Because she could type, take dictation, and manage an office, she was able to get a job in the secretarial pool at Republic. When John Wayne made *Stagecoach,* St. John went out of her way to congratulate him on his success. Duke was impressed and appreciative. He told her if he ever needed an assistant he'd remember her. True to his word, when he established his own production company in 1946, Mary St. John became his private secretary. A pillar of unbending loyalty, she saw him through his successes and failures, his marital difficulties, his triumphs, his defeats, and his political controversies.

The second person to enter Wayne's entourage was James Edward Grant, a former Chicago newspaperman who went to Hollywood after the advent of sound in motion pictures. As a screenwriter, Grant had enjoyed such hits as *Boom Town* and *Johnny Eager,* the film which won a 1942 Best Supporting Oscar for Van Heflin. When John Ford introduced Jimmy Grant to Duke Wayne in 1940, the two became fast friends.

In early 1946 Grant wrote a script for Duke's production company called *The Angel and the Outlaw.* It was an offbeat Western about a gunfighter who renounces violence after falling in love with a beautiful Quaker girl. Grant told Duke he'd like to direct the picture himself. Duke recalled how John Ford had given him a chance. And since Grant was a friend, Duke agreed to give him the same sort of chance.

Renamed *Angel and the Badman,* the film gave nice supporting roles to old friends Harry Carey and Bruce Cabot. Duke hired Yakima Canutt to coordinate the stunts and serve as second unit director. Archie Stout, who had shot many of the Lone Star and Republic Westerns, signed on as cinematographer. And for the role of Prudence, Duke paid Paramount a lofty $125,000 for permission to cast Gail Russell. "She was just so beautiful," recalled Catalina Lawrence, the film's script supervisor. "No one, not even Elizabeth Taylor, was as beautiful as Gail."

Rumors that Duke and Gail Russell were involved in a love affair were loud enough to incur the wrath of Chata. The truth of this story seems to depend on who is telling it. Duke always denied an affair, insisting he and Gail were never more than good friends. But by all indications the two were enormously attracted to one another.

Harry Carey Jr.

"The on-screen chemistry Duke had with Maureen O'Hara was very special. But I think it was most special with Gail Russell in

With Gail Russell in *The Angel and the Badman* (1947)

Angel and the Badman. My father was in the picture, and my mother was there with him while they were filming in Sedona. My mother said he and Gail definitely had tremendous chemistry between them. Yet I don't think it ever got into a big affair. Maureen and Duke offscreen didn't have anything like that. They were good friends. That's all. But according to my mother, he had a definite attraction to Gail."

What is certain is that Gail Russell was a vulnerable, fragile, and insecure young woman, and her extreme beauty was fodder for some of the industry's more lustful power brokers. Duke treated her with a kindness and gentleness she had not experienced from many males in the picture business. Not surprisingly, she became emotionally and physically attracted to him.

Duke, We're Glad We Knew You

John Wayne and Gail Russell would work together again in
1948 as the ill-fated lovers in *Wake of the Red Witch*. As in *Angel and
the Badman,* the screen chemistry between the two was riveting.
Before she died in 1961, at age thirty-six from complications of
alcoholism, she told a producer "the one word that defines Duke
is 'honest.' He's an honest man. He can't be otherwise." Whatever
the nature of their relationship, she looked up to Duke and he, in
turn, wanted to protect and take care of her. "Gail, you just got to
say no to some of this shit," he would constantly remind her. Duke
was deeply saddened by her early death and her tragic life.

Angel and the Badman was not a big box office draw. Perhaps the
lack of sustained and substantial action so true to most John
Wayne films proved a detriment. Nevertheless, the picture was an
appealing low-budget Western which, according to the *New York
Times,* was "different from and a notch or two superior to the
normal sagebrush saga." On the whole, Duke was satisfied with the
results.

Angel and the Badman may not be the typical Wayne shoot-'em-
up adventure yarn, yet the story has a compelling warmth not
seen in many Westerns. As Quirt Evans, the injured and tired
gunman who falls in love with Prudence, Duke adds a new and
different strength to his hero image which made him all the more
appealing.

There was one small problem. John Wayne, of course, was
called "Duke" by practically everyone he worked with. But now
he was at the production end of the business for the first time.
The crew thought perhaps he could be called "Mr. Wayne" as a
matter of respect. The problem was solved the first day of shooting when someone said "Mr. Wayne" four times before receiving
an answer from Duke. Wayne remained "Duke" no matter what
level he attained in the industry.

From 1947 through 1950, John Wayne's performances in such
films as *Red River, Fort Apache, She Wore a Yellow Ribbon, Sands of Iwo
Jima, Wake of the Red Witch, Three Godfathers,* and *Rio Grande,* saw
him gain increasing favor among mainstream moviegoers. By
1950 he emerged as Hollywood's top box office draw. He remained
on Hollywood's top-ten list for sixteen consecutive years.

On October 8, 1949, eight John Wayne pictures were playing

around the country simultaneously. Moreover, for perhaps the first time, critics began to appreciate that John Wayne was a darn good actor.

"John Wayne turns in a first-rate portrayal of a ramrod, wreckage and ruin Colonel estranged from his wife and compelled to send his son on a dangerous mission," wrote the *New York Herald Tribune* in its review of *Rio Grande* (1950).

In 1946 Howard Hawks, one of the industry's top directors whose list of credits included *Sergeant York, The Big Sleep,* and *To Have and Have Not,* declared his independence of the Hollywood studio system and formed Monterey Productions. In a distinguished career dating back to the silent era, Hawks had made pictures ranging from action and adventure to crime and comedy. But he had never made a Western. He purchased the film rights to Borden Chase's story, "The Chisholm Trail," which he hoped to make into an epic Western about the first cattle drive along the Chisholm Trail.

Originally Hawks had leaned toward Gary Cooper for the part of Tom Dunson and Cary Grant for the part of Cherry Valance—a more significant role than the one eventually played by John Ireland in the movie. However, Cooper found the role too violent for his liking and Grant simply did not want to take second billing to anyone. So Hawks offered Duke $75,000 and a share of the film's profits to play Tom Dunson. For the role of young Matthew Garth, Hawks turned to Broadway and signed an outstanding actor from the New York stage by the name of Montgomery Clift.

The film was *Red River,* and it was a defining moment in John Wayne's career. *Stagecoach* made Wayne a star, but *Red River* truly made Duke an actor. His Tom Dunson is an incredibly complex man who ages in the glint of the camera's eye.

Today *Red River* stands as one of the true Western classics. The film also stars Joanne Dru, Walter Brennan, John Ireland, Harry Carey, Harry Carey Jr., and twenty-six-year-old Shelly Winters. It received Academy Award nominations for writing (Borden Chase and Charles Schnee) and editing (Christian Nyby). Also in the cast was Pierce Lyden, whose illustrious career as a B Western bad guy spanned three decades.

Eighty-eight years old, Pierce Lyden was recently awarded a

star on the Palm Springs Walk of Fame. During his career he appeared in hundreds of films opposite the likes of Roy Rogers, Gene Autry, and Bill Boyd (Hopalong Cassidy). He was on the receiving end of punches thrown by "Wild" Bill Elliott and Johnny Mack Brown. But he has never forgotten working with John Wayne in *Red River.*

Pierce Lyden

"It was just a small part that I had in *Red River.* I was a scout for the wagon train and when John Wayne tries to pull out I try to stop him. I had some good dialogue but unfortunately most of it landed on the cutting room floor. Yet Duke and I rehearsed a couple of times together and I found him to be a very nice guy. I was a darn good chess player, too, and [I] had lots of matches with Duke during the filming. I never won once. Just rehearsing my lines of dialogue with John Wayne was one of the great thrills of my life. For a long time I felt *Red River* was a very underrated Western. Now, of course, it is considered a classic.

"Mongtomery Clift was a good actor who came from the New York stage. Howard Hawks had been in New York, had seen him in a stage show, and liked him. Hawks wanted him to come to Hollywood. Then of all things he put him in a Western. Well, he [Clift] had to be trained for everything. They were fortunate in getting my friend Richard Farnsworth to help out.

"Richard was one of the great stuntmen, who later became a top-flight actor. He was nominated for an Academy Award in the movie *The Gray Fox* in the early nineteen eighties. Richard looked just enough like Mongtomery Clift so they could shoot all the close-ups. He taught Montgomery Clift how to roll a cigarette and how to ride a horse. He [Farnsworth] made Clift in the film. Clift may have been an excellent actor, but I believe Richard Farnsworth should have and could have played that part."

Bosley Crowther in his *New York Times* review of October 1, 1948, called *Red River* "one of the best cowboy films ever made,"

Wake of the Red Witch
would also team Duke
with Gail Russell

and he praised Duke for "a withering job of acting. . . . This consistently able portrayer of two-fisted, two-gunned outdoor men, surpasses himself in this picture. You wouldn't want to tangle with him!"

Similarly, *Variety* called John Wayne's performance "magnificent," while *Showman's Trade Review* called Duke's portrayal "one of the most potent characterizations of which Hollywood can boast." It was a difficult role and Duke made it work beautifully.

Duke's performance in *Red River* finally made a true believer of John Ford as well. Playing a rough, weather-beaten, middle-aged man with an axe to grind, Wayne showed Ford he had finally become an actor of merit and depth with broader range and scope than many believed possible.

Now it was Ford's turn again. Between 1947 and 1950 Ford made five Westerns under the Argosy banner: *Three Godfathers, Fort Apache, She Wore a Yellow Ribbon, Wagonmaster,* and *Rio Grande.* All were enormously popular and helped revive interest in the film

In Howard Hawks's *Red River* with Montgomery Clift and Walter Brennan

Western. With the exception of *Wagonmaster,* each starred John Wayne. Ford's Cavalry Trilogy—*Fort Apache, She Wore a Yellow Ribbon,* and *Rio Grande*—which ranks among the director's most famous works, provided audiences a panoramic landscape of the American West that has rarely been duplicated.

The first of the three was *Fort Apache* in 1947. The film called for a generous $2.5 million budget. To ensure adequate payback, Ford chose his actors with uncanny precision. Henry Fonda was cast as Major Owen Thursday and Duke as Captain Kirby York. Other roles went to Ford regulars Anna Lee, Ward Bond, Victor McLaglen, Jack Pennick, and Pedro Armendariz. Ford's old friend George O'Brien, who starred for him many years earlier in the silent film *Iron Horse,* was given a strong supporting role as Captain Cullingwood.

To enhance the film's romantic theme, Ford chose an adult Shirley Temple as Philadelphia Thursday. Temple still had great box office appeal and was paid the same amount of money ($100,000) as Fonda and Wayne. Ford also cast Temple's tall, handsome, athletic husband John Agar as Lieutenant O'Rourke, her romantic interest in the film.

Agar, the son of a Chicago Family that made its fortune in the meatpacking business, was a physical education instructor in the Army Air Corps in 1945 when he became engaged to Shirley Temple. He was first signed by *Gone With the Wind* producer David O. Selznick before Ford cast him in *Fort Apache.*

Agar would have starring roles in two more Wayne films: *She Wore A Yellow Ribbon* (1948) and *Sands of Iwo Jima* (1949), which earned Duke his first Oscar nomination. Divorced from Shirley Temple in 1949, Agar has been married more than forty years to his present wife, Loretta. After a twenty-year lapse, he appeared three more times with John Wayne in the late 1960s and early 1970s. He has never forgotten those earlier films and the enormous help and support Wayne gave him.

John Agar

"I worked with Duke three years in a row—1947, 1948, and 1949. In those days I was a young leading man. Many years later I worked with him again in *The Undefeated, Chisum,* and *Big Jake.* Duke was with me all the way in each movie I made with him. He'd always extend that much-needed pat on the back. I had nothing but the greatest affection for him. What a wonderful feeling it was because I admired him so much as a kid. What was especially nice was that he never treated me like a beginner who didn't know a thing. To the contrary, he always tried to help me out.

"Of course, I saw him on the screen long before I ever got in the business myself. I would see him on Saturday afternoons in *The Three Mesquiteers* when I was growing up. That was when he was making some of those quickie Westerns. He did a lot of those at Corriganville, Crash Corrigan's ranch. We filmed *Fort Apache* there.

73

"I was really flabbergasted when I first met Mr. Ford and he put me in *Fort Apache*. It was my first movie. What I remember about Duke was that he was very helpful and very kind. Remember, I was working with what I considered all these big stars, guys like Ward Bond, Victor McLaglen, Henry Fonda, and George O'Brien. It is no secret that Ford was pretty tough on people at times. I always thought he was a kidder of sorts, but he got rough with me a couple of times. Duke would come over to me and say, 'Don't worry about it. He's done that to me, he's done that to Fonda, he's done that to everybody.'

"I always felt John Wayne was like a big brother. Of course I worked three films with him one right after the other: *Fort Apache, She Wore a Yellow Ribbon,* and *Sands of Iwo Jima.* It was very thrilling because there is no doubt in my mind that Duke was the last of the heroes in the motion picture business. We don't have them anymore.

"I feel strongly that Duke should have been nominated for an Academy Award for his role in *She Wore a Yellow Ribbon.* He was just brilliant. Remember, too, I have a lot of scenes with him. He played a guy twenty years older. We shot that in 1948. At the time, Duke was forty-one and was playing a guy in his late fifties or sixties. To me *Yellow Ribbon* was the best thing Duke ever did. He was also great in *Sands of Iwo Jima.* He won his first Oscar nomination for that film, and I was lucky enough to have a leading role.

"When I was in the business—even today I consider it a business—Duke was very unique. He was in the top ten box office draws for close to thirty years. Nobody [else] ever did that. The big thing about Duke was that he was honest. He portrayed the parts he played with honesty and conviction. He always told me you should listen not only with your ears, but with all your senses and that a good actor pays attention to what is coming from other people he is working with. Duke was very good at that. He didn't even have to say anything and you knew where he was coming from. He always did this when he was doing a scene. Because of his listening ability, his reactions were very honest and true. He played so well off the other people he was working with. I think Gary Cooper was the same kind of actor.

The Hawks Connection

The Duke's immortal sole

"And Duke was a damn good actor, absolutely he was. I saw that right away. The actors back then put their personalities into the roles they played. Then Brando and Dean came along and tried to use method to lose their personalities in parts. I never believed in that form of acting. Look, the sincerest form of flattery is imitation. They used to imitate a lot of those people back then. Who do they imitate now? Very few—Bob Mitchum and Clint [Eastwood]. That's about it.

"Duke has endured like no one else. One of the reasons for this, I feel, is that he did a lot of Westerns. Westerns are very basic to this country and have had great staying power. Duke did a lot of movies with John Ford, and working with Ford always meant toeing the mark. My feeling has always been that Duke realized at all times that he could not have had a career without Ford. Remember, *Stagecoach* made a star of Duke. I think Duke always kept that in the back of his mind. He had tremendous loyalty to Ford. He'd be loyal to Ford even if Ford was wrong.

"I recall that Duke and Mr. Ford used to play two-handed bridge. Unlike a lot of the guys, I wasn't a card player. Duke did have strong political feelings. He was a conservative Republican, as I am. I think Duke was very much a believer in the original intent of the Constitution, as I am. He never believed much in all the things which have been added on to it. Duke was a real patriot. Don't let anyone tell you differently. The press may have gotten on his case because during the Second World War many people went into the service and Duke didn't. But he was almost thirty-eight years old and had four kids. He had a family.

"Duke Wayne was one of the most unforgettable people I have ever known. When I see him in films today, it brings back memories of one of the finest people I ever had the privilege to know. I feel extremely fortunate that I was able to work with him. He was a special guy."

Film critic Bosley Crowther called *Fort Apache* "a rootin', tootin', Wild West Show full of Indians and the United States cavalry. . . . John Wayne is powerful, forthright, and exquisitely brave." Harold Barnes in the *New York Herald Review* lauded Duke's performance as well. "John Wayne is excellent as a captain who escapes the slaughter and protects his superior's name for the sake of the service."

It was while filming *Fort Apache* that John Ford first took notice of a young wrangler and stuntman who doubled for John Agar in the picture. Ford thought no one had ever looked better on a horse, so he turned to Duke and asked the wrangler's name. The wrangler wasn't a stranger to Duke; he had doubled for him a number of times in the past. "His name's Ben Johnson," Duke said. "He's married to Fats Jones's daughter." (Fats Jones Stables, in the northeast San Fernando Valley, was one of the two biggest horse suppliers during the heyday of Westerns.)

The following year Ford cast Johnson in *Three Godfathers,* then followed by casting him in the plumb role of Sergeant Tyree in *She Wore a Yellow Ribbon.*

Filmed in Monument Valley and released in July 1949, *She Wore a Yellow Ribbon* is easily Ford's most sentimental picture, and Captain Nathan Brittles was arguably John Wayne's finest role. Also starring Joanne Dru, Victor McLaglen, Mildred Natwick, George O'Brien, and John Agar and Harry Carey Jr. as Lieutenants Cohill and Pennell, the film made an Oscar winner of Winton Hoch for his color cinematography.

Yellow Ribbon deserves to be watched and rewatched, if for no better reason than to see a composite John Wayne. It's all there: maturity, strength, sentiment, and dignity. Nowhere is it better viewed than in the scene where his troops give Captain Brittles a watch as a remembrance on the day of his retirement. Brittles fumbles nervously for his glasses, and fighting to hold back tears, reads the simple inscription: "Lest we forget. . . ." It was surely one of Duke's finest hours on the silver screen. As Bosley Crowther wrote in the *New York Times:* "Mr. Wayne, his hair streaked with silver and wearing a dashing mustache, is the absolute image and ideal of the legendary cavalryman."

Duke had not only matured beautifully as an actor, he had also become a mentor to younger actors like Agar, Carey Jr., and Johnson. When Ford made *Rio Grande,* the final film in his celebrated Cavalry Trilogy, Duke's costar was Maureen O'Hara. It was the first of five teamings of Wayne and O'Hara, who eight years earlier starred in Ford's Oscar-winning masterpiece *How Green Was My Valley.* Wayne and O'Hara would go on to become one of the most celebrated screen couples, reaching a high point two years later in *The Quiet Man,* the film for which Ford won a record fourth Best Director Oscar.

Duke gave another stellar performance as Lieutenant Colonel Kirby Yorke. Why Ford gave Duke's character the same name he had in *Fort Apache,* has never been quite determined. Certainly the two characters are different, and Ford teased a bit by adding an *e* to Yorke's name. Ford cast Claude Jarman Jr., who six years ear-

With Harry Carey Jr. in
Three Godfathers (1948)

lier had won the hearts of audiences as Gregory Peck's young son in *The Yearling*, to play Duke's estranged son Jeff, who enlists in the army after flunking out of West Point only to be assigned to his father's command as an ordinary trooper.

Rio Grande also features Harry Carey Jr., Victor McLaglen, and Chill Wills. But there are those who argue it was former stunt-man-wrangler Ben Johnson who stole the screen as Tyree, the trooper trying to stay one step behind the Indians and one step ahead of the hangman and a trumped-up manslaughter charge.

Johnson's story is an interesting one. Born in Foraker, Oklahoma, in 1919, he was working on a cattle ranch in 1939 when Howard Hughes came to Oklahoma to buy a carload of horses for filming *The Outlaw* with Jane Russell. Hughes hired the rugged young cowboy to bring the horses back to California. "When I left

Wayne, Harry Carey Jr., Ben Johnson, George O'Brien, and John Agar in *She Wore a Yellow Ribbon* (1949)

Oklahoma," Johnson would later say, "I wasn't even sure what direction Hollywood was, but I could ride a horse pretty good." Once there he began working as a stuntman, wrangler, and double for such people as Wayne, Jimmy Stewart, Henry Fonda, Joel McCrea, Alan Ladd, and Gary Cooper. He soon became one of Ford's most appealing discoveries, making his acting debut in *Three Godfathers* in 1948.

Johnson's commanding presence and distinctive Oklahoma drawl helped him become one of the top Western character actors in the fifties and sixties, with important roles in such first-rate Westerns as *Shane, One Eyed Jacks,* and *The Wild Bunch.* The only person ever to win both a World Rodeo Championship and an Oscar, Johnson stole the show at the 1972 Academy Awards when he accepted his well-deserved Oscar as Best Supporting Actor for

The Last Picture Show. He put away his unfinished speech and told the audience ". . . the longer I worked on it, the phonier it got." Then he held the shiny statue in his right hand and declared, "What I'm about to say will start a controversy around the world. This couldn't have happened to a nicer fellow."

From the carefree young man eager to ride, laugh, and fight in those marvelous Ford Westerns to his touching portrayal as an old rodeo star rescued from a retirement home by his son in *My Heroes Have Always Been Cowboys* (1991), Ben Johnson rode to film stardom with few stops. And along the way he managed to become a genuine screen icon.

A veteran of many of the best Western films ever made, Johnson, who died earlier this year, worked with John Wayne in six movies, including Duke's later pictures *The Undefeated* (1969), *Chisum* (1972), and *The Train Robbers* (1973). He spoke of Wayne with genuine respect.

Ben Johnson

"Duke was the Rock of Gibraltar for me. He helped me a heck of a lot in the picture business. I doubled for Duke way back in the nineteen forties, right after I first came out here. He was very professional and he was a great guy to work with.

"Duke was from the old school. It was honesty, realism, and respect. He had a lot of respect for himself and a lot of respect for women and children. I like that philosophy, and that's what I live my life by. I was always glad someone else felt and thought the same way. He sure helped an awful lot of people throughout the years. He was an all-around good fellow and helped a lot of kids all over the world, lots of under-privileged kids. I liked that, too.

"I made a number of movies with Duke and also spent time with him in his various cattle operations. That's how I know Duke was an honest man. I watched him make a lot of deals and a lot of swaps, and he was always an honest man. But he could get pretty mad. If someone tried to beat him out of something or be dishonest, he'd get mad. I saw him get into fights when he was mad about something.

"I was much better with horses than I was with acting, but watching John Wayne and watching John Ford direct him made it easier for me in the picture business. It's a shame there are not a lot of people around today like Duke. A lot of the younger people don't even know what honesty means.

"And old Duke was real good to work with. Anybody who would try, he would try to put up with them. If they didn't work, well, they didn't last very long. One of the toughest pictures I have ever been on was *Three Godfathers.* We were working in the sand dunes all the time. Sometimes I thought Ford was trying to destroy us. It was my first movie and Duke was real good to me. 'Ford is a mean son of a buck,' Duke would say. 'But he's my son of a buck.' If you listened to him, he was a good education. I learned a lot from him.

"I really enjoyed working with Duke in *Yellow Ribbon* and *Rio Grande. Yellow Ribbon* was one of Duke's best parts. He was real convincing. It was a good movie, a good clean movie, something you could take your family to see. We had an awful lot of fun doing it. I got a lot of pleasure running from the Indians in that one. Then in *Rio Grande,* we had quite an experience with the Roman riding [riding two horses, standing, with one foot on each horse's back]. I always liked to ride a horse and did a lot of riding in that picture. We were supposed to come up with some riding we could use in the picture to beat the upper crust. Dobe [Harry Carey Jr.] and me came up with the Roman riding and took the prize.

"We were making *The Train Robbers* in 1972. That's when they called me from Hollywood and said I better get back there because I might win an Academy Award. Well I was a cowboy and no cowboy had ever won an Academy Award, so I knew I couldn't. Well, anyhow, Duke lent Ann-Margret and me his new airplane to go to the awards. We come up there and I win that old Oscar. That's the big thing in my life. I'm the only cowboy who ever won a World Championship in the rodeo and won an Oscar in the movies. I don't know if it means anything or not, but I like to hear myself tell it anyway.

Duke, We're Glad We Knew You

"Duke had strong opinions, especially about politics. I liked that very much about him. He was an American and he didn't mind telling you he was. The last time I saw him is when he was making a commercial on the East Coast. It was for Great Western Bank, I believe. Somebody had misplaced his saddle. He called me and I brought a saddle out there. One of the horses he used was from the Donnally Ranch. So I helped furnish one of the last horses John Wayne ever used. About two weeks later he called me up early one morning to tell me that he had found his saddle. Somebody had put it under his bed in his motor home.

"When I heard he died, it was like losing part of [my] family. I felt kind of the same way when John Ford died six years earlier. But unlike Duke, I got to see John Ford when he was on his deathbed. The last thing he said to me was 'Ben, don't forget to stay real.' I never forgot that."

In the 1948 *Motion Picture Herald* poll of Hollywood's most popular stars, Wayne ranked thirty-third. By 1950 he was number one. This was due in part to Duke's marvelous work in *Sands of Iwo Jima,* one of the best war films ever. To say it was an important film for Wayne would be an understatement.

It was in 1948 that producer Edmund Grainger ran across the phrase "sands of Iwo Jima" in a newspaper and thought instantly of Joe Rosenthal's famous photograph of a group of marines planting the American flag at the summit of Mount Surabachi. The Marine Corps encouraged the making of movies about marines, and justifiably. The army, navy, and air corps had been glorified in such films as *The Story of GI Joe, Thirty Seconds Over Tokyo,* and *They Were Expendable.*

Yet a cinematic classic about the marines was sorely missing. After some initial reservations about Republic's ability to deliver a first-rate war film, the marines signed on with the project, promising Grainger the use of Camp Pendleton as the location for filming and all the equipment and technical advice that was available.

Directed by Allan Dwan, this superb picture is enhanced by some of the most stunning actual combat footage ever filmed. John Wayne portrays the hard-nosed sergeant who tries to mold his young recruits into Marines. The recruits hate his unyielding

Wayne was nominated for a Best Actor Oscar for *Sands of Iwo Jima* in 1949 but lost to Broderick Crawford for his performance in *All the King's Men*.

toughness, but he finally wins their respect when he leads them into combat.

Duke became fully committed to the role of Sergeant Stryker. He continually badgered the film's technical advisors, observing and studying the movements and behavior of a tough drill instructor. As he did with the role of Ethan Edwards in *The Searchers,* he *became* Sgt. Stryker in *Sands of Iwo Jima,* his assistant, Mary St. John, recalled. The plaudits for Duke's performance were near unanimous. "John Wayne may be everybody's idea of a good actor. He was immense in *Iwo Jima.*" wrote Walter Winchell, the most influential columnist in America at the time.

The *New York Times* also jumped on Wayne's bandwagon. "Wayne is especially honest and convincing, for he manages to dominate a screenplay which is crowded with exciting battle scenes. His performance holds the picture together. . . ."

John Agar, one of Duke's costars in *Sands of Iwo Jima,* recalls Wayne's performance with clarity.

John Agar

"I played Pvt. Conway, one of the hostile recruits Stryker won over. In the beginning, Conway gives Stryker a lot of trouble. He is in the marines only because his father and grandfather had also been marines. He resents his father and hates Stryker because of his connection with his dad. Then as the picture goes on, he realizes what a jerk he has been and how right Stryker has been all along. Stryker gets killed at the end, and it is Conway who pushes the troops forward.

"I had great affection for John Wayne, which helped me play off him as well as some people say I did in the picture. In one scene when I am reading a letter from my wife, who is played by Adele Mara, a grenade lands by me and he pushes me out of the way to save my life. Then in the end when Duke is shot by a sniper, I finish reading his unfinished letter to his son.

"Sergeant Stryker was right down Duke's alley. It showed the tough part about him, [and] the soft part about him. It was really very much like him. His eyes expressed such conviction that when I spoke my lines it just seemed as if [we were having a regular conversation]. He was very encouraging at all times and told me repeatedly what a good job I was doing. I've never forgotten that."

Sands of Iwo Jima was nominated for four Academy Awards: Best Story, Best Editing, Best Sound, and a long-awaited Best Actor nomination for John Wayne. He joined Kirk Douglas (*Champion*), Gregory Peck (*Twelve O'Clock High*), Richard Todd (*The Hasty Heart*), and winner Broderick Crawford (*All The Kind's Men*) as the year's nominees. It would be twenty years before Duke would receive another Oscar nomination. But his peers had finally taken notice.

7. The Producer: Boetticher and "The Bullfighter and the Lady"

> I remember once he said to me, "Hank, you old son of a bitch. Always tell it how it is. Because then tomorrow you won't be wondering what you were lying about yesterday."
>
> — Hank Worden, *Standing Tall*
> 1989

On March 3, 1952, *Time* magazine made Duke the topic of its cover story, trying to put a spin on some of the reasons for his enormous popularity. After all, his legs were not as pretty as Betty Grable's; his voice was not as sweet as Bing Crosby's; and he was not nearly as funny as Dean Martin and Jerry Lewis. Duke's response to the puzzle was probably the best anyone could offer. "All I do is sell sincerity, and I've been selling the hell out of that ever since I got started."

He was forty-four years old, a craftsman who had learned his trade, and a businessman who truly believed in the product he was selling. Moreover, he exercised as tight a control over his films as any big-name star. He insisted on simple stories and sympathetic parts that best fit his personality and the dialogue he used so effectively. It worked. By mid-1950 when the movie industry was at a low point, nine Los Angeles theaters were showing different John Wayne movies. The March 3, 1952, issue of *Time* quoted one weary producer's outburst about the gripings of his associates: "What they're all trying to say is that there's nothing wrong with this damned industry that a dozen John Waynes couldn't cure."

John Wayne made ten pictures between 1947 and 1950, of which seven were Westerns. By contrast, between 1950 and 1956

Boetticher and "The Bullfighter and the Lady"

With Maureen O'Hara and Claude Jarman Jr. in *Rio Grande* (1950). The last of Ford's Cavalry trilogy, this was the first of five Wayne films with O'Hara.

he made eleven films, but only *Hondo* (1953) was a Western. He was ex-boxer Sean Thornton in *The Quiet Man,* a down-and-out football coach rebuilding the fortunes of St. Anthony's College in *Trouble Along the Way,* a civilian army transport pilot who brings his plane down in icy uncharted territory in *Island in the Sky,* and a disgraced copilot whom fate lends a second chance in William Wellman's *The High and The Mighty.*

With an all-star cast, *The High and the Mighty* was nominated for six Academy Awards, more than any John Wayne film except *Stagecoach, The Quiet Man,* and *The Alamo.* The film won for the musical score of Dimitri Tiomkin, who also scored *Red River, Rio Bravo,* and *The Alamo.*

During this period, Duke was also a producer at Republic. His first venture into production had been *Angel and the Badman* in

1947. In 1949 he produced *The Fighting Kentuckian* for Herb Yates. In 1952 he teamed with Bob Fellows to form the Wayne-Fellows Production Company, which produced *Big Jim McLain* in 1952, and *Island in the Sky* and *Hondo* in 1953.

In 1950, a thirty-four-year-old former bullfighter named Budd Boetticher needed financial backing for a proposed film venture. He gave the script to his friend Andy McLaglen, who in turn handed it to John Wayne's favorite screenwriter, James Edward Grant. Grant liked the script and set up a meeting with Wayne. Wayne then arranged for Herb Yates at Republic to finance the film. The film, *The Bullfighter and the Lady,* was instrumental in making Budd Boetticher a distinguished and respected director.

While the association between Wayne and Boetticher was fraught with confrontation and combat, it was also based on mutual respect.

Today Budd Boetticher ranks among the greatest living directors. His films are studied in film schools both here in the United States and abroad. In fact, Boetticher has become a cult figure in many circles. In Europe his films are enormously popular and critically acclaimed. Boetticher recalls those halcyon days of the early nineteen fifties when he was as close as anyone to John Wayne. While they had many verbal "shootouts" Boetticher makes one point clear: "Had it not been for John Wayne there might not have been a Budd Boetticher. I probably would have been Oscar Boetticher Jr., making B pictures the rest of my life."

Budd Boetticher

"I knew about Duke long before I met him and he helped produce *The Bullfighter and the Lady,* the film which really launched my career. The best way to describe my association with Wayne was that he was my best friend or my deadliest enemy according to how he woke up in the morning, but I loved the guy. In fact, when they were honoring me in London last year, someone said to me, 'Mr. Boetticher, if you had one thing to do over again in your career what would it be?' And I said I would probably be a lot

Wayne and family circa 1951.

nicer to John Wayne. Because I fought him. But that's been my personality.

"Duke actually produced two of the very best of my fifty-two films: *The Bullfighter and the Lady,* and *Seven Men From Now.* That's the film which started Lee Marvin's career and was the first of seven films I did with Randolph Scott. Five of those were written by Burt Kennedy.

"*The Bullfighter and the Lady* was quite an experience for me. Duke and I fought all the time. But without him I wouldn't have had a career. This is a story I like to tell which really shows the good side of Duke.

"It was the first day of filming. I usually like to start with a sensitive scene instead of the physical stuff. Now Bob Stack was the richest boy in Bel Air, but he couldn't get a job. He had no career until *Bullfighter and the Lady*. Well, he was standing on the porch doing a scene with a couple of other actors. Duke came around right in the middle of the first scene and grabbed Bob around the lapel and said, 'Jeeze, if you're gonna play the part, play it like a man!' Duke wanted him to play it like John Wayne, and the part didn't call for that.

"Well, Duke did that about five straight times. So talk about stupidity! Here I was Oscar Boetticher Jr., but I told Duke Wayne I wanted to talk with him. He said, 'What's the matter, Bood?' (That's what he called me.) I said to him, 'Do you think you can direct the picture better than I can? You walked right in front of the camera and I'm the director. I'm nobody yet, but I am going to be big one day. And if you think you can do the picture better than I can, considering I've been a bullfighter and have really written the script—Duke cut me off. 'Or?' he said. 'Or I'll go home,' I said.

"So he went out, God bless him, and he stood in front of my crew and said, 'Ladies and Gentlemen. I have implicit faith in my young director here and what he says goes! He suggested that I go home, and I'm going home. And I'll be back when we give a party for you after the picture.' And he did. That was pretty great!

"I met Duke at the airport about three weeks before *The Bullfighter and the Lady* was about to start. Whenever Duke and Chata went to the airport to go to a foreign location, they never got there together. If they had to wait for an hour to get on a plane, they would go to the bar. Duke arrived in Mexico City, and when he got off the plane, he was alone. He had had a few belts. He had this big cowboy hat and his Western suit. He really looked more like John Wayne than anyone else in the world.

"So we arrived at the hotel and went downstairs to the bar. It was quite crowded for a Saturday night. This guy comes in the bar. We later found out he was from Kansas City. Anyhow, he looks at Wayne and says, 'I'm great at names. I know you, but I don't know who you are. But I'll associate you with a city, and I'll tell you in five minutes your name.' Well, Duke looked at him and said, 'That would really be great.' So he had another martini. It seems everybody in the bar knew Wayne except this guy. So the conversation went something like this:

THE GUY: Hey, buster! Spend any time in the West?
DUKE: I live out West.
THE GUY: In San Francisco?
DUKE: I've been there.
THE GUY: It still doesn't ring a bell, but don't tell me.

"So we have another drink. I have a beer. Duke has another martini. When he drank and he was sitting down, he got taller and taller and taller. Now he is about 6'4" and is furious and wants to kill this guy. Everyone is in on this except this idiot they should never have let out of the country. So the fellow continues:

THE GUY: I'm going to take another shot at you. This is like trying to think of a song at night, it drives me crazy, goddammit. I'll get it. Any time in the East.
DUKE: I've been all over the East.
THE GUY: Boston?
DUKE: Nope.
THE GUY: OK. I'll tell you.
DUKE: OK Do that.

"So we go another five minutes and the fellow says: 'Last shot! Spend any time in the Middle West?'
DUKE: I've been all over the Middle West. Pick a town.
THE GUY: I give up! What's your name?

"Now, God, Duke's been waiting for this.
DUKE: John Wayne.
THE GUY: Cincinnati, maybe?

91

"Well, I fell on the floor. I said, 'Come on, big shot! Nobody knows you down here. It didn't mean a thing to this idiot from Kansas City.'

"Anyway, Wayne was Wayne, and I probably knew him better than anyone else over a period of a few years, and then I never saw him again. He ended up not liking me. I fought for what I stood for and we got into it a few times.

"Now, Duke really couldn't box. But if he ever hit you, he was one of the strongest man I've ever seen in my life. And when we were drinking, he'd really hate my guts. He thought I was cocky and wasn't as good as I thought I was. One time we were standing in front of a big new Electrolux refrigerator which was as tall as Duke. And he reared back to hit me. He had what we called a bourbon and a glass. He never put anything in it except for a little ice. He reared back and telegraphed his punch. I was a boxer and slipped to one side and he hit my refrigerator and sprung the door. I gave the refrigerator to [actor] Walter Reed, and that was the great thing in Walter's house. Duke's fist was implanted in the refrigerator. Tyson couldn't have matched that. It was like the Angel Gabriel slept here.

"Jimmy [James Edward] Grant was Svengali as far as Duke was concerned. Jimmy was such a problem that he became president of Alcoholics Anonymous in Los Angeles. You had to have been a hell of a drunk to do that. We were in Mexico, and Jimmy had a thirty-six-page treatment of a script. Duke and Chata and Katy Jurado and me were sitting in the bullring one day. Jimmy Grant had disappeared for two weeks. We couldn't find him anywhere. Duke says, 'Well he does this kind of thing. He holes himself up, but he'll come up with a good script.'

"There were eleven seats to our right in the front row in Plaza, Mexico. In those days the women wore damned near evening gowns and fur coats, and the men were in suits or uniforms. It was very formal and these eleven seats were empty. All of a sudden there is a hustle and bustle behind us and here comes Jimmy Grant with ten hookers, and he had been living in a whorehouse. Chata turns to Duke and says, 'If you even smile at one of those women, I'm going to slap you.'

"Duke had a preference for Latin women. I think this is because he was very uncomfortable with American women. I think the Latin women were brought up to be more subservient. They were brought up in the Catholic Church. Men were their idols, and John Wayne was an idol. He had three wives. They were all Latin women: Josephine, Chata, and Pilar. Guys like Frank Sinatra and John Wayne are both bastards and both [saints]. Most people, I think, were totally in awe of the guy. He was absolutely great, but he did have warts which could make him difficult.

"One of the funniest stories told to me about Duke was when he was making *The Green Berets* in 1968. Duke was having some trouble with the technical people from the Green Beret units. In fact, the studio called and was going to bring the picture home because, as a director, Duke could be difficult and some of the Green Beret people didn't want to work with him any longer.

"So the studio sent for Mervyn LeRoy who was head of Santa Ana Racetrack. Mervyn was a distinguished old director. Well, Duke heard about it in about five minutes. He was waiting for Mervyn to show up on the set. Mervyn showed up from his private plane, walked in from behind, and said 'Hello, John!'

"Of course, anybody who called Duke 'John' didn't know him very well. Duke asked him what he was doing here. He replied that the studio thought they might help him. Duke told him to go you-know-what. So Mervyn turned around and headed for the plane. Michael [Wayne] ran up and said, 'J.W.' (he called [his dad] J.W.) don't you realize that's our last shot here? If he goes home they're going to cancel the picture. 'Well, what do you want me to do?' Duke replied. Michael told Duke he had to go to the airport with him and apologize.

"Well, apologize was a word Wayne never bothered to look up. He says, 'Jeeze, Jeeze Christ!' So they get in the car and arrive at the airport. Mervyn LeRoy is walking up the gangplank. Duke says, 'Merv, where are you going?' Well, John, I'm going home,' he replied. Wayne said, 'For Christ's sake, why?' Merv said, 'You told me to go f— myself!' Duke says, 'I tell everybody to go f— themselves, what's so special about you?' Mervyn LeRoy burst out laughing and came back.

"When Duke's production company, Batjac, wanted to make *Seven Men From Now*, which was released in 1956, Duke called Burt Kennedy and me. Burt wrote five of the films we did with Randolph Scott. They are classics now. They teach them in cinema [classes]. I've seen them lately in tributes to me and they're wonderful shows. And they started the careers of guys like Lee Marvin, Pernell Roberts, James Coburn, and Craig Stevens. We made a new star every time.

"In *Seven Men From Now* we had a scene in the river when Walter Reed was washing a horse with Randy [Scott]. Duke called us in the office and I don't think he knew that I knew a hell of a lot more about horses than he did. He told us we were going to get calls from all over the United States. How could we do a thing like that? I asked him what he meant. He said we couldn't wash a horse in the river. 'Who says?' I answered. 'Do you think we carry buckets? If the river's there, we put horses in the river and wash the horse, Duke!' Duke just raised hell. Of course, we never got letters. And the film was a fantastic hit.

"I think Duke was always sorry he didn't play the hero [in *Seven Men From Now*]. I recall that Duke came in to have coffee with Burt [Kennedy] and me one morning. He said, 'Bood and Burt, who do you think should play this fellow in the picture?' Out of respect for him we said, 'Duke, we want you to do it.' But for some reason he suggested Randolph Scott. So we made seven fine films with Randy Scott.

"As an actor I thought he [Wayne] was wonderful. As a performer, there was no one in the world like Duke. He played John Wayne better than anybody in the world. The man had style. He was Duke and he was fascinating and he was tough. But I don't think I could have directed him. I couldn't have lasted halfway through a picture with him. Either I would have quit, or Duke would have fired me. But he did produce two of my best pictures, *Bullfighter and the Lady* and *Seven Men From Now*. In Europe, some people think of *[Seven Men From Now]* as the best Western ever made.

"Although I was really just close to him for a couple of years in the early fifties, I always knew he would just get bigger and bigger. They had to give him an Academy Award for *True Grit*. They finally realized he had slipped past them and he had to have it. I think his pictures with Howard Hawks were wonderful. *Red River* and *Rio Bravo* were two of his best. But Wayne could push his weight around better than anybody but John Ford. I thought Hawks and Ford got the absolute best out of Duke as an actor.

"He played well on the screen with a lot of leading ladies, but I think his screen chemistry with Maureen O'Hara was very special. Maureen made a picture with me, and of all the leading ladies I had, she was head and shoulders above all of them. She was my big, big favorite. But I think he was more fond of Gail Russell than any of them. And I think Duke had a crush on her. She was my leading lady in *Seven Men From Now*. In fact, he wanted her in the picture. I think she was the one leading lady that he really cared about in anything but a professional way.

"I'll tell you when we stopped talking to each other. I was across from Universal one night at my prop man's bar. My friend Eddie Keyes had a bar across from Universal. I had a new Jaguar and it was getting its ten-thousand-mile check. So I was waiting for them to deliver it to me. I was down at the bar with this big, long mirror, and the bar was empty. I was sitting with Eddie Keyes and in comes Duke's chauffeur with an actor I didn't know. I said, 'How are you, Murph?' He said, 'How are you, sir.'

"Murphy asked me when I was going to join Duke's little group of guys. I told him I was a lousy tenderfoot scout and had quit the Boy Scouts in two weeks. Duke was a true patriot, but I thought he waved the flag a little too much. I was an officer in the navy during World War II, but Duke could be pretty stubborn on certain things. I couldn't get into his flag-waving as much as a lot of other guys, and this is what eventually severed our close friendship.

"No one has sustained himself after death like Duke. First of all, he had that God-given size. He had a personality that was as dogmatic and opinionated as you can get. And he could terrify anybody except John Ford and me, I guess. Remember I had been a bullfighter, so when people ask me I just say, 'What could Wayne do that is as frightening as those bulls?'

"He had that personality that every kid in the world wanted to [have]. You know, when I introduced my beautiful wife to him and he shook hands with her, his hand actually encompassed hers and you couldn't see a finger. She said she'd never shaken hands with anybody like that in her life.

"I hate the expression, but Duke Wayne really was bigger than life. I think Andy McLaglen was on target when he said the two people he never thought would die were his dad and Duke Wayne. You didn't think Duke could die. He was a very, very special man. Although we didn't end up very good friends, I would have done anything in the world for him because I really loved him. I go back to what I said earlier: If it had not been for John Wayne, there might never have been a Budd Boetticher. And yes, I wish I had been nicer to him."

The Budd Boetticher-John Wayne connection is well-chronicled by veteran actor Walter Reed. Reed, whose résumé includes more than four hundred television shows and 150 movies, began his acting career as a leading man, playing opposite the likes of Lucille Ball, Anne Shirley, and Paulette Goddard. Unlike many leading men, however, he made the transition to character roles early in his career and soon became one of the best known and most successful character actors in the business.

Like John Wayne, Reed wasn't a cowboy per se but fit in with cowboys very well. In addition to *Seven Men From Now,* he appeared with Wayne in *The High and the Mighty* and Ford's *The Horse Soldiers* with William Holden. Reed also spent more time with Duke as an offscreen pal. Now eighty-three years old, Walter Reed lives in Santa Cruz, California.

Walter Reed

"I'll never forget the first time I met Duke Wayne. I was with Budd Boetticher, and Duke was at Budd's home. Before then, while I was certainly aware of him, he was just another actor to me. I was impressed with his work. I'll tell you something. When Duke was around, on or off the screen, you knew he was there. He was a very, very natural guy. Not a phony bone in his body. He told it like it was. He liked hanging around the stuntmen a lot. And at times he was just like a little kid. He really liked to have fun. And if you were good, he told you so. I always liked that.

Boetticher and "The Bullfighter and the Lady"

"Well, getting back to that first time I met him, Duke had put up some money for Budd's film. It was *The Bullfighter and the Lady.* As I said, Duke was over at Budd's house and we had a lot of fun that night. The next night he calls and says, 'Hey, I want to talk with you again, Budd.' So he came over and we all had a few drinks. Then a little before ten he says, 'Hey, I'm hungry, let's go out to eat!' So Budd and his wife and me and my wife went to the Tail of the Cock restaurant with Duke. It was located in the Valley. It was just as they were closing, so Duke suggested we go over to a little Italian place across the street.

"Budd and I were busted. It wasn't a good time financially for either of us. But we went to that Italian restaurant with Duke and had a wonderful dinner—lots of drinks and all kinds of good food. After dinner we had a few more drinks. We were all laughing and feeling great. Then all of a sudden Duke disappeared. I said, 'My gosh, where's Wayne?'

"The guy at the door tells us Duke left, that Duke was 'feeling no pain.' He told us Duke had a deal with the cops. If he thought he had too much to drink, they would take him home. It was a very smart deal. He did shows and charity things for the cops, so if he ever got so crocked he couldn't drive, they would take him home.

"We were petrified. I only had two dollars, and Budd's wife had a dollar. My wife didn't have a darn cent with her. So we got to thinking about it. I said, 'As long as we are going to wash dishes, why don't we have another drink?' So we ate the fancy desserts and had a few fancy after-dinner drinks.

"Finally, my wife said, 'Well, I guess the time has come. Who's going to wash dishes and who is going to dry and stack them?' We were laughing. The moment of truth had come. I said to the waiter, 'Our bill, please.' And the manager came over and said, 'There's no bill. Mr. Wayne left a blank check!' From then on I loved Duke. This was my introduction to John Wayne.

"I went over to his house in Encino a couple of times with Budd Boetticher. One night it was raining like mad, and after we said good night to Duke we got stuck in the mud. We couldn't get the cart out. The cops came. They asked us what we were doing and we replied that we had been visiting John Wayne next door.

The cop said, 'John Wayne? He wouldn't live in a place like this.' It wasn't a fancy place, so how could the biggest movie star in the country live there? So they went to the door with us. We ring the bell and Duke opens the door. Now Duke wore a little hairpiece sometimes. And the cop says, 'These fellows say they were with John Wayne.' He says, 'Well, I'm Duke' in that inimitable style. The cop says, 'You don't look like John Wayne.' And Wayne says, 'What the hell do you want me to do? Go in and put my hairpiece on?' Well, the cops came in and got a couple of autographs. Then they helped pull us out of the mud.

"In 1954 I did *The High And The Mighty* for William Wellman. I was the guy who put the small boy on the plane. Wellman's son Mike played my son in the picture. I say to the boy something like, 'Tell your mother there shouldn't be an ocean between us.' Then the boy sleeps on the plane all through the picture.

"Actually, I had been up for another part—a bigger part opposite Laraine Day. Andy McLaglen had me come to Wellman's home to have me interviewed. Since Duke was producing the picture, we went over to Batjac to get the script. I went there and stood outside Bob Fellows's office. He had produced *Bombardier* ten years earlier when I was the leading man to Anne Shirley. I heard him say to the assistant director: 'Walter Reed! I don't want some stock boy doing this part.' He came out stammering and said something like the script wasn't ready yet. Then he talked Wellman out of using me. Wellman gave me another part that wasn't nearly as big.

"So after I got through with the scene, Wayne comes over to me and says, 'Wellman's really mad.' I asked him why. Duke said, 'He really liked you in the scene and why did he let that jerk talk him out of using Walter Reed?' He [Wellman] couldn't stand John Howard, the fellow who did the scene. He thought he was stiff. Wellman took a liking to me now. A short time later he arranged for one of his friends to give me the lead in a sleeper of a picture called *Macumba Love*, which we filmed in Brazil.

"Duke also produced *Seven Men From Now*, which is the best film I ever made. Duke produced it, but Randy Scott starred in the picture. After Wayne saw it, he wished he had done the part himself. He would have been magnificent in it. Batjac produced a lot of stuff, and I really don't know why he didn't take the part after reading the story. Duke was very hurt because Warner Brothers released it as the second end of a double feature behind some English space movie. It was released very badly. It was a very good film that somehow did not get feature billing. Budd Boetticher directed it and a great writer named Burt Kennedy wrote it.

"I thought Duke was wonderful in *The High and The Mighty*. It was a good story and was written by one of his good friends [Ernest Gann]. It was a big hit. You know Duke always gave you a cup when you worked with him. It would say, 'To Walter from Duke.' And on the back it would have the name of the film. I gave one to a neighbor of mine years ago because he was such a big *High and the Mighty* fan. I'm sorry I did this because Wayne is such a big legend now. I gave another one to the University of Wyoming. Chuck Roberson, his stuntman and a very good friend of mine, had more than thirty of them.

"Yet as good a performance as he gave in *The High and the Mighty*, it was a bit too straight for me. I liked him better in Westerns. I liked him in a cowboy outfit. Duke was some kind of person. Like me, he wasn't a Westerner in the traditional mold, being born in the Midwest and raised in Southern California. But he learned all the Western skills very well. He was a natural. And when you got to know him he was a very funny guy with a great sense of humor.

"Wayne always wanted to be a director. When we did *The Horse Soldiers*, he'd try to second-guess Ford. Right before a scene he'd say, "Walter, why don't we do it this way. You do this. . . .' I'd say, 'Duke, if the old man. . . .' He'd look at me and say, 'Shhh!' He didn't want the old man to hear anything. He didn't want me to say to Ford, 'Well Mr. Wayne told me to do it this way' or something to that effect.

"It was funny because Duke didn't do it maliciously. He had ideas—a lot of good ideas. Duke would kind of smile at me and say, 'Don't tell him.' Ford was the only guy who could tell Wayne anything. He had a lot of respect for the old man. But some of Duke's ideas were so good that if Ford called me on it, I'd tell the old man something like 'I thought *you* wanted it that way.'

"I got to liking Wayne very much. We'd go to Duke's house to drink with him and play poker. He was a good guy to drink with. But it's a funny thing. He would not drink or anything when we were working. He kept in good shape during the week. It showed. He never missed lines. He was prepared when he went on there. He just loved to have fun. Yet he wasn't a ladies' man. And he wasn't a womanizer. He married all his women except Pat Stacy, and she was like a wife to him. She did everything for him when he was sick. Whenever he was on a show, instead of going out each Saturday, he ran an all-night poker game. He just plain liked that.

"I've always admired Wayne because he stood for what he believed. He could have gotten into a lot of trouble with people in the industry who didn't share his beliefs. For example, if someone like Jane Fonda was producing she could have cooled him. It was never any phoniness with Duke. Like Ford, he was a real patriot. Remember that wasn't a popular position back then. I came from a military family myself. My father retired from a military career in 1923, and my son flew thirty-seven combat missions in Vietnam. He said it may have been the wrong war, but the politicians wouldn't let us win it. That's basically what Duke was saying during Vietnam.

"There were two schools of thought. But I really admired Wayne's courage to stand up for something that may have killed him in the business. Much of the political left used the same kind of McCarthy tactics in the sixties that were used against them in the fifties. At times Wayne may have punched things a bit too hard to get his point through. But when you were with him, he didn't say anything like 'Walter, let's go salute the flag.' What he said was always out in the open, and I respected that.

"There are so many great stories that people tell about Wayne, and granted that they are second hand, they are probably true. One of my favorites is about a Gillette ad. They wanted Wayne to do a razor ad. It was on a boat, a merchant ship, and there was a young lieutenant in the scene with him. They offered Duke a million dollars to do the thing. He wanted to know who the young lieutenant would be. They said they would get a stock actor to do it, a guy they could pay minimum. Duke says, 'I'll tell you what! I'll do it on one condition. You give the million dollars to Pat [his son, Patrick] and give me scale instead.' It's a great way of giving your kid money without it being inherited.

"There's another story about when he was directing *The Alamo*, which I like to tell. When they were filming the picture, there was a barrier where cars had to stop before they could proceed any further. Well, one guy goes right through the barrier, right past the guy who is signaling him to stop. It was a Cadillac, and when Duke sees this he is furious. He gets into a jeep with some other guy and goes over there.

" 'What the hell are you doing?' he yells. Well, this big Texan gets out of the Cadillac, and boom, he hits Duke. Duke falls all the way across the street on his back. He gets up, brushes himself off and says, 'OK, let him go.' I don't know if it is a true story for sure. But it's a great story. Because it would be just like Duke. He would say, 'Hey, this guy is pretty good!'

"I can't place the exact qualities which have made Duke such a lasting legend. You know it's there, but it's hard to pinpoint. I'm not sure anybody really can. His way of talking was very simple and direct. He didn't give long soliloquies, and he had the ability to listen. He never tried to upstage anybody. If it was your scene, he let you be the star. Of course, he was going to get those close-ups, because Ford was going to see [to] that.

"Duke Wayne was a straight shooter, a real straight shooter. If he liked you, he was loyal as all hell. But he didn't like ass-kissers. He could see right through you. He never went around with a swelled head like some of these guys today. In the old days we would have thrown some of these people off the set. Duke liked genuine people. Jimmy Stewart was another one just like Duke. They really liked each other because neither guy was a phony.

"John Wayne was a real good guy, a real professional, and a very good actor. Don't let anybody tell you differently. He could act. And he really was bigger than life. What a friend once said about Lawrence Welk in the music business can be applied to Wayne: 'I don't know what he had, but he sure had it.' Duke had it then. And he has it now. Even with Gary Cooper and people like that, it just wasn't the same.

"Maybe the best word I can use is *stature*. Wayne had stature. That's an important word for a hero. And he never lost that stature, not even when he was ill at the Oscar ceremony a couple of months before he died in 1979. To the very last, Duke Wayne had stature. I think that's what people see today."

8. Hondo Lane and "The Quiet Man"

> One of the best things you can say about Duke is that he was a swell guy when he was making fifty bucks a week, and he's an even better guy now that he's making a half a million a year.
>
> — Actor Grant Withers, *Time*, March 3, 1952

In 1952 Dwight D. Eisenhower was elected the country's thirty-fourth president, and peace and prosperity loomed ahead. Bob Mathias captured his second successive decathlon Gold at the Olympics in Helsinki, Finland, and a Texas schoolboy named Dean Smith won a Gold Medal for the United States in the one-hundred-yard dash. The year 1952 was also the year of *The Quiet Man*, which would make John Ford the only four-time Oscar-winning director in cinema history.

Rarely has a film been afforded as many accolades as *The Quiet Man*. St. Patrick's Day can't go by without movie fans around the land being privy to this splendid film. As Sean Thornton, John Wayne gives a definitive portrayal. Few films have ever been more fun to watch.

Thornton is a prize fighter who, after killing a man in the ring, retires to the tiny Irish hamlet where he was born. He quickly falls in love with a fiery redheaded colleen named Mary Kate Danaher, played by Maureen O'Hara. This was the second teaming of Wayne and O'Hara, who worked together for the first time two years earlier in *Rio Grande*.

From the moment their eyes lock early in the film, the chemistry is electric. Rarely has a love scene been played out on the screen so well as when Sean and Mary Kate are caught in the rain. The looks on their faces tell all they want to say but dare not speak. The screen chemistry between John Wayne and Maureen O'Hara

Hondo Lane and "The Quiet Man"

With Maureen O'Hara in *The Quiet Man*

can be matched by only a few screen couples such as Alan Ladd and Veronica Lake, Spencer Tracy and Katharine Hepburn, and Humphrey Bogart and Lauren Bacall.

"My father was a major movie star, and I think you have to kind of explode off the screen to be larger than life. And I think Maureen was the woman who could match him on the screen," says Michael Wayne. "Something happened on the screen. There was an electricity there. She could match John Wayne kiss for kiss, punch for punch, stride for stride."

Harry Carey Jr. knew Wayne and O'Hara well and worked with both of them.

Harry Carey Jr.

"Maureen and Duke offscreen didn't have anything going on like the attraction between Duke and Gail Russell. They were good friends, that's all. Nevertheless, Chata came down to the location because she was worried about Duke and Maureen. Chata had nothing to worry about because Duke took marriage seriously. A lot of girls used to come on to him, but he never really paid any attention to them."

The Quiet Man began in 1933 when the *Saturday Evening Post* published a simple short story by Maurice Walsh. Ford purchased the screen rights from the author for $10 and promised more if he ever made the film. Ford, who was born Sean O'Feeney, felt a strong kinship toward his Irish heritage, but his early attempts to create the movie repeatedly fell on deaf ears.

In 1945 Ford approached Maureen O'Hara, who had played his heroine in *How Green Was My Valley* four years earlier, about doing *The Quiet Man*. Born in Ireland herself, O'Hara was enthusiastic from the start and accepted the role of Mary Kate immediately. But despite Ford's other successes, the studios didn't seem to have much faith in *The Quiet Man*.

Finally, Ford hit pay dirt at Republic, an unlikely choice. Herbert Yates, Republic's studio head, was known to run a tight budget. But Republic did have an asset no other studio had—John Wayne.

Hondo Lane and "The Quiet Man"

O'Hara and Duke shared an on-screen romantic chemistry but were never more than good friends.

Yates also had hopes of upgrading his film catalog and was anxious to have a director of Ford's stature in his camp. He signed the three-time Oscar winner to a three picture deal. However, Yates, too, questioned the box office appeal of *The Quiet Man* and refused to do it unless Ford and Merian Cooper first provided him another picture which would make money. That film was *Rio Grande*.

Ford, of course, used many of the same actors over and over to great success. Wayne, O'Hara, Victor McLaglen, Ward Bond, and Arthur Shields were already seasoned Ford staples. But it was Shields's brother Barry Fitzgerald—already a big star and an Oscar winner for 1944's *Going My Way*—who stole *The Quiet Man* as Michaeleen Flynn, the village marriage broker and bookie.

Ford's decision to film on location in Ireland was a wise one—it would have been impossible to match the green of Ireland anywhere else in the world. Winton Hoch, who won an Oscar for his color cinematography in *She Wore a Yellow Ribbon*, was behind the camera again.

Duke's whole family spent the summer in Ireland while he was making *The Quiet Man*. Since it was summer, Duke decided to take all four of his children with him. His oldest son Michael and oldest daughter Toni were in their teens and have vivid memories of that summer of 1951 on the Emerald Isle.

"We lived in California all our lives with palm trees. All of a sudden there's a huge castle there. There's a great big river there. It was absolutely fabulous," recalls Duke's daughter Toni La Cava. "It didn't have a lot of the modern conveniences. My father had a bathroom. Jack [Ford] had a bathroom. I think Maureen had a bathroom. But the rest of the crew and everybody had to share this one big bathroom area and one big shower area."

Ford gave cameo roles to all of Duke's children. "I think actually what he wanted was Patrick and Melinda who were in the cart with Maureen," Toni recalls. "And then I think he thought, 'Those two lost souls, they need to be in it, too.' So we all dressed up in costumes and Michael and I are standing on either side of the cart, and Maureen is in the cart with Patrick and Melinda."

The Quiet Man remains one of Duke's crowning glories. The film was nominated for seven Academy Awards, including Best Picture of 1952. Winton Hoch and Archie Stout won an Oscar for the brilliant color cinematography and John Ford garnered an unprecedented fourth Academy Award as Best Director. Victor McLaglen was also nominated for Best Supporting Actor, but why Oscar bypassed Wayne, O'Hara, and Fitzgerald remains a mystery.

At the same time, however, Duke's personal life was in shambles. Chata had gone to Ireland with Duke and his kids in 1951 for the filming of *The Quiet Man*. But the marriage was already beyond repair. Encumbered by an uncontrolled alcohol problem and an alcoholic mother who was her constant companion, Chata left Duke in February 1952.

The well-publicized divorce proceedings were ugly and filled with charges and countercharges. "Chata was reckless. She simply told the wildest stories," Mary St. John recalled. The divorce became final in 1954.

Chata disappeared from Duke's life, surfacing only a few times the following year to create legal problems. A short time later she

Trouble Along the Way

died in Mexico City of an apparent heart attack. She was thirty-two. Years later Duke would say his divorce from Josephine and marriage to Chata two weeks later was a big mistake.

Throughout the ordeal of his divorce Wayne kept busy with work, making *Trouble Along The Way* and *Island in the Sky* in 1953. Then on November 27, 1953, Warner Brothers released *Hondo*, Duke's first Western in nearly four years. The role of Hondo Lane was another vintage part for John Wayne and one which is sometimes overlooked.

Based on a story by Louis L'Amour, with a screenplay by James Edward Grant, and directed by John Farrow (the father of actress Mia Farrow), *Hondo* is one of Wayne's best performances. Offset by the gimmickry of the 3-D process, it is still an action-filled Western.

One of the film's major liabilities is that it was released the same year George Stevens's epic Western *Shane* was released by Paramount. Arguably the greatest Western ever, with a stunning career performance by Alan Ladd in the title role, *Shane* stole the Western thunder that year. *Hondo* was a good picture. *Shane* was a superb one.

Hondo costarred Geraldine Page, fresh from the Broadway stage, as Angie Lowe, a lonely woman abandoned by her husband and living on a ranch with her small son Johnny, played by Lee Aaker. Page received a Best Supporting Actress nomination in this, her movie debut.

Aaker was just ten years old when he made *Hondo*. He would soon go on to TV stardom as Rusty in the *Rin Tin Tin* series which ran from 1954 to 1959. Now fifty-three, Aaker still recalls the thrill of working with John Wayne.

Lee Aaker

"Thinking back to *Hondo,* I can only say I wish I would have been a little older because John Wayne to me is an idol, a real idol. I wish I would have been able to go out with him and talk or have a beer instead of being the little kid. I would have loved doing more than just scenes with him.

"In one scene he picks me up and throws me in the water. I have a nice eight-by-ten-inch autographed picture that says, 'Lee, some day I'll give you a real swimming lesson.' *Hondo* was the first big 3-D movie. We were in Mexico for three months doing it. One thing I do remember well was on July 4th when we were filming the picture, Mike Wayne and I bought some sky rockets. We lit one and it went way down to the bottom of the swimming pool blowing out the bottom of the whole pool. Geraldine Page left the stage to do the picture and was nominated for Best Supporting Actress. But most of all, I remember John Wayne as being very nice to me."

Hondo Lane and "The Quiet Man"

Hondo, with Geraldine Page and Lee Aaker, was shot in 3-D (1953). Page was nominated for an oscar for this, her first screen role.

Glenn Ford was originally slated for the title role in *Hondo*, which Wayne was producing. Farrow and Ford, however, had worked together before, and Ford had no desire to work with Farrow again. Wayne refused to fire Farrow, and on reading the script again, decided to play the title character himself.

The cast also included Ward Bond and Paul Fix, and a rugged thirty-year-old actor with the physical stature of John Wayne by the name of James Arness. Leo Gordon also appeared as Ed Lowe, Page's estranged husband. Gordon appeared in three films with John Wayne: *Hondo, The Conqueror,* and *McLintock!*. Born in Brooklyn and trained on the stage, Gordon since *Hondo* has played mainly villains. He also has written screenplays for more than fifteen films, including *Tobruk* and *The Tower of London,* as well as numerous scripts for television.

109

Leo Gordon

"I was born in Brooklyn and was not a trained cowboy when we made *Hondo*. I was doing a stage play with Edward G. Robinson—*Darkness at Noon*. Somebody who was a famous artist saw me and thought I'd be a good prospect and they signed me up. I went back to New York and a couple of weeks later I got a call and one of the questions was 'Do you ride?' The only horses I had ever been close to were those pulling the Borden milk wagon. But I said, 'Hell yes, I can ride!' So the following day I rented a horse in Central Park and rode for eight hours. I spent the next couple of days in a bath with Epsom salts.

"My agent told me I had a couple of weeks on a picture with John Wayne which was going to be shot in Mexico. The film was *Hondo*. The next thing I knew I was on a plane heading to Mexico. My instructions were to take a taxi to the location, which was a little town where they were shooting the film. Then I found out the town was 110 miles away and I thought they really didn't mean I should take a taxi for a hundred-mile ride. So I grabbed a local bus, with chickens and pigs aboard, and took the 110-mile trip. Everybody got quite a laugh out of that because the taxi fare would have been something like ten bucks. I took the bus and I think it cost a buck and a half. This was the first time I met John Wayne.

"I had a couple of run-ins with him. Nothing of great importance. In the fight scene at the bar I grabbed his shirt and he said, 'Hey, easy on that. These shirts are not easy to come by.' I threw a sharp right at his jaw and he said, 'Cut, cut, cut. Don't you know how to throw a punch?' And he demonstrated by dropping his right arm way back and making a roundhouse. I said, 'Hell, you do that and I'll nail you three times before you can get it up there.'

"The next run-in was my death scene where he shoots me at the water hole. He shoots me and I'm lying on my right hip and I just buckled forward, and he says, 'Jeeze Christ, don't you know when you get hit with a damn slug, you fly backwards?' So this time I was a little pissed off and I pulled up my shirt and indicated where I had been shot. I told him I had caught two in the gut once and that I fell forward. 'Well, it looks better for the camera,' he shot back at me.

110

Hondo Lane and "The Quiet Man"

With Donna Reed in
Trouble Along the Way

"When we were shooting, Frank McGrath and I are knocking and whacking on the damn horses to get away from the Indians. We go down to the gully and up on the other side. I made some comment like, 'I'm doing the best I can.' So Wayne says, 'If you can't ride the son of a bitch, then carry him!' But that was meant in a humorous way.

"Wayne kind of gave Geraldine Page a bit of a hard time. It was her first picture and she even won an Oscar nomination. But she had come from the Broadway stage and I don't think he was too high on what he called 'New York' actors.

"But I liked the guy. He was what you'd call a roughhouser. It was kind of the feeling that on every picture he'd pick one actor and really get on his ass. For example, in *The Conqueror* it was Lee Van Cleef. Each time Lee would come on a scene on horseback, Wayne would yell, 'Watch yourself, fellows, loose horse,' which means a rider can't control his animal. That just might have been a page from the John Ford text.

111

Duke, We're Glad We Knew You

"*Hondo* was the first big 3-D movie and they had that great big camera that was the size of a small truck. They used to have to get what they called 'the lilly' after each shot to see if the color balance was correct. It was the second picture I made. Wayne and I had the same agent. I had a choice between *The Robe* and *Hondo*. I had never been to the interior of Mexico and I thought, 'Hell, I'd rather go to Mexico than go to the 20th Century-Fox lot and do *The Robe*.' So that's how the film came about for me.

"The film still holds up. Like most films made in that period, it is superior to what they put out today. Wayne was a real professional. There is no way of getting away from that. John Farrow was the director and when Wayne would say something, he would perk up both ears and listen. The same thing happened on *The Conqueror*. Interestingly enough, Dick Powell directed the picture—a man who you would not juxtapose against Duke Wayne, [but who] would argue Wayne up against the wall.

"Dick would really stand up to him. One shot, Dick was standing and Wayne was on the horse. The horse's head was near Powell and [Powell and Wayne] had some damn discussion. Suddenly Wayne just yanked the reins and swung the horse's head around, forcing Powell to jump back. Powell came back up to him and said, 'Don't you ever do that to me again!' Wayne just kind of looked at him and smiled and rode the horse back.

"I'm one of the few survivors who made the film [The Conquerer]. Most of the people involved in it died of cancer. I don't know the actual figures, but I think 90 percent of them are gone. It was filmed in St. George, Utah, and they [test] dropped a nuclear bomb not far from there. I was up there a number of weeks. To add insult to injury, I was back just about a week and my agent called to say I was going back to Utah to do another picture called *Santa Fe Passage*. So I had another four weeks over there.

"I worked with Wayne three times over a ten-year period from *Hondo* in 1953 to *McLintock!* in 1962. I never noticed any real change in him. But that was before his first bout with cancer. There was one joke on set, and this was that Andy McLaglen was the only one Wayne looked up to. The reason for this was that Andy was 6'7".

Hondo Lane and "The Quiet Man"

With George Chandler in *High and Mighty* (1956)

"I've also worked with a lot of big people in the business. Wayne was Wayne. Unique. [He was] one of a kind, both on and off the screen. He's had a sustaining power among leading men that is unmatched by anyone. To analyze this off the top of the head, I think he personifies what every American male would like to think of himself as. The persona and the image is what we all like to fulfill. Wayne's preference was for Latin women. All three of his wives were Latin. I think he was intrigued with the lifestyle and the mores, so to speak, of the Latin countries. You could be macho down there and it was respected. Up here they wanted you to put your left hand on your hip and hold the pumpernickel.

"I never got to know him that much personally. He would hang out a lot with the stunt guys, Chuck Roberson and the whole bunch. Usually they'd love to play hearts or poker. He had his own little entourage. After *McLintock!*, I had a couple of meetings with him discussing a script which never went anywhere. Up in his office, he'd come in with a sports jacket and slacks and the whole bit, and he might as well been wearing a Stetson and a holstered gun. He was Wayne!

"When I am asked why the industry has changed so much, I can only answer, 'Why has the country changed so much?' I'll tell you I get as nostalgic as hell sometimes thinking back to the fifties and sixties. It really gets to me at times. That might be one of the reasons for Wayne's legacy. As I said earlier, I believe John Wayne remains not just a parcel of what American males would like to be, but males everywhere. I tend to identify Wayne with Westerns. Other than *The Quiet Man,* his non-Westerns never clicked with me like his Westerns did. Because he was so deep into Westerns, I think the legacy has endured to what it is today.

"It is the Westerns and what the Western has meant as an art form which has so much to do with his success. It is like [what] one of the great producers—maybe it was [Samuel] Goldwyn—said about Gary Cooper. 'Cooper without a hat, you lose money. Put a Stetson on him, you make money!' I think that Stetson may have had a lot to do with John Wayne's success!"

In 1953, Duke made his first television appearance on *The Milton Berle Show.* Of course, "Uncle Miltie" was Mr. Television back then. By the mid-fifties our TV sets kept us in the saddle with a number of television Westerns. Most were popular, but none had the staying power of *Gunsmoke*. It stayed on the air for twenty years, from 1955 to 1975, and made household names of James Arness, Amanda Blake, Milburn Stone, Ken Curtis, and Dennis Weaver.

John Wayne introduced *Gunsmoke's* first episode on September 10, 1955: "Good evening. My name is John Wayne. Some of you have seen me before. I hope so—I've been kickin' around Hollywood for a long time. I've made a lot of pictures out here, all kinds. Some of them are Westerns, and that's what I'm here to tell you about tonight—a Western. A new television show called *Gunsmoke*. I knew there was only one man to play it—James Arness. He's a young fella and may be new to some of you. But I've worked with him and I predict he'll be a big star. And now I'm proud to present *Gunsmoke*."

John Wayne recommended Arness for the role of Matt Dillon after having worked with him earlier in *Big Jim McLain* and *Hondo*. It has been said CBS first offered the role to Wayne himself but he turned it down. Many dismiss this as wishful thinking, suggesting CBS never offered the role to Duke but only solicited his opinion on who could play the part.

"Not so!" said Robert Totten, who directed numerous *Gunsmoke* episodes—and acted in a few—during a ten-year period starting in the mid-sixties. Called a young John Ford by some of his colleagues, Totten won an Emmy and a Peabody Award for directing the television versions of *The Red Pony* and *The Adventures of Huckleberry Finn*. An actor, writer, and director, Totten also directed *The Sacketts,* which was named the Best Western of the nineteen eighties (film or TV) by the National Cowboy Hall of Fame. According to Totten, who died in 1995, CBS was dead serious when it offered the Matt Dillon role to John Wayne.

Robert Totten

"It's true. Actually, Charles [Bill] Warren really believed John Wayne would take a stab at it himself. They knew they couldn't use Bill Conrad, who did it on radio. They were looking for a larger-than-life figure who could also match Conrad's voice. Well, they were talking about one guy—the one and only!

"So they went to John Wayne, and Duke didn't scoff at it at all. In fact, he once told me they flattered him by coming to him that way. But he knew a young guy who really needed a break. Television was new and so was Jim Arness. So Duke pushed for Jim, and you know the rest of the story. Duke did make a piece of the film when he introduced *Gunsmoke*."

Duke, We're Glad We Knew You

Wayne as Ghengis Khan in *The Conqueror,* a film best forgotten.

As the popularity of TV grew, Duke began to appear periodically on the small screen, sometimes to promote a film. He was a frequent guest on Rowan and Martin's *Laugh In* in the nineteen sixties (appearing once as the Easter Bunny). He also appeared on *I Love Lucy* and *The Dean Martin Show* and made appearances on many of Bob Hope's specials.

But the movies remained his big vehicle. By 1956 John Wayne had made 115 pictures. That year, Wayne made perhaps his best and most critically acclaimed film, *The Searchers,* as well as what is arguably his worst picture, *The Conqueror.*

9. From Ethan Edwards to Genghis Khan: A Study in Contrast

I didn't know until recently the kinds of things they have been saying about my dad in the papers and magazines. The ones that don't know him sure irritate me. He doesn't talk or act brash like they say. You should see how gentle he is when he wakes up my little sister and me."

— Ethan Wayne, the *Saturday Evening Post,* (1976).

Nineteen fifty-four was a watershed year in John Wayne's personal life and professional career. A short time after his divorce from Chata, Duke married Peruvian actress Pilar Pallete. The two met when Duke visited the set of a movie being filmed in Peru. Pilar was the leading lady. The attraction was immediate and Duke was particularly intrigued by the fact that she was basically unfamiliar with his work.

In January, Duke's business partner, Bob Fellows, separated from his wife Eleanor. Convinced a divorce was imminent and that he would need to liquidate his assets, Fellows asked Duke to buy him out. Wayne agreed. It was Michael Wayne who suggested the name Batjac for Duke's new company. Batjak was the name of the Dutch shipping company featured in *Wake of the Red Witch.* A secretary's typographical error resulted in the *k* being changed to *c.* On May 25, 1954, the former production company of Wayne-Fellows officially became Batjac Productions.

There is little to say about *The Conqueror* which hasn't been said before. It was simply a bad film, arguably Duke's worst. In 1950 Wayne and RKO boss Howard Hughes signed a deal to do three films. The first was *Jet Pilot,* which began shooting in 1950 but wasn't released until 1957. The second was *The Flying Leathernecks,* a well-acted war film with Robert Ryan. And the third was *The Conqueror.*

Shooting began in the summer of 1954 in St. George, Utah. Hughes hired Dick Powell to produce and direct the film, and RKO budgeted four million dollars for the project. The screenwriter, Oscar Millard, originally wrote the part of Genghis Khan with Marlon Brando in mind. To his credit, Powell tried everything he could to get Brando on loan from Fox, but Brando was unavailable. John Wayne signed on with a surprising degree of enthusiasm.

With the exception of some impressive stuntwork in the battle scenes, the picture warrants little attention except for its unusual contribution to film lore—most of the cast and crew of *The Conqueror* eventually died from cancer. Coincidental or not, it must be noted that *The Conqueror* was filmed at a location not far from the army's nuclear test site. Neither cast nor crew was aware of this during filming.

John Agar, for one, links the cancer deaths to the nuclear testing: "I believe [Duke] could have lived longer. Everybody got sick because of the radiation. A lot of the people in the film eventually died of cancer: Susan Hayward, Agnes Moorehead, Pedro Armendariz, Dick Powell, who directed the picture, and Duke, too." Pilar Wayne isn't so sure. She feels there was a more obvious factor—all the victims were heavy smokers.

Another person from the film who is still around is eighty-three-year-old Yvonne Wood, who designed the male costumes for the picture. A heavy smoker even today, she lives in the town of Solvang, about one hundred thirty miles north of Los Angeles. Over her distinguished career as a designer and sketch artist, she designed costumes for some of Hollywood's most esteemed actors and actresses, including Carmen Miranda, Linda Darnell, Henry Fonda, Jimmy Stewart, Shirley Jones, Danny Kaye, James Mason, Basil Rathbone, Alan Ladd, and Marlon Brando. She well recalls *The Conqueror* with some levity.

Yvonne Wood

"John [Wayne] was a highly educated man, and what he didn't learn in college he learned afterwards. In fact, John Wayne and

A Study in Contrast

Charlton Heston were among the brightest and best-educated film stars I ever met. He was difficult when we first started the project, but originally I think the script scared him half to death. He was forty-seven years old and the story starts when Genghis Khan was seventeen. I also think he thought, 'Jeeze, a woman designer. I'm going to look like a Chinese fag.'

"The first time we met he brought his makeup man. Somehow they came to a parting of the ways many years later. We started talking measurements. It was mainly discussion. I hadn't done many sketches because I wanted to meet him first. When Wayne finally saw the sketches, he was delighted because I made him look like a man and not what he thought I'd do.

"When I was called for an interview and handed a script I was ecstatic. For years and years, Genghis Khan was my favorite historical character. That's somewhat funny because I'm not a blood-thirsty person and Genghis Khan certainly was. I had read two or three books about him over the years, so I got out my books to see what [he] may have worn.

"But then I read the script. Dick [Powell] asked me what I thought. I told him I understood they were rewriting it. Well, I thought that man was going to topple through the floor, he was laughing so hard. I couldn't say it was a great script. I just couldn't. It was awful. And every rewrite got worse. I think they all had a money contract they had to live up to and that is why they did the picture. Mr. Hughes had sucked them in. And if you have a contract for a certain amount of time, you do what there is and get it over with.

"As a designer, you sketch your views and put them on paper. You go no further without approval. But realistically what could you do about Mongolian costumes of a thousand and a half years ago? Nobody has anything authentic except some engravings. But John [Wayne] was very pleased with the designs and how they looked on him, which was wonderful for me. Many things can go wrong between the original sketch and the finished product. But from that point, he was in my corner.

"The thing I discovered right away was that Wayne was tough. He was real tough. He couldn't tolerate people who didn't deliver what they were supposed to do. He was a perfectionist

119

and a real professional. After two days on location, we'd stand there on the back of the truck during the noon hour, grab our food, and eat. Then you start changing six hundred or eight hundred Mongols into Tartars. Not that there was that much difference.

"At first you couldn't tell who was winning during the battle scenes, so I concentrated on headgear which would distinguish the Mongols from the Tartars. Now at least the audience could separate the two. That went over well with Wayne. Both Wayne and Powell had air-conditioned trailers. I had a lot of fun talking and discussing things with Wayne. We had one big thing in common. We both loved the same jellied lunch dish, and it was always frozen when we tried to eat it at lunch time. These were some of the lighter moments.

"And we had some good times. On Saturday nights we would see the rushes. Once we watched *The Pearl,* John Steinbeck's great story. Another time we looked at *Hondo,* which Wayne had just made. Otherwise our entertainment was the baseball games in town. They were great fun. Various groups around Hurricane [Utah] rode in to play ball. I had loved baseball since the Depression days. I had an apartment near the baseball diamond and when [my husband] came down to visit, we would barbecue every weekend and watch the games.

"Finally the St. George All Stars, the local team, decided to challenge the cast and crew of *The Conqueror* to a ball game. Everyone played in the big game: John Wayne, Pedro [Armendariz], Susan Hayward, and her two sons—although I'm not sure about Dick Powell. The stands were full, and there were great big washtubs full of beer. All of the Mormons gathered.

"The prop men had a clown routine, and they managed to throw in everything. It didn't take long to find out that it wasn't a very serious game. Everybody was clowning. Wayne played, Pedro Armendariz played, then comes Susan with her ten-year-old twins. It was a long-lasting baseball game. The only thing I ever saw that was close to this was a big soccer game in Durango, Mexico. You can't beat the movie crews for fun. Wayne brought his boys Michael and Pat along. They were in the picture as extras. I've always liked those two boys.

120

A Study in Contrast

"I worked on many Westerns, including *One Eyed Jacks,* but I never worked professionally with John Wayne again. I was supposed to do *Rio Lobo* but then they postponed it, and when they started shooting, I was working on something else. But after *The Conqueror,* he wrote me a beautiful letter which, unfortunately, I didn't save. It was a short letter and he congratulated me. He said he was going to do his best to see that I was nominated for an Academy Award. But you don't get nominated for a turkey. And that picture was voted the worst picture around for about ten years until something worse came along. It was really bad.

"John Wayne was loyal to his friends, loyal to a fault, sometimes even to the wrong ones. In my opinion, he had a tendency to overdo loyalty. I think one of his business partners almost ruined him once. The only other person I knew with that type of loyalty was my friend Linda Darnell. When I came back into the business after being away from it for four and a half years, John Wayne was the only man I wanted to call. He tried to help line me up with Paramount Studios, but they had their own people.

"All told, I was in Utah for six weeks filming *The Conqueror.* I know lots of people died among the cast and the crew. Among the local people there was an increase in cancer, too. For years I got lots of questions about this. One guy called me and talked for a while asking the same question over and over again. Finally he said, 'Incidentally, how are you feeling?' I said, 'I was feeling pretty good until you called.' He never called me again!"

Duke's next picture, *The Searchers,* is one of the great Westerns of all time. Released on March 13, 1956, *The Searchers* has been credited with influencing the work of contemporary directors such as Steven Spielberg, Martin Scorsese, and George Lucas.

The Searchers reunited Wayne with John Ford for the first time since *The Quiet Man* four years earlier. It was also the first Western they had done together since *Rio Grande* in 1950. It is a haunting story of two white men (Wayne and Jeffrey Hunter) searching for a girl (Natalie Wood) who was kidnapped by Comanches. As director, Ford offers a tougher, less optimistic view of life than in his previous films. Never has the wilderness seemed so brutal and

With Jeffrey Hunter in *The Searchers* (1956)

threatening than in this biting but tender masterpiece. The role of Ethan Edwards was also a new challenge for John Wayne.

Film critic William Zinsser noted in the *New York Herald Tribune,* "Wayne is fascinating for his sheer hardness. There's no kindness in his nature—he is crafty and arrogant and his eyes are as cold as ice."

Harry Carey Jr. had already made four pictures with John Wayne dating back to *Three Godfathers* in 1948 and had known Duke a good part of his life. But he saw a different John Wayne in *The Searchers.*

Harry Carey Jr.

"The first scene I was in with Duke, I discovered my family's prize bull had been slaughtered, When I looked up at Duke during rehearsal, it was into the meanest and coldest eyes I have ever seen. I don't know how he molded that character. Maybe he had known someone like Ethan Edwards as a kid. Now I wished I had asked him.

"Somehow, Duke became Ethan Edwards, on the screen and off. He was even Ethan Edwards at dinner time. He didn't kid around on *The Searchers* like he did in the other pictures. But we got along great on the picture. I played a kid named Brad Jorgensen. When Duke comes to tell me he found the girl I loved dead, I run off and get killed. He said, 'What do you want me to do, draw you a picture? I wrapped her up in my coat and buried her with my own hands.' It was a great line which Duke did particularly well. It was one of the most intense scenes I ever did with him.

"Natalie Wood was sixteen when we made the film. She was so pretty and a real nice kid. She was absolutely gorgeous. At the end of the film when Duke picks her up in his arms and says, 'Let's go home, Debbie,' it always makes me cry. They showed that scene quite a bit when Duke died in 1979.

"I've worked with a bunch of big stars since 1948, but never one who gave as much in a scene as John Wayne. He was a pain in the ass sometimes because he changed things, but I'd rather do a scene with John Wayne than anyone I ever worked with in the business.

"My mom, Olive Carey, played my screen mom, Mrs. Jorgensen, in *The Searchers*. My mother and John Ford went back a long way. They had known each other since she was eighteen and he was nineteen. The movement Duke made when he closed the door at the end of the picture was a tribute to my father. That was John Ford's idea. But the idea of Duke putting his left hand over his right elbow, that was his own idea. He was to look and then just walk away. But just before he turned, he saw my mom, the widow of his all-time hero, standing behind the camera. He raised his left hand, reached across his chest and grabbed his right arm at the elbow. My dad did that a lot in movies when Duke was still a kid in Glendale. It was just one take, as natural as anything. My mother was deeply affected. Duke loved my mom. In fact, he worshipped her."

Duke's performance as Ethan Edwards is the thread that holds *The Searchers* together. Based on a short novel by Alan LeMay,

Duke, We're Glad We Knew You

Frank Nugent's screenplay was written with John Wayne in mind. Ford was precise in his casting as usual, with Jeffrey Hunter as Martin Pawley and Vera Miles as his sweetheart Laurie Jorgensen.

To offset some of the books' original grimness, Ford added two new characters to provide the film some comic relief: a somewhat senile old man named Mose Harper, played by Hank Worden, and the Rev. Sam Clayton, played by the reliable Ward Bond. Ken Curtis—a former singer who would soon have a long run as Festus in *Gunsmoke*—played stammering Charlie McCorry, who was a more solid character in the book than in the film. Duke's catch-phrase in the film, "That'll be the day," immediately entered the jargon of teenage slang, inspiring singer-songwriter Buddy Holly's 1957 hit of the same name.

Not then recognized as the classic it has become today, *The Searchers* was ignored at Oscar time, though it generally played to excellent reviews.

Bosley Crowther in the *New York Times* called Wayne's fine performance "uncommonly commanding . . . [a man] whose passion for revenge is magnificently uncontaminated by caution or sentiment." *Look* magazine called the film "a Western in the grand manner, the most roisterous since *Shane*. The *Hollywood Reporter* went even further, calling *The Searchers* "undoubtedly the greatest Western ever made."

On March 31, 1956, Pilar gave birth to a daughter named Aissa. At age forty-nine with four grown children, John Wayne had started a second family. When a son was born on February 12, 1962, they named him John Ethan in tribute to Duke's days as Ethan Edwards in *The Searchers*.

Buddy Holly's hit song "That'll Be the Day" leaped to the top of the pop charts in 1957. Rock and roll was here to stay. In 1957 John Wayne turned fifty. A new generation of Americans had come of age since World War II. To enhance his appeal and broaden his audience among these rock and rollers, Duke cast teenage heartthrobs in his next few Westerns: Ricky Nelson in *Rio Bravo* (1959), Frankie Avalon in *The Alamo* (1960), and Fabian in *North to Alaska* (1960).

Rio Bravo was Duke's first venture with Howard Hawks since *Red River* ten years earlier. And while Hawks would emerge as John

124

A Study in Contrast

Ford's principal rival among Western directors, the two men differed immensely in style. Ford was the poet, the romantic, the sentimentalist. Hawks was the antiromantic, a traditional straight-shooting director with an original touch and a flair for comedy.

Both Wayne and Hawks had been critical of the film *High Noon*, despite its wide acclaim. Wayne objected to the portrayal of a town where the citizens and institutions lacked courage and moral fiber. Most historians of the American West tend to agree, and evidence suggests that in times of trouble, most people stood by their lawmen. Duke considered *High Noon* a specious depiction of Western character. In a 1971 interview with *Playboy*, he minced no words on the issue:

> Everyone says *High Noon* was a great picture because Tiomkin wrote some great music for it and because Gary Cooper and Grace Kelly were in it. In the picture, four guys come in to gun down the sheriff. He goes to church and asks for help and the guys go, "Oh well, oh gee." And the women stand up and say, "You rats, you rats." So Cooper goes out alone. It's the most un-American thing I ever saw in my whole life. The last thing in the picture is ole Coop putting the United States marshal's badge under his foot and stepping on it.

The film annoyed Hawks, too. He considered a sheriff running around town looking for help, finding none, then being saved only by his Quaker wife utter nonsense. So, in defiance of this theme, Hawks made *Rio Bravo*. It is an extraordinary picture with Duke letter-perfect as Sheriff John T. Chance. It is the antithesis of *High Noon*. Duke is a lawman who arrests a murderer and holds him in jail pending trial. When the going gets rough, he gets help from many quarters, including his deputies—a crippled old man (Walter Brennan) and a drunk (Dean Martin)—and from a young gunslinger (Ricky Nelson) and a gambler named Feathers who becomes Duke's love interest (Angie Dickinson).

A superbly crafted Western, with music composed and conducted by Dimitri Tiomkin, the film tapped the previously unrecognized dramatic talent of Dean Martin, who for many years was considered the lighter end of the comedy team of Dean Martin and Jerry Lewis. As Chance's alcoholic deputy Dude, Martin was superb in a role Hawks had originally slated for Montgomery Clift. He also won Wayne's respect during the shooting, and a warm friendship developed between the two that continued until Wayne's death.

With the exception of Ford, no director could pull a performance out of Wayne like Hawks. Duke respected Hawks. More important, he listened to him, something he did with few directors. The admiration was mutual: "John Wayne represents more force, more power, than anybody else on the screen," Hawks would later say.

Director Peter Bogdanovich points to a defining moment in *Rio Bravo* which he feels conveys Wayne's most enduring qualities. The scene has Duke walking down the steps of the sheriff's office toward a group of men riding up to meet him. Bogdanovich notes:

> Hawks frames the shot from behind—Wayne striding slowly, casually away from camera in that slightly rocking, graceful way of his—and the image is held for quite a long while as if to give us plenty of time to enjoy the sight: a classic familiar figure—unmistakable from any angle—moving across the world of illusion he has more than conquered.

In 1959 John Ford made *The Horse Soldiers* starring Wayne and William Holden. The final film of the great cowboy star Hoot Gibson, *The Horse Soldiers* marked the twentieth time Wayne and Ford had worked together and brought Wayne's film total to 122.

In 1959 Humphrey Bogart and Errol Flynn were already gone. Gary Cooper and Clark Gable also would soon belong to the ages. By 1962 Jimmy Cagney simply decided he had had enough and retired. But John Wayne was here and bigger than ever. As the century was about to enter its seventh decade, few could have predicted the turbulence looming ahead.

10. "The Alamo": A Noble Dream

> I met Duke in 1952 when we made a movie together,
> and it was Duke who suggested me for Matt Dillon in
> the television series *Gunsmoke*. He was a real friend. He
> was honest, strong, independent, and proud. He's
> exactly the kind of man he portrayed in *The Shootist*.
> We didn't know it then, but John Wayne was telling us
> the rules he lived by, on screen and off.
>
> — James Arness, in *Standing*
> *Tall* 1989

The torch has been passed to an new generation of Americans."
Such were the words of forty-three-year-old John F. Kennedy as
he became the country's youngest elected chief executive in 1960.
What followed was the most tumultuous decade the nation had
known since the Civil War.

Like everyone else, John Wayne was caught in the clashing
political and cultural currents of the changing times, starting with
The Alamo in 1960 and ending with his Oscar-winning role in *True
Grit* in 1969. But it was *The Green Berets* in 1968 which tested the
mettle of Duke's conservatism and patriotism, putting him at odds
with many Hollywood power brokers and most of the liberal rank
and file.

John Wayne was fifty-two when filming of *The Alamo* began in
1959. For more than fourteen years, his dreams centered around
this endeavor. He insisted on directing because he had guided the
project through its infancy and had nurtured it through each stage
of development. And when he finished *The Alamo*, he told Hedda
Hopper, "I wanted to direct from the first time I set foot in a studio.
I was sidetracked for something like thirty years—I finally made it."

The story of the Alamo, and the courageous men who fought
to the last in its defense, was well-known. For Wayne, working on

Duke, We're Glad We Knew You

With Linda Crista (Flaca) in *The Alamo*

The Alamo was as much a statement of personal conviction as it was the creation of an epic film. Wayne's views on patriotism were always well-defined and clear, leaving no room for ambiguity.

As early as 1947, Duke brought the idea for a film about the Alamo to his pal screenwriter Jimmy Grant. The two traveled to San Antonio and hired a research group to provide every written word about the Alamo and its defenders. Duke had often pitched the idea to Herbert Yates, his boss at Republic Pictures. Yet Yates was reluctant to do another film on the Alamo (Republic had done a small-budget film on the Alamo in 1939 called *Man of Conquest*). Eager to please Duke, his top star, Yates held out the carrot for years but was never willing to finalize the deal.

When filming finally began, it was largely because of the

"The Alamo": A Noble Dream

late James T. "Happy" Shahan. Shahan owned a twenty-two-thousand-acre ranch six miles north of Bracketville, Texas. Because of the popularity of Westerns, he felt the area would make an ideal film site and for years had tried to lure the Hollywood brass to Brackettville.

It was Happy Shahan who finally convinced Duke to abandon Durango, Mexico, as a location site in favor of his Brackettville cattle ranch. Shahan contracted for the construction of an elaborate set. With the help of art designer Al Ybarra, whom Wayne had hired in 1949, a completed Alamo compound and a town of nineteen buildings was ready for the scheduled arrival of actors and crew in mid-1959.

At the start of that year Duke was not yet sure of his casting. Originally, he had wanted to play Sam Houston (Richard Boone's part) and devote his remaining energies to production and directing. However, United Artists said they would only help budget the film with the condition that Duke play Davy Crockett. United Artists insisted this was the only way to secure a good box office gross.

Three years earlier Wayne had talked to Argentine-born actress Linda Crystal about the role of Flaca, his romantic interest in the film. Duke could also count on his stable of buddies: Ken Curtis, Hank Worden, Chuck Roberson, Jack Pennick, and his son Patrick for important secondary roles.

Early press releases named William Holden and Rock Hudson to play Jim Bowie and Col. William Travis. Holden and Wayne had become good friends in the early fifties and wanted to work together in a film project. Holden had formed his own production company, William Holden Productions, and in 1959 Wayne and Holden starred together in Ford's *The Horse Soldiers*. But when Batjac and Holden Productions couldn't come to terms on shooting schedules and other matters, Holden bowed out.

For the part of Colonel Travis, John Ford ultimately sold Wayne on a newcomer from England named Laurence Harvey. Harvey's performance in the 1958 film *Room at the Top* earned him an Oscar nomination and worldwide recognition. Harvey's bisexuality was a bit of a problem for Duke at first, but he learned to respect Harvey's grit and toughness, and the two got along fine.

With Walter Reed in *The Horse Soldiers* (Courtesy Walter Reed)

After signing Harvey, Duke again turned his attention to the all-important role of Jim Bowie. Names like Charlton Heston and James Arness surfaced from time to time. But by summer Duke had decided on Richard Widmark. Widmark, who once was assistant to the head of the drama department at Lake Forest College in Illinois, won acclaim as the psychopathic thug Tommy Udo in Henry Hathaway's 1948 film *Kiss of Death*. It was Widmark's first screen appearance and garnered him a Best Supporting Actor nomination.

Wayne admired Widmark's acting versatility and felt that as Bowie he could provide a proper character balance between the boisterous Davy Crockett and the priggish Colonel Travis. A man of enormous intellect and ego, Widmark would be at loggerheads with Wayne during much of the filming. But Wayne respected Widmark's talent, and reports that Wayne hated Widmark and once threw him against a wall in anger are untrue.

"The Alamo": A Noble Dream

Harry Carey Jr.

"I've known Widmark for fifty years almost, about as long as I've known Duke. Richard Widmark is an extremely private man, one of the most private men I've known. He doesn't like to express his feelings much. But back in the nineteen sixties when we were younger he always had me around with him. He's very bright. Outside of John Ford and my father, he's probably the brightest man I've known in the picture business. But when you first meet him it's like you're meeting the devil himself.

"God, everybody knows there was animosity between Duke and Widmark on the set of *The Alamo*. That's not even a secret. Widmark, as I said, is highly intelligent but he also has a very short fuse. And Wayne could get excited. Wayne had his whole gang with him on *The Alamo*: Denver Pyle, Ken Curtis, Chuck Roberson, Hank Worden—the whole gang.

They had one big run-in, I'm told. But then there was a tremendous amount of pressure on Duke. Duke was using bad language and there was a bunch of kids and nuns on top of the hill. According to Kenny Curtis, Duke yelled to Widmark, 'Let's see if you can come down those goddamn stairs.' And Widmark grabbed an axe handle and said, 'I want you to apologize to everybody on the set. Don't ever yell at me again. Apologize to all those people!' Duke just kind of looked around and said, 'What did I say?' But then again, I got this all secondhand."

Since *The Alamo* was to be filled with action and some of the largest battle scenes ever filmed, Wayne employed one of the largest groups of stuntmen ever assembled. Cliff Lyons, Duke's friend and a legendary stuntman from early Hollywood days, was second unit director.

Whatever mistakes were made in the film, it's impossible to fault the musical scoring. Composer and arranger Dimitri Tiomkin had written the scores for some of Hollywood's best known films, including *Mr. Smith Goes to Washington*, *Friendly Persuasion*, *Duel in the Sun*, and *Cyrano de Bergerac*. Tiomkin won Oscars for scoring *The High and the Mighty*, *The Old Man and the Sea*, and *High Noon*, for

131

which he also won an Oscar with lyricist Ned Washington for Best Original Song, "High Noon (Do Not Forsake Me Oh My Darlin')."

Wayne and Tiomkin became acquainted when Tiomkin wrote the score for *Red River,* and over the course of their careers the two men would work together six times. Although born in Russia, Tiomkin had gained a reputation as one of the best Western music composers in the film industry.

For *The Alamo,* Tiomkin's music was given lyrics by his old associate Paul Francis Webster. John Wayne knew the musical score of a film is often remembered long after the film is forgotten. Few movies have been scored with more skill than *The Alamo,* and few songs have sounded better on-screen than the soft melodic strains of "The Green Leaves of Summer," sung by Jester Hairston. And Tiomkin's use of the thematic melody in the film's final scene has rarely been duplicated.

The Alamo was nominated for seven Academy Awards, including Best Picture, Supporting Actor (Chill Wills), color Cinematography (William Clothier), drama Score (Dimitri Tiomkin), and Original Song (Tiomkin with Paul Francis Webster). But at Oscar time the picture won only for Best Sound (Jack Solomon).

John Wayne had put his all into *The Alamo.* Incredibly, he managed to shoot the film in just eighty-one days. But he lost thirty pounds in the process, and his cigarette smoking reached five packs a day. No producer ever tried harder to gain Oscar nominations for a film. Perhaps he tried too hard. Duke took out full-page ads in the trade papers *Variety* and the *Hollywood Reporter.* Batjac Productions threw parties with Alamo themes, spending lots of money in an obvious attempt to woo votes.

The kiss of death, however, came when Chill Wills campaigned for Best Supporting Actor by buying trade paper ads calling for his "cousins" in the Academy to vote for him. One particularly galling ad had the cast and crew standing in front of the Alamo set. The text read:

> "We of *The Alamo* are praying harder than the real Texans prayed for their lives in the real Alamo for Chill Wills to win the Oscar. Cousin Chill's acting was great!
> "Your Alamo Cousins"

"The Alamo": A Noble Dream

Bad taste, you bet! And Duke knew it. He put out a series of ads of his own denouncing Wills campaign, stating he thought Chill Wills's intentions were not as bad as his taste. Nevertheless, the Academy responded more to Groucho Marx's now classic ad which read: "Dear Mr. Wills, I'm delighted to be your cousin, but I'm voting for Sal Mineo."

In the presidential election of 1960, Wayne enthusiastically supported Richard Nixon for his tough anticommunist position. He despised the Kennedys for what he called their "lace-curtain arrogance and unctuous liberalism." Hoping to boost Nixon's chances and promote the film, he scheduled *The Alamo*'s premier for San Antonio, Texas, at the end of October to coincide with the final stages of the 1960 presidential campaign.

The affair was a star-studded event. But the reviews were generally lukewarm. Wayne had expected as much from the New York critics and media who were increasingly panning his work. *The New Yorker* accused Wayne of having "turned a splendid chapter of our past into sentimental and preposterous flapdoodle. . . ." *Newsweek* called it ". . . the most lavish B picture ever made . . . B for banal."

At the San Antonio premier, John Ford said *The Alamo* was "the most important motion picture ever made. It's timeless. It's the greatest picture I have ever seen. It will last forever—run forever for all peoples, all families—everywhere." But Ford's accolades met a sharp rebuff by film critic John Cutts: "May I humbly suggest to Mr. Ford," he wrote sarcastically, "that the film only *seems* to last forever."

It is wrong to dismiss *The Alamo* as the long-winded flop many critics would have us believe it to be. The film had flaws to be sure. But as a period war saga locked into the sentiment and drama of its time, it's a fine film. Moreover, *The Alamo* was not the financial disaster some have assumed. To the contrary, on its release, *The Alamo* grossed $8 million, making it one of the year's top-grossing films. It set a foreign film box office record in Japan, topping the record previously set by *Ben Hur.*

The Alamo also established box office records in London, Paris, Stockholm, Rome, Denmark, and San Juan, Puerto Rico. And while John Wayne did not personally realize profits from the film, United Artists and MGM/UA reaped millions from releases and

133

redistribution rights. The critics aside, the film did receive seven Oscar nominations and one Academy Award. It also won awards from organizations such as Western Heritage, *Good Housekeeping* magazine, and the Foreign Press Association.

While the Oscar eluded a deserving Dimitri Tiomkin, *The Alamo*'s musical score was popular and profitable. Both the Academy Award–nominated song, "The Green Leaves of Summer," and "The Ballad of the Alamo," performed by country star Marty Robbins, reached the Top Forty in the pop charts. Three albums and nineteen single recordings were issued from music of *The Alamo*, performed by such artists as Frankie Avalon, the Brothers Four, Nelson Riddle, Mantovani, and Hugo Montenegro.

For John Wayne, *The Alamo* was a mixed bag of sorts. The reviews were not what he had hoped for, and he incurred heavy personal debts. But he settled his financial problems when he sold the film to United Artists. He was still in the top ten list of box office earners, and offers for new roles kept coming in.

If Duke felt betrayed or cheated of rewards at Oscar time, he never said so publicly. It was not his style to do so. He had fulfilled a long-standing dream to produce and direct this picture. He had done his best, which was all he ever asked of himself or anyone else. When he sold *The Alamo* to United Artists in 1961, he shut the door on a project which consumed much of his energy and time for sixteen years. Michael Wayne took over as president and owner of Batjac Productions, and Batjac returned to making films in 1963.

A few years after its original release, Duke stated, "I wish they would rerelease *The Alamo* today. There's more to that movie than my damn conservative attitude." The passing years have proven him correct. Through the remainder of the sixties John Wayne did not lose an inch of popularity. He would appear in twenty more films during that decade, giving definitive treatment to three more roles: Tom Doniphon in *The Man Who Shot Liberty Valance*, George Washington McLintock in *McLintock!*, and Rooster Cogburn in *True Grit*.

Among the twenty stuntmen working on *The Alamo* was twenty-seven-year-old Dean Smith. A relative unknown in the film business, prior to *The Alamo*, Smith had won a Gold Medal for the United States in the 1952 summer Olympics in Helsinki. In 1957 he signed with the Los Angeles Rams in the National Football League. Smith was elected to the Texas (Sports) Hall of Fame

With Dean Smith in *The Alamo* (Courtesy Dean Smith)

in 1985 with baseball great Nolan Ryan, football's Mean Joe Greene, and golf's Harvey Pennick.

One of the industry's premier stuntmen, Smith has worked with the best in the motion picture business for more than thirty years. But the biggest and best of them all, he insists, was John Wayne, whom he appeared with in many films. Born and raised in Texas, Smith considers his career as a stuntman and actor a boyhood dream come true.

Dean Smith

"The first big picture I ever did was *The Alamo*. It was done in Texas and being a Texas boy who was involved in sports all my life, it is still my favorite picture. It was the most fulfilling job I ever had.

John Wayne and a brunette Angie Dickinson in *I Married a Woman*

This was the first time I met John Wayne and I have been friendly with the Wayne family ever since. It was also the first time I met John Ford. I ran and jumped over a horse and he saw me. From that time until he died, I worked on all his pictures.

"To make a long story short, the way I got on the picture was through Bob Mathias who was under contract to Wayne at Batjac. Bob Mathias was one of the greatest athletes in the world. He won the decathlon Gold Medal for the United States in the 1948 and 1952 Olympic Games. Mathias introduced me to Bob Morrison, Duke's brother. Through Morrison I met Cliff Lyons and that's what enabled me to work on *The Alamo*.

"I doubled Frankie Avalon and had about fifteen different costumes in the picture. This is the most exciting picture I ever made and the first time in my life I ever had real money in my pocket. John Wayne really took a liking to me and they really utilized my talent. I did a bunch of fancy jumps and all kinds of stuff. It was just a picture I will never forget and a very memorable moment for me. I had one little part in *Rio Bravo* when nobody knew who Dean Smith was. I was just working in the background.

"I grew up in Texas and I loved those old B Westerns. Like the other kids I lived on a farm and learned to ride at a very early age. I knew how to raise chickens and take care of things. But our big thing was to go into town on Saturday and see these cowboy pictures. Gene [Autrey] was my first hero, and then came Roy [Rogers], Tex Ritter, and all those guys. Then I started realizing there was Clark Gable, Gary Cooper, and John Wayne. I have never forgotten the compliment Roy Rogers gave me. 'Dean,' he said. 'If you had been here when Gene and I got started, with the abilities you have, you would have been a big B Western acting star.'

"While I didn't meet John Wayne until we did *The Alamo*, I had seen him many times before. Once he came to Austin, Texas, to make an appearance for *The High and the Mighty*. Oh, hell, I had hero worship even then. He got off the plane and had one of those tweed jackets on. [The plane] was one of those DC-6s. I'll tell you what, he was bigger than life!

"I had my picture taken with Duke once in *Texas Monthly*. He was wearing a bracelet from an elephant's tusk on his wrist. He smoked so many of those cigarettes that he had nicotine all over his hand. He used to smoke the hell out of those Camel cigarettes. I was just a young kid and he would rib me quite a bit. But he always had me around. I was on all those later jobs. Wayne was a hard worker and he had so much to do on the picture. They just don't make guys like that any more. I've been very blessed to have worked with Duke Wayne.

"Duke had wanted to make *The Alamo* for a long time. Somehow Happy Shahan in Brackettville and people in San Antonio came up with the money, so he was able to make it. The financing would be prohibitive now. But he had a love for *The Alamo* and the history of the Alamo and the building of Texas. He was a real professional and was always prepared to work. And you damn well be ready to work, too. He had little patience for anyone who didn't give it their best. I think it's great to love your work and want to be meticulous about it.

"Wayne liked and respected Howard Hawks. Don Seigal and Andy McLaglen could do a hell of a good job with him in the later

137

years. But I think it took a guy like Ford to get all there was to get out of John Wayne. I'm sure Wayne was very beholden to Ford because of *Stagecoach*. He started gaining strength and popularity after he did that. I'm sure Ford taught John Wayne a lot of things. These guys were real professional and first class. He was loyal to me, and his family still is.

"When Wayne and Ford and those others started dying out, I think they lost the recipe and ingredients that made those kind of pictures. For example, John Ford could go to a place like Monument Valley and do a scene where Wayne—or anyone else for that matter—could be standing in front of those big buttes or riding a horse, and it looked like he painted it on film. He not only had the ability, he had the knowledge to be able to put Indians and horses, artillery, and columns of soldiers on film. And he knew how to put excitement and music into his films.

"Ford could be tough on all of us, even Duke. There wasn't any of us he didn't put a bite on sooner or later. He made my life miserable, too. He accused me of giving out his phone number to some green-eyed Mexican that I didn't even know. He was either trying to make a patsy out of me or see if he could get my goat. He damn near succeeded!

"John Wayne used to scare the daylights out of me when I was around him at the beginning. We all wanted so hard to please him, because it was such an honor to work with him. Because of this you always wanted to do your best. And we had fun working with Duke. It was a wonderful experience doing a John Wayne picture because it was like family. At the end you had fulfillment. You were satisfied. You felt you were achieving something. You work on these films today, and it's like going down to the corner and getting on the bus.

"I had acting parts in *Rio Lobo* and *Big Jake*. And I turned down doubling Robert Redford in *Butch Cassidy and the Sundance Kid* to work on *True Grit*. That was because old man Hathaway told me he was going to give me a part. Hell, I only had one line in the damn picture and I doubled Robert Duvall. I also doubled Jay Silverheels in that hanging scene out there in the middle of the courthouse. I'm glad I got to know old Tonto [Silverheels] before he died. He worked out in the same gym with me in Woodland Hills.

138

"The Alamo": A Noble Dream

"Henry Hathaway and Wayne were able to work together well. Hathaway was the most miserable son of a gun that you ever saw at times, but I kind of liked him. We had a lot of fun with Duke. For example, he would call Cliff Lyons 'Mother Lyons.' I remember we were playing cards one time in a big motor home. Duke, Glenn Campbell, Chuck Roberson, and me. Now I really didn't know much about the game of 'hearts.' But somehow I ran the game and didn't even know how I did it. Duke said, 'Shit, you little devil you! How the hell did you manage to do this?'

"Another time we were making *Rio Lobo* down in Arizona. It was nighttime and we had been working. Well, Duke and Jack Elam were playing [liar's] poker and Elam was just kicking Duke's butt all over the place. I happened to have a dollar bill with a whole lot of numbers on it. I forget the numbers but I think they were sevens or eights. I slipped Wayne that old dollar bill, and he just kicked Elam's butt. He got a big kick out of that. Certain things like that you remember.

"I also recall when we were doing *True Grit,* a bunch of us were doing a lot of talking. We'd get to talking. I think by then Duke kind of knew that sooner or later one of these days the Western was going to go downhill, the ways things were changing and everything. And of course, he was right.

"A lot of people ask me why I just wanted to work in Westerns. Of course, I've done lots of other work, but the Westerns were special. And no one was more special than Duke. I was a country boy and grew up watching these fellows. They were like kinfolk to me. When one of them dies, it's like losing a relative.

"I liked just about all of Duke's work. But I thought he was best as Rooster in *True Grit.* I believe he deserved the Oscar for that. The other picture I always mention is *The Shootist.* I didn't work on that one, but I visited Duke on the set. It was the last time I ever saw him. Both roles show the mature side of the guy. I liked him in *McLintock!,* too. And he was outstanding in *She Wore a Yellow Ribbon* when he had his hair grayed and played an older man. In fact, everything Wayne did with Ford was well-orchestrated.

"Duke Wayne had an image unlike anybody else's. He was able to tower above the others. He had longevity, he had strength, and he had courage. I think his strength was what we all have carried

139

on. He was every man's father, grandfather, and great-grandfather. He's what we'd like to think everybody should be in this country. Not like these guys around today. And I don't mind saying that. This is because I have already worked with all my heroes. These guys were a crop of men whom we ain't getting replaced. I wish we could bring them back."

11. Pappy's Last Hurrah

> I consider [John] Wayne one of the great movie actors
> of all time—a view not universally held among my
> fellow film critics, and the folks back East. Wayne has
> special meaning for me not just as a critic and movie
> buff, but as an American and as a woman.
>
> — Molly Haskell, in *The Ladies'*
> *Home Journal* (July 1976)

By the time the nineteen sixties rolled around, the young actors of the nineteen forties like Ben Johnson, Harry Carey Jr., and John Agar had become seasoned pros. Director Andrew McLaglen had risen through the ranks to become one of the top directors of Western film and television. Wayne was again becoming mentor of sorts to a new generation of performers such as Edward Faulkner, Robert Donner, and Christopher Mitchum, each of whom, like Dean Smith, worked with Duke in a number of pictures.

During the nineteen sixties John Wayne made two final films with John Ford: *The Man Who Shot Liberty Valance* (1962) and *Donovan's Reef* (1963). While the first was a top-notch effort, the second showed signs of decline for the great director. Through the remainder of the decade it was Howard Hawks and Henry Hathaway who guided Duke through his best work, and in Hathaway's case, helped Duke through his toughest personal battle to date.

On November 5, 1960, while Ford was busy working on *Two Rode Together* in Brackettville and *The Alamo* had just opened in theaters around the land, Ward Bond—in Dallas to attend a football game—suffered a heart attack and died. It was a stunning blow to both Ford and Wayne.

Just the year before, Duke had been unnerved by the suicide of his old friend and drinking partner Grant Withers. After five failed marriages Withers had become a lonely alcoholic. He swallowed a lethal does of barbiturates that he washed down with a bottle of vodka. He left a note asking his friends for forgiveness for letting them down. Now it was Ward Bond. Bond and Wayne were like irascible brothers for years.

They had been together all their professional careers, with a friendship dating back to their USC football days. They appeared together for the first time in *Salute* way back in 1928. Bond worked in nineteen films with Wayne, including some of Duke's best: *The Long Voyage Home, The Shepherd of the Hills, They Were Expendable, Fort Apache, Three Godfathers, The Quiet Man, Hondo, The Searchers,* and *Rio Bravo.* Of all the actors who shared the screen with Wayne, only three—Yakima Canutt with thirty, Chuck Roberson with twenty-seven, and Paul Fix with twenty-five—can be seen in more Wayne movies.

A bereaved John Ford made the funeral arrangements. Ward Bond's body was placed in a flag-draped casket with uniformed honor guards and a white flag carried at half-mast. At the funeral, the Sons of the Pioneers sang "The Song of the Wagonmaster," and John Wayne, his voice cracking and his eyes filled with tears, delivered the eulogy. "We were the closest friends from school days right on through," Duke recalled. "This is just the way Ward would have wanted it—to look out on the faces of good friends. He was a wonderful, generous, big-hearted man."

According to Randy Roberts and James S. Olson in their comprehensive 1995 biography *John Wayne: American,* Wayne was uncomfortable in the role of Tom Doniphon in *The Man Who Shot Liberty Valance.* This despite the fact that it was one of Duke's strongest performances. "Ford was a monster on the set," actor Ken Murray recalled. It was reputed that he was particularly nasty to Wayne because Ford was upset that Duke did not use him more on *The Alamo.* It has also been suggested that Ford might have become a bit jealous of Duke by this time in their respective careers.

The reviews were generally lukewarm at best, although the film has grown greatly in stature with the passing years. In 1962 *Variety* wrote that *"Liberty Valance* falls distinctly shy of its innate story. . . ." But by 1986, film critic Tag Gallagher hailed it as a "masterpiece" with Ford "at the apex of his career." Whatever interpretation one accepts, it is obvious the film lacks the romantic optimism so vivid in Ford's earlier work. His earlier films celebrated the Western way of life, *Liberty Valance,* on the other hand, seemed to mourn its passing.

Years later, Duke complained to Dan Ford how difficult the film had been for him. "He [Ford] had Jimmy Stewart for the shit-kicker hero. He had Edmond O'Brien for the quick-witted humor. Add Lee Marvin for a flamboyant heavy, and, shit, I've got to walk through the goddam picture."

Tom Doniphon was out of step with his time, and while Duke played the part perfectly, he just wasn't ready for such a characterization. He was more comfortable with such a part a few years later when he played Wil Andersen in *The Cowboys* and John Bernard Books in *The Shootist.*

In 1960 Ron Talsky was a twenty-five-year-old trainee at Western Costume Company, earning a dollar an hour and parking cars on Sunset Boulevard to make ends meet. Before his death in 1995 at age sixty, his career as a film costume designer spanned forty years. He worked with all the great stars and most of the top directors.

Over the years he got to know John Wayne quite well, working with him on such films as *The Alamo, The Man Who Shot Liberty Valance,* and *McLintock!.* He was also the costumer for the 1979 Academy Awards when Wayne made his final public appearance.

Ron Talsky

"I was working for Frank Beetson and learning my trade at Western Costume Company, when Mr. Beetson was preparing a film called *The Alamo.* He asked me how would I like to go out and work on it as a trainee. So I went to work on the set of *The Alamo* and that is where I met John Wayne.

"I was a costumer, but I had never worked on a film. I spent three years at Western Costume learning to distinguish one type of coat from another, putting stock away, fumigating, dyeing, cleaning, and shining boots—all those things. Just training. There are two ways to learn your craft: on-the-job training such as with Western Costume Company or going to some sort of art school.

Duke, We're Glad We Knew You

"So I got to meet Duke when I went to Brackettville, Texas, to do the film. Mr. Ford came out there, too, to help Duke with the second unit. The next year I worked with Mr. Ford again on *Two Rode Together* with Richard Widmark and Jimmy Stewart. Then it was *How The West Was Won,* where I worked on the John Ford segment with John Wayne. Then I did *Liberty Valance* and *McLintock!.* The John Ford segment on *How The West Was Won* was the Battle of Shiloh where Duke played General Sherman. His appearance was brief and it was the most critically acclaimed segment of the film.

"Of course, *The Alamo* was Duke's pet project. He financed it, he put it together, and he busted his butt for it. I was there and we worked hard. We would leave Fort Clark Guest Ranch at one o'clock in the morning with five wardrobe people. We'd go to the Alamo and dress six thousand as Santa Anna's army.

"At 1:30 A.M. they started bringing them out in waves and trucks. So at lunchtime we would all lie down in the dirt, no matter where we were. Duke would come up and say, 'Wardrobe!' And we'd just open our eyes and say, 'Working on it!' He just loved it. Whenever he called us, or whatever he said, we said 'Working on it,' and he just loved that. We didn't even know what he wanted. He just beamed. He had the kindest, beamingest grin you've ever seen on a man.

"People made a lot about the difficulties he had with Richard Widmark. But you can step on that. I never saw it. I admire and respect Widmark, whom I have worked with six times. Duke had a lot of pressure on the film and Widmark appreciated that point. He was acting and directing, with six hundred extras sitting out there, some half drunk, in the field. So you really couldn't expect Duke to be of good cheer every moment of the day.

"But they did have some disagreements. One time Duke snapped in the direction of Widmark. There were some extras behind Widmark. Widmark said, 'Don't talk to me like that!' Duke said, 'I wasn't talking to you!' But I guess it looked like he was. On another occasion Duke flipped a cigarette and it happened to land at Widmark's foot. And that ticked Widmark off. But Duke had a big undertaking, and Widmark didn't want to give any leeway for abuse whether it was directed at him or anybody. Without [my having] any discussion with Dick, I thought he just wanted to see that things didn't get out of hand. But I can also see how people could have thought otherwise.

"It was a long filming, about five months, which was monumental back then. I was there every day of the filming, including the day when the cannon fell and hit Laurence Harvey's foot and he couldn't walk for a while. I went up to Duke and said I was the same size and if he needed a stand-in for Harvey for a while he should let me know. He said, 'God, I really appreciate it.' This was a guy we all wanted to die for.

"I did *The Man Who Shot Liberty Valance* for Mr. Ford, and it meant working with Duke again. I thought *Liberty Valance* was one of the better jobs, not only from my end but in all aspects. The picture got nominated for Best Costume [Design] (black-and-white). Originally, it was designed by me and sketched by me for color. Then they went to black-and-white about two weeks before filming. I designed it for color and it worked for black-and-white.

"Lee Marvin had always been a renegade and one of my favorite people. This was Lee's first job with Mr. Ford. This was a very big undertaking with an all-star cast. We all got to be very good pals. Mr. Ford always kept a barrel on stage as kind of a punishment, and you never knew whose turn it would be to be in the barrel that day and that included Duke. When Andy Devine was designated for the barrel, we lined up the prop people to get him an oversized one. Andy kept saying, 'You're never going to get me in the barrel because I'm too big.' But the prop people found one and in went Andy.

"We even had a dunce hat. It was like Edmond O'Brien's paper hat that he wore in the printer's shop [in the film]. It was made of newspapers and [looked] like a pirate's hat. I was designated to wear it for a couple of days until I was told to take it off. Duke had a part in this.

"There was a costume ball called the Adam and Eve Ball, which was held at the Beverly Hilton. I had arranged for two tables to accommodate the cast. Of course, Mr. Ford came to me on Friday expecting me to meet him at the door. So here I am sweating. I'm still a young kid. He arrives and I take him through the kitchen. We got lost going through the lobby, and I don't know how I ended up in the kitchen. Well, they announce for Mr. Ford to come out to take a bow and give Duke his Adam and Eve Award. So Mr. Ford gets up. He has this eye patch and the room isn't well lit. Well, he trips down the two stairs momentarily, braces himself, jumps right up, and gets to the microphone. Then he announces Duke's award.

"So Duke walks up, and he, too, rolls down the two steps in order to back up Ford's actions. Everybody thought this was all in fun and they had a good laugh. On Monday I was in the dunce hat. I was blamed for Mr. Ford falling down since I didn't go to the table and escort him to the stage. I didn't know I was supposed to do that. So I had to wear the dunce hat for three days.

"The truth was that Duke did the same thing as Ford to make it look like that was what he was supposed to do all along. He did it to cover up Ford's bad sight. The audience just loved it. It was a validation. But he did this to take away the embarrassment from Ford. And I was blamed for the whole thing happening.

"One of the best stories I tell about *Liberty Valance* deals with costuming the picture. It was one of the largest all-star casts at the time [with] Duke, Jimmy Stewart, Lee Marvin, Edmond O'Brien, Woody Strode, Andy Devine.

"I was designing everybody's clothes. Mr. Ford was not well one day and he went home. He sent word to me to get the sketches quickly and take them over to his house. He wanted to see what I was doing. So I had a sketch artist come over to Western Costume where all the clothes were made, aged, and revamped. So all the clothes were sketched and taken over.

"Meanwhile, Duke had called up and said, 'Ron, I have all my old clothes and I don't want to come in for a fitting.' I said OK. About a week later Mr. Ford said he wanted to see Duke dressed in the office at Paramount. So I called him and said he should bring the stuff in. He said, 'Sure, Ron, no problem.'

"Now I had learned a trick from Mr. Beetson. Sometimes it was best when you had made-to-order clothes, to take the labels out, wash them several times, and throw them in the corner of the dressing room and let the actor or director pick them up. It's a trickery method and one we used a lot which many people don't know about.

Pappy's Last Hurrah

"I had done exactly that for Duke's clothes in *Liberty Valance*. I had already made them. So I go over for my designated time and appointment to meet Duke who is bringing in a box of clothes to show Mr. Ford. We go into an office down the hallway into Paramount, Duke with his box and me. He asked me what I thought of it. I said 'Fine. If you like it, I like it.' He proceeds to put the clothes on. Well, he can't button his shirt. He can't button his pants. He says, 'My God, what are we going to do?' I told him to wait just a minute. I called over to Western Costume, which was adjacent to Paramount. The man working there said we should bring the clothes over to Western Costume.

"I put them in a paper bag and brought them over. 'Try these,' I told Duke, handing him a new suit of clothes. He put them on and said, 'God, these fit me nice.' I had already gotten his recent measurements from his last job. So I knew we were making things that had a chance of fitting. He tried them on and he was just pleased. 'Wow, these are great,' he said. 'Where did you get them?' I told him I found them at Western Costume. 'These fit perfect,' he said again.

"He went in and showed Mr. Ford. He was real pleased. 'That's the idea,' Ford said with approval. Duke replied, 'Yes, Mr. Ford.' Duke would always say, 'Yes, sir!' or he would call him 'Pappy' or 'Mr. Ford.' There might have been a time or two he called him by his first name, but I don't recall it. It was always in the strictest of respect.

"Anyhow, we went back into an empty office and Duke says, 'Only one thing I want, Ron, is a cuff.' I asked him why—the pants weren't too short. He said, 'Lengthen it!' I still couldn't get his message. But if you recall his movies, he wears a turned-back cuff on his canvas pants. So I added a piece there and got them up. He said, 'Good, now don't forget, I want a bandanna!' I said, 'OK, what color?' He said, 'Coffee.'

"Three days later I met him on the set, and he said he had everything but the bandanna. I told him that I had it in my back pocket. He said to give it to him. So I reached in my pocket and gave him a bandanna. 'There you are,' I said. He looked at me like I was crazy. 'That's black,' he said. I told him he said coffee, and I drink my coffee black. He just looked at me again. Then from the other back pocket I pulled out a tan bandanna.

147

"That's my one highlight story I tell about Duke. He was ready to jump all over me, and when I pulled out the right bandanna, he just broke up and roared. He really roared. He had that great sense of humor.

"I used to have a boat and I'd go over to Catalina Island. He'd take his little outboard and come over with his little kids and visit. He was a good guy, one I was always proud to say hello to. I don't want to blow smoke and be a Hollywood story. But when you see a guy in Catalina and the makeup is gone and the guy just comes over to bullshit with you, this is one terrific guy. He was my kind of guy."

In 1963 John Wayne and John Ford made their last picture together. It was *Donovan's Reef.* Set and filmed in Hawaii, the picture costarred Lee Marvin, Jack Warden, Elizabeth Allen, and Mike Mazurki. On the set with Mazurki were his two teenage daughters.

Today Michelle Mazurki works for a movie talent agency in Southern California. She had longed for a career in the movie business since 1962, when her father was working on *Four For Texas* with Frank Sinatra and Dean Martin. During filming, she happened onto the set of *To Kill A Mockingbird* and walked by the tree where, in the film, the character Boo Radley left gifts for the kids. From then on, she was hooked.

Michelle Mazurki recalls having the time of her life in Hawaii making *Donovan's Reef* with John Wayne and Lee Marvin. But more important, she also had an unexpected role in making the film. Now, more than thirty years later, she looks back through the eyes of a teenager to vividly recall Wayne and John Ford in their last film together.

Michelle Mazurki

"My father was a well-known character actor, and he appeared in many of Wayne's movies. In 1962 he got this job on *Donovan's Reef* and somehow he arranged that my sister and I could go to Hawaii for the filming. He even managed to get us jobs as extras. We lived

Pappy's Last Hurrah

With Elizabeth Allen in *Donovan's Reef* (1963)

in a beautiful villa, which was paradise. We'd work in the morning doing a beach scene. We'd have beautiful, lavish buffets, then we would go home and swim and surf all day. It was a total vacation, plus we were getting very good money.

"I remember we were filming on the most beautiful estate on Kawai. I saw the movie on TV and marveled on how beautiful it was. One day we were all standing around doing whatever, and they needed a stand-in for John Wayne. John Ford was there with that patch over his eye and with his hat on, and he's looking around.

"He's yelling for John Wayne's stand-in. Everyone is looking bewildered and kind of nodding at each other. Somehow they managed to forget to arrange a stand-in for John Wayne. Ford looks around and he decides that because I was the tallest person, I would stand-in for Duke. All of the extras were dark-haired natives who were five feet or under. My sister and I were both over six feet tall and we were blond. John Ford was running up and down the set and took one look at us and goes, 'Put hats on those two.' So they are looking for a stand-in and he points to me and goes, 'You, you'll be John Wayne's stand-in!' So I became the only woman who ever stood in for John Wayne in a movie.

"John Wayne was a very big man in stature, and he was very polite. He was just very immense in every way. He was an amazing man. He was down-to-earth. What you saw was really the way he was. I was a teenager then and he definitely was very macho. He used to walk very straight. He was very purposeful in his walk. Oh, he was very manly. My father was very manly and they were the same type. You knew he was a star just by his presence. You kind of kept your distance.

"Not long ago, I was watching a rerun of that interview with Barbara Walters. It was when he had cancer and he knew he had cancer. I remember thinking that regardless of his politics, he was straight on. He said what he believed. He was a true American. He was very patriotic. Basically, there was no bull about him. He was a real meat-and-potatoes kind of guy. I got to thinking that he had basically stood for the best this country had to offer back then. I admired him more and more as I got older. I could see so many [more] fine qualities in him than I did when I was younger. I really admired him for what he stood for. Right, wrong, or indifferent, he had firm convictions. On the screen he conjures up that picture even now.

"It was great working on *Donovan's Reef*. It is still one of my favorite John Wayne films. Not just because my father was in it, but because it was more contemporary. There was also some humor. It was very much a family affair. Most of the people had their kids. When we weren't filming we were by the pool. I remember going over on the plane. Lee Marvin was very funny. He was a funny, funny guy. All the stars were in first class and all the family members were in tourist. My sister and I were sitting next to Lee Marvin's wife and kids. Lee had all these little towheaded kids.

"We were young and impressionable, and somebody was slipping us some champagne. So my father walked back with a glass of champagne. He said, 'I want my girls to taste this because I don't want you having any back here.' So we said, 'OK, Dad!' We tasted the champagne and said, 'Oh, this is terrible. Don't worry about us Dad, we won't have any of that.' So he left and we kept drinking champagne. We were giggling all the time during the flight.

"I recall watching how well Duke and Lee Marvin played off each other and how they seemed to have genuinely liked each other. They were old pros. Unlike some other films, there was no friction on the set. Everyone seemed to get along fine. But I'm seeing this through a young girl's eyes.

"John Ford was very imposing, a very imposing man. When he said something, people listened. I was aware of his reputation as a director. But to see him in person he was really quite remarkable. Growing up, we were always around a lot of movie people. Whenever my father was making a movie, or was in town, we'd go to the set. There was always a lot of people around. You were aware that it was something special.

"John Wayne had that same star quality. One day we were all sitting for lunch. The lunches were beautiful. They would bring in those long, long tables, and the cast and crew would sit down and have beautiful fresh fruit, rice, chicken, and fish. It was just gorgeous. I was sitting next to my father and John Wayne was across from me and over one. He turned to my father and said, 'She looks like Marlene Dietrich.' Well, you can imagine how flattered I was. John Wayne and Marlene Dietrich had a thing many years before, I had heard, and he told me I looked like her.

"I tracked her down once in New York and told her the story. I now have this beautiful photograph of Marlene Dietrich, autographed 'To Michele, my lookalike.'"

12. "McLintock!," Maureen and Majesty

> As much as I couldn't stand some of the old moguls—
> especially Harry Cohn—these men took an interest in
> the future of their business. They had integrity. There
> was a stretch when they realized that they made a
> hero out of a goddamn gangster heavy in crime
> movies, that they were doing a discredit to their
> country. So the moguls voluntarily took it upon
> themselves to stop making gangster pictures. But
> today's executives don't give a damn.
>
> — John Wayne, *Playboy*
> (May 1971)

Duke admired Darryl Zanuck and had considered him a friend for many years. Zanuck began his career writing stories for *Rin Tin Tin* before becoming production chief at Warner Brothers in 1931. He cofounded Century Productions in 1933 which in 1935 merged with Fox Studios where he was vice president in charge of production from 1935 to 1952. After ten years as an independent producer, in 1962 he became executive president of 20th Century-Fox and massed a string of achievements matched by few in the movie business.

From the day Zanuck first read Cornelius Ryan's bestselling book *The Longest Day*, he was determined to bring it to the screen. Since production costs would be enormous, Zanuck hoped to save money by having members of his all-star cast make only cameo appearances throughout the film.

His international cast was a grand array of top-line talent, one of the most impressive ever assembled for a single film: Robert Mitchum, Henry Fonda, Robert Ryan, Red Buttons, Richard Burton, Rod Steiger, Sean Connery, and more.

Zanuck originally signed almost everyone he wanted except

152

With Peri Alcaide and Howard Hawks on the set of *Hatari* in 1962
(Courtesy Peri Alcaide)

John Wayne, with whom he had fallen out a couple of years earlier after his tirade against *The Alamo*.

In a printed interview, Zanuck railed against actors who were
exerting increasing control over screenplays, salaries, and directors by forming their own production companies. He criticized Burt
Lancaster, Kirk Douglas, and Marlon Brando, but he was particularly hard on John Wayne who he said had no right to produce,
direct, *and* star in *The Alamo*. He went on to say he pitied "poor old
Duke Wayne" for his incompetent producing talents. While "poor
old Duke" was breaking box office records, he was nevertheless
deeply hurt by Zanuck's attack and the tone of his invective.

Zanuck now needed Duke for the part of Lt. Colonel Benjamin
Vandervoot who led the heroic 82nd Airborne Division through
the Normandy Invasion. When he first came to Wayne, Duke

couldn't have cared less. Even an appeal to Duke's patriotism wouldn't budge him. Duke finally agreed to take the role, but for $250,000—an amount far greater than the $30,000 other big stars were getting for their cameo parts. While Duke knew it was an excessive demand, he never figured Zanuck would agree. But Zanuck swallowed his pride and agreed to pay Duke $250,000 for four days work, with a stipulation that Duke could delay filming if Pilar, now pregnant with son Ethan, gave birth.

Years later Duke talked about taking all that money. "Poor old Zanuck," he commented. "I shouldn't have been that rotten, I guess. . . . I always liked that son of a bitch, but I was goddam mad at his attack on me. But you know, it was nice that when I got over there on location, old Zanuck was decent to me. He was so pleasant that I kinda wished I hadn't charged him that much money. That had to be the most expensive interview a movie producer ever gave."

The Longest Day was a critical and box office smash. It won a number of prestigious awards and received five Academy Award nominations, including Best Picture. It captured Oscars for cinematography (black-and-white) and special effects. Duke appeared eight times in the film for a total of twelve minutes and thirteen seconds, and his name topped billing for the all-star cast. It marked one of the few times that mighty Zanuck was forced to eat humble pie.

Soon after the funeral of Ward Bond, Wayne traveled to Tanganyika in East Africa to shoot *Hatari* for Howard Hawks. Despite his depression over Bond's death and his less than successful promotion campaign for *The Alamo,* the months in East Africa lifted his spirits. Pilar and the children made the trip with him, and Hawks was a director he respected and trusted.

Hatari (the name means "danger" in Swahili) did well at the box office, grossing more than $14 million. East Africa's scenic beauty reminded Duke of the austere beauty of southern Arizona where he and Hawks made *Red River.* David Bongard, film critic for the *Los Angeles Herald-Examiner,* praised the film for its "thrilling and believable bit of photography engineered by producer-director Howard Hawks and cameraman Russell Harlan." The film captured an Oscar for Best (color) Cinematography.

Peri Alcaide was one of the top foreign movie correspondents based in the United States. Interviewing John Wayne on the set of *Hatari* was among the major plums of her career—not just because he was big box office here in the United States, but because he was America's top movie attraction in her native Turkey. Peri and actor Chris Alcaide, her husband of more than forty years, once owned and operated an art gallery in West Hollywood which for many years catered to stars and collectors alike. She remembers John Wayne as a real man and a gentleman.

Peri Alcaide

"I was a foreign correspondent from Turkey and represented five papers at the time, including the *Istanbul Express* for which I wrote a column every week. In Hollywood I worked as a foreign correspondent for twenty-five years. I was treated so very well. I socialized with the best of them, the big ones like Jimmy Stewart and Jimmy Cagney, both of whom were fine men.

"John Wayne was a hero in Turkey. He was a hero everywhere. [In] Europe, he was the king. Clark Gable was called the king, but John Wayne *was* the king. Whenever I think of American men, John Wayne comes first, as much as George Washington. He [Wayne] was a good American, too. We always loved to see his movies. I told John Wayne and Howard Hawks they should come and make a picture in Turkey and the Turkish Government would give up a whole army for them.

"John Wayne was one of the most down-to-earth people I ever met. I had never thought of him like that, so I was really quite surprised. The first time I met John Wayne was at a department store. He was buying patio equipment and he was [there with] his whole family. It was in Akron. They used to sell the most beautiful things for less money. They were all laughing and were having such a good time. I said that one of these days I was going to come down to the studio and do an interview and have my picture taken with him. John Wayne said, 'Anytime, anytime.'

"I found him to be so much the gentleman. I had no idea he could be so kind. He had that same nice quality as Gregory Peck. John Wayne gave me the impression he was a very strong man, a gentleman. I expected a very rough man and found the opposite. He could remember everything he made, every picture. It shows me what he did was not just for fame and money, it was for art. You use everything that is in you to make a picture meaningful.

"Although *Hatari* was filmed in Africa, there were still lots of animals when they [continued filming] in the studio. I interviewed him on the set of *Hatari*. Both Wayne and Howard Hawks treated me so good that I felt I had known them for a hundred years. I was deeply impressed with Howard Hawks. He was a very modest man. I could see that Wayne respected Howard Hawks very much. He would even defer to Mr. Hawks. He brought out what was best in John Wayne. If an actor doesn't like his producer and director, it usually shows.

"The guy was a straight guy. Like you say, he was a straight shooter. There was nothing phony about him. This is why I admired him so greatly. You would never know he was such a big actor and star. He was just a real man, and that's what I admire. I love America and I love American men. But I think in this country women often expect too much from a man. To keep a man is an art. John Wayne represented what a man should be: strong, gentle, honest, and very polite to women. He was real. He was the 'Real McCoy!'"

In the summer of 1961 Duke signed a ten-picture deal with Paramount, which included a $6,000,000 advance. Consequently, most of his money problems, incurred while making *The Alamo*, vanished. During the next thirty months he made six pictures for Paramount. These included *The Man Who Shot Liberty Valence*, *Donovan's Reef*, and *McLintock!*.

Shooting ended on *Donovan's Reef* in August 1962. In late September Duke took his family and headed to Arizona to shoot Andy McLaglen's *McLintock!* for Batjac. McLaglen's association with John Wayne had been a long and positive one, and it was fitting that Duke should star in his first major Western film. Because of his long friendship with Victor McLaglen, Duke had literally watched Andy grow up in the business, so working with him was a real pleasure.

In certain ways *McLintock!* was like a family affair. Duke's two oldest sons had a big hand in the project. Michael was producing, and Pat had a leading role. Pilar was on location and Aissa had a bit part in the film. Chuck Roberson, Duke's good pal and favorite stuntman, played the sheriff. His longtime pal Bruce Cabot also had a part. And Bill Clothier, another old friend, was cinematographer.

Clothier, who died in 1996 at ninety-three, was behind the camera in no less than twenty-five Wayne films between 1950 and 1973, picking up an Oscar nomination for *The Alamo* in 1960. Of all cinematographers, only Archie Stout, whose career began in the nineteen thirties, shot as many pictures as Clothier.

What Duke enjoyed most was being teamed again with Maureen O'Hara. O'Hara was one of the few women with whom Duke felt completely comfortable. She was a special friend who stood by him through thick and thin, during his bad times with Chata, then later with Pilar. Fortunately, the friendship never resulted in marriage. Mary St. John once said, "They are the two strongest people I have ever known. They would have been like oil and water as man and wife." *McLintock!* again radiates with their screen chemistry.

McLintock! combined action and comedy for a real treat. As George Washington McLintock, Duke is cattle baron, banker, and leading citizen of the territorial town of McLintock.

McLintock! featured a mudhole scene which was one of Duke's favorites. The script called for a huge brawl at the edge of a mudhole, with dozens of people sliding down the hill into the muck during the fight. This free-for-all sequence cost $50,000. It all began when Duke took a swipe at bad guy Leo Gordon. Duke's challenge to Gordon after taking his shotgun from him provides perhaps the film's most enduring moment and one of his most unforgettable lines:

"I haven't lost my temper in forty years, but pilgrim, you caused a lot of trouble this morning, mighta got somebody killed and somebody should belt you in the mouth. But I won't. The hell I won't!"

Leo Gordon

"I recall that day well. [John] Ford came down and was visiting one day and you'd have thought the real big mucky muck of the world was there the way Wayne catered to him. I was the one he called 'Pilgrim' in that classic scene. I'm the guy he knocks down after he says, 'The hell I won't!' The interesting thing about that is they used a drilling material called bentonite in the construction of the hill, making it slippery as hell. It is a clay derivative used in drilling oil wells and making chocolate syrup. They needed two tons, which they mixed with water, and the bentonite was constantly reheated.

"So the first guy to go down there is my double. He cracked the hell out of his head and was bleeding all over the place. So I had to do it the next shot. And before it was over, they had everybody doing it, including Maureen O'Hara. No doubles at all. We spent a week in that goddamned thing. It was cold as hell."

13. C for Courage: The Duke's Finest Hour

> There it was—the rumor, and after a while the headlines. "I licked the Big C," John Wayne announced, as John Wayne would, reducing those outlaw cells to the level of any other outlaws; but even so, we all sensed that this would be the one unpredictable confrontation, the one shootout Wayne could lose.
>
> — Joan Didion, the *Saturday Evening Post* (August 1965)

John Wayne may have been the immortal Duke to movie fans and even some of his friends, but five to six packs of cigarettes a day is not a prescription for good health. What was extraordinary about his ugly bout with cancer was Wayne's courage in handling the disease and his decision to go public with it. This might well have been Duke's finest hour.

After discovering the tumor on Duke's lung, the physicians at Scripps referred him to Dr. John E. Jones and the surgical team at Good Samaritan Hospital in Los Angeles. It was September and Wayne bluntly asked Dr. Jones if he'd be ready to film *The Sons of Katie Elder* in November. The doctor was candid. "No way, Duke. . . . You'll have to reschedule the movie." Surgery was performed on September 17, 1964. The tumor was the size of a golf ball. Doctors removed Duke's left lung, part of his right lung, and a rib. The recovery was tough and painful. The good news, however, was that the tumor was self-contained, and the cancer had not spread.

At the time of the surgery Wayne's closest advisors reached a consensus on what to tell the press. Batjac released a statement explaining that John Wayne was in Good Samaritan to repair an old ankle injury he had incurred during the 1957 filming of *Legend of the Lost* and reinjured on *Circus World*.

Duke, We're Glad We Knew You

John Wayne was human. Finding out about the cancer, he said, was "like somebody hit me across the belly with a baseball bat. It wasn't just the fear of death. It [was] the helplessness. I couldn't see myself lying on a bed, not able to do anything for myself, no damned good to anybody. I felt like a jerk."

But if there was one thing he hated, it was to mislead people. His health had become a hot topic in Hollywood in the fall of 1964, and rumors abounded. At the time, singer Nat "King" Cole was also being treated for lung cancer at St. John's Hospital in Santa Monica, and a reporter had bribed a technician for the truth about Cole's illness. The last thing Duke wanted was for America to discover his cancer the same way. His image revolved around candor and honesty. He decided it was time to go public.

On December 29, 1964, Duke gave an exclusive interview to his friend, syndicated columnist James Bacon. The interview took place in the den of Wayne's Encino, California, home and appeared in the *New York Times* the following day. In part, Duke said:

> "I wanted to tell [the truth] right from the start but all the statements were given out while I was doped up under sedation. By the time I got on my feet the damage was done. . . . My advisors all thought it would destroy my image, but there's a lot of good image in John Wayne licking cancer—and that's what my doctors tell me. . . . I had the Big C, but I've beaten the son of a bitch. Maybe I can give some poor bastard a little hope by being honest. I want people to know cancer can be licked. . . . I feel great now. On January 4, I'll go to Durango, Mexico, to start *The Sons of Katie Elder.* It's a typical John Wayne Western, so you know I have to be in good health. I didn't get famous doing drawing room comedies."

As soon as Duke completed the interview, he drove to St. John's to see Cole. He did his best to encourage the great singer, and they had a pleasant visit. But while Duke's cancer had been contained, Cole's had spread to the lymph nodes. Nat Cole died on February 15, 1965, slightly more than a month later.

C for Courage: The Duke's Finest Hour

Writer James Bacon reported that after the surgery Duke received more than fifty thousand letters. Less than four months later he was back at work, heading south to Durango to start filming *The Sons of Katie Elder* for Henry Hathaway. The crusty Hathaway had survived colon cancer himself and was not about to soft-soap Duke. Hathaway was a tough taskmaster, and refused to go easy with him. Later Duke would credit Hathaway for pushing him through.

"Duke had the greatest respect for Henry both as a director and as a man," says Luster Bayless, who was Wayne's personal costumer and close friend. "In fact, Duke told me later that Henry had helped save his life because he hadn't shown him any damn sympathy following his surgery. Henry made him work like nothing had happened."

Hathaway worked him hard and Duke managed to survive the filming on little more than sheer willpower. The result was perhaps the last family-type western. *The Sons of Katie Elder* teamed Duke once more with Dean Martin as brothers John and Tom Elder, who are reunited with younger brothers Matt (Earl Holliman) and Bud (Michael Anderson Jr.) at the funeral of their mother, Katie.

Press coverage for the film exceeded that for *The Alamo*, but if the press hoped to find signs of a faltering and sick John Wayne, they were sadly disappointed. What they saw was a leaner John Wayne who appeared in better shape than in his previous few films.

A straightforward Western yarn full of action and adventure, with an exciting musical score by Elmer Bernstein, *The Sons of Katie Elder* was John Wayne's 135th picture and Henry Hathaway's 84th. It also marked the final time Wayne wore a double-breasted shirt, the type he had worn in almost all his Western films since *Stagecoach*. While Hathaway spared Duke little comfort, he still made sure Duke could finish filming at the remote locations. It took real grit and courage, but Duke survived the rigorous action scenes intact.

Despite their strong political differences, John Wayne and Kirk Douglas greatly respected each other's professional abilities, and their contrasting styles were well-suited for the big screen. In 1966 Duke and Douglas appeared together in *Cast A Giant Shadow* which Duke also helped produce through his Batjac Production Company, much to the delight of writer-director Melville Shavelson.

161

It is the story of Col. David Marcus (Douglas) who forms a ragtag Israeli army into a first-class fighting unit to face the Arabs after the birth of Israel in 1948. Duke's role is a small one. He plays General Randolph, who tries to stop Marcus, still technically an officer in the American army. Although he appears on-screen for only eleven minutes, he plays his sequences with appealing subtlety and conviction, particularly when Marcus shames the general into personally inspecting the Nazi death camp at Dachau. Duke says little, but his eyes tell volumes of what he feels.

In 1967 it was Wayne and Douglas once more in *War Wagon*. Again the interplay between Wayne and Douglas is first-rate, with Duke as Taw Jackson, who is out of jail on parole and determined to gain revenge on the man who defrauded him (Bruce Cabot). Douglas plays Lomax, the gunman who is hired to kill Jackson but instead is won over to Jackson's side for a hefty sum.

War Wagon was one of two Westerns Duke did for writer-director Burt Kennedy. One of the genre's most entertaining directors, Kennedy also directed Wayne in the 1973 Western *The Train Robbers* with Ann-Margret and Ben Johnson.

Kennedy is a former radio and TV writer who made his name in film by penning the best of Budd Boetticher's outstanding Westerns of the fifties. Kennedy himself turned to directing in the nineteen sixties. He is one of the few Western directors to film a successful Western spoof, *Support Your Local Sheriff* (1969) with James Garner. Kennedy's other works include *The Rounders* (1965) and *Support You Local Gunfighter* (1971). His association with John Wayne dates back to 1953.

Burt Kennedy

"I met John Wayne in 1953, and soon after that I went to work for his company doing a script. Duke kind of took me off the streets. My folks were in vaudeville years ago, and they worked for a guy named Bob O'Donnell who owned a bunch of theaters down in Texas. Duke told me himself that it was Bob O'Donnell who told him to look me up and maybe do something for me. I worked

C for Courage: The Duke's Finest Hour

for his company for two months. After that he put me under contract, and I remained under contract to him for about seven years. Then I left him in the early sixties when I started to direct.

"The first script I wrote for him was called *Seven Men From Now*. That's the one Budd [Boetticher] and I did with Randy Scott. Duke used to say to me that he should have his throat cut for not acting in it himself. The problem is that I came in as this little guy and they had just paid a fortune for a script called "Quality of Mercy" by Ben Hecht. They paid a lot of money for it. I think my script was about $1,500, so they reasoned that it probably wasn't that good. It wasn't until Bob Mitchum offered me a lot of money for the script because he wanted to do it that Duke said, 'Wait a minute, let me take a look at it.'

"So they sent it to Warners and Jack Warner read the script and told Duke he wanted him to do it. Duke had just done *The Searchers* and didn't want to do another Western right away. Then it fell to Budd and they did the picture. *Seven Men From Now* is a good picture, a very good story. Budd and I are both proud of it. But it's not on video. It's owned by Batjac and they haven't released it. I don't know why.

"I wrote another script for Duke. It was called *The Tall T*. But when Bob Fellows and Duke split up, part of the settlement was that the script for *The Tall T* went to Bob. So he turned around and sold it to Columbia for Randy Scott to do. Budd directed it, and the film still gets outstanding reviews. So I wrote two scripts with Duke in mind that Randy Scott ended up doing for Budd and me.

"I directed Duke twice—in *War Wagon* and then later in *The Train Robbers*. He was fine to direct, except sometimes he'd get ornery. I always said that when Duke thought he was at his best, he was at his very worst. And only Ford, who would actually grab Duke and push his face around, was in total control. He really directed him. He couldn't make a move that Ford didn't yell at him. Duke tells a lot of stories about Ford getting on him. He really molded Duke into what Duke was and there are very few of us— especially me—who could match him.

"I always describe Ford as the Ty Cobb of the picture business— anything to get a hit. Ford was like that. The work was rough but he helped a lot of people. A guy came into Ford's office one time

163

and wanted to borrow money because his wife was sick, and Ford bawled the shit out of him. The guy went away and Ford sent his manager after him. He gave him a thousand bucks, sent a car to pick up his wife, paid the bills, that kind of stuff.

"Duke borrowed a lot from Ford. He mimicked Ford in a lot of things, a lot of good things, too. Duke could be the greatest guy on earth and the biggest jerk you ever saw. He and Budd didn't always get on that well. Budd had a giant ego and Duke had a giant ego. But that's part of what this game is about.

"The great anecdote I tell about filming *War Wagon* has to do with Duke and Kirk. In Kirk's book [*The Ragman's Son*] he said I was afraid of Duke. Well, everybody's afraid of Duke. At the very first shot in the picture, Kirk was playing the dandy. He had a glove with a little ring on his little finger. Duke came up to me and said, 'Jeeze, you see that goddamn ring? He looks like a faggot. He'll ruin the goddamn movie!'

"So I said, 'Well, it's the first shot so I better get it off of him.' Duke said OK, so we both walked over to Kirk. I said, 'Kirk, don't you think the ring is a little much?' Kirk says, 'No, I think it's good. What do you think, Duke?' Duke says, 'No, I think it's fine!' That's kind of the way it went the whole picture.

"Duke wasn't a very good gun bearer. He'd nudge you into doing something. Then he wouldn't back you up. But Duke and Kirk got along as well as they were supposed to. The story is about two guys who didn't like each other but were in it for the money. Their politics, of course, were different. But only one time did Kirk get a little miffed. We took time out and I shot a little something for the governor's race, a little blurb for Ronnie Reagan. He was running for governor at the time. Kirk sat beside me and made some comments. 'The sun's up and here we are doing this shit!' But they were fine. I don't think they had any trouble at all.

"The fact is that when we made *War Wagon* they were trying to get Rod Taylor. I gave up half my salary for Kirk Douglas to make the picture, because he and Duke were always good together. They had great conflict just walking down the street. With *The Train Robbers,* I didn't have the people in it I wanted. I didn't want Rod Taylor, I wanted Jack Elam who had just done *Rio Lobo* with Duke. But Duke wanted Taylor.

164

C for Courage: The Duke's Finest Hour

"I think Duke was at his very best in *Red River* and *The Searchers*. To me, those are the best pictures he made. He also did some wonderful work in non-Westerns. *They Were Expendable,* which he did with Ford, was a great picture. They made that at the end of the war. Duke always liked *The Long Voyage Home* and so did I. *Trouble Along the Way* was a good one. So was *The High and the Mighty.* In fact I loved it. I was working for him at the time, and when I first saw it without the musical score, it was not a particularly good picture. But with Tiomkin's score it became great. I loved Duke's character, especially when he walks away at the end whistling that damned thing.

"Tiomkin was great. I did a movie called *Welcome To Hard Times* with Henry Fonda, and Tiomkin was going to score it. He came in and we ran this picture together. He said he loved this picture and he wanted to do it. I said, 'You'll do it unless you get a bigger one to do.' And he did. He scored *War Wagon* for me.

"Duke was kind of a giant, not just in stature. He had this unmistakable presence. I remember one time I walked on stage when they were making *El Dorado,* and Duke and Bob Mitchum were standing together. And in the middle was James Caan and it looked like he wasn't there. People just disappeared when they were around those guys. Lee Marvin was another one of those guys who just had it when he walked in front of the camera.

"I was visiting the set when they were doing *Rio Bravo.* Ricky Nelson had a guitar and Dean Martin was singing a song about 'My Rifle, My Pony, and Me.' I said to Duke, 'You know that's the theme from *Red River.*' Tiomkin wrote the score for both films. Duke was tone deaf and said, 'Like hell it is.'

"There is another story Duke told me that nobody has heard before. After he did *Stagecoach* he invited Sol and Moe Siegal, who were executives at Republic, to a showing of the film. *Stagecoach* was produced by United Artists but Duke had his contract with Republic. When it was over, they went across the street. Duke sat there but the Siegals didn't say a word about it. Finally he got up and went over to their table and said, 'What do you think?' And Sol Siegal said, 'From now on you better let Republic make the Westerns.' And it went on to be nominated for seven Academy Awards and lost out only because they did *Gone With the Wind* that year.

165

"I went to visit Duke at UCLA hospital. A friend of mine did a sculpting piece on him, and we went down to give it to him. He looked very drawn but he was up and around. Then I saw him again in the hospital and he really looked bad. I knew he was going. I was with Al Murphy and we were waiting in the hall. Now Al Murphy was a little guy whose real name was Silverstein. It was not uncommon back then for people with Jewish names, or for that matter for people with other ethnic-sounding names, to change them for professional reasons. Anyhow, Duke would always kid Al about that. It was his way of showing that he liked you.

"Well, when Michael [Wayne] said we could go in and see him, as sick as he was he started giving us this Irish-Jewish routine. Almost till the end he kept that great sense of humor of his. That great sense of humor, that wonderful sense of humor is the big thing I'll always remember about him. And when you'd tell him a story, he'd actually fall down laughing sometimes. But I knew when I left him that day I would never see him again. This was just about a month before he died. You could see how sick he was.

"But during those later years none of us really saw him that much. He didn't hang out except when he was doing a picture. I loved Duke, but he could be many, many guys. I can leave you with one line. I had such a rough time with Duke in *War Wagon*. He was going to begin *The Green Berets*. Some people were asking if I'd like to direct him in *The Green Berets*. I told them other things being equal, I'd rather *join* the Green Berets!"

War Wagon was filmed in the fall of 1966 and released in May 1967. Just a month later *El Dorado* hit the screen. Howard Hawks began filming *El Dorado* in the fall of 1965, pairing Duke and Robert Mitchum for the first time. However, Paramount did not want the film to conflict with the opening of *Nevada Smith* in the summer of 1966, so the studio did not release the film until June 1967.

El Dorado was the fourth teaming of Wayne and Hawks and in some ways was a recycled *Rio Bravo,* though Hawks denied any such contention. But the real fun was in watching Duke Wayne and Bob Mitchum play off one another while limping along side by side on crutches.

166

With Robert Mitchum in *El Dorado* (1967)

El Dorado was one of the first films for actor Robert Donner. Stationed on the West Coast during his stint in the navy, Donner decided to stay in California. He worked as a bartender, a shipping clerk, and an insurance investigator. Then an actor and his wife moved into Donner's apartment complex. They became friends, and before the struggling actor lost his option at Universal, he suggested Donner might pursue acting himself. He told Donner he had the voice and appearance and ought to give it a try.

Donner eventually followed through. By that time his actor friend had become a popular TV star in a Western series—*Rawhide*. The actor's name was Clint Eastwood.

After appearing in *Rawhide*, Donner went on to appear in such pictures as *Cool Hand Luke, The Man Who Loved Cat Dancing,* and *High Plains Drifter*. He worked in four pictures with John Wayne: *El Dorado, The Undefeated, Chisum,* and *Rio Bravo*.

Robert Donner

"My first recognition of Duke was when I'd go to the movies as a kid. There he was, twenty-five feet tall on that screen. Even more interesting is that I found him to be just the same when I actually met him.

"I first met John Wayne when we were down in Old Tucson making *El Dorado*. Basically, Howard Hawks was the one who introduced him to me. When I first looked at him, he had recently come back from lung surgery. I looked at him and I saw the moves he was making with his shoulder, the way he turned around. I said, 'My God, this man is a caricature of himself.' You see him on a twenty-five-foot screen and he moves so largely. Then all of a sudden you see him [in person], and you realize this is the way he really moves, and that it works.

"I'll never forget the first scene I was in with him. We were down in Old Tucson filming *El Dorado*. I had met the other guys in the cast, Bob Mitchum, Chris George, all of them. But I hadn't met Duke yet. It's the scene where I'm going to bushwhack him when he comes out of this cantina. I'm hiding behind the barrel waiting to bushwhack him. It was my first scene and I really didn't understand what was going on.

"The problem is that I'm hiding back there, but the audience has to see me hiding. I have to be hiding in front of the window, so the audience can see back there. But it's not getting through to me. All of a sudden, here comes Duke and he picks me up by the shoulders and he places me in front of the window. And he says, 'If the little guy will come up in front of the window, maybe somebody will see him.' And he walks off.

"Well, 'the little guy' comes up in front of the window, so they can see him. Cut: Print. It was OK. Well, I swallow my testicles

C for Courage: The Duke's Finest Hour

which are up in my throat, and I walk up to Duke and say, 'Excuse me, Mr. Wayne. But this little guy's name is Robert Donner.' And he turns around and says, 'Oh, hell, I know that!' And he gives me a little slug on the shoulder and walks away. And that was the end of it. But this was [my] introduction to Duke.

"After *El Dorado*, we did *Undefeated*. We did it down in Durango, Mexico. We are standing in the middle of town, a place out in the sticks. The mountains and rocks appear to be a giant pipe organ, and the wind is blowing. We're Confederates. Duke is a northerner but we join forces because the banditos are coming in. Now I'm standing with Merlin Olsen and someone says we are going to do scene 246 or something like that. I look down and I say, 'I think I'm in the wrong boots.' Now Duke hears this. And he just turns around and says, 'If they're just checking your boots, cowboy, we lost them.'

"There's a scene in the picture where Ben Johnson and I get into a fight. We're sitting and fishing and the next thing you know we are fighting. Now it was cold in Durango, but Andy [McLaglen] would go down there and feel the water. He'd say, 'No, no, not today.' The water wasn't cold enough for him. As I recall, he'd drag Duke into it. 'Duke, what do you think?' Duke would say, 'No, No! It's not cold enough.' So this went on for days. Well, one day they decided it was cold enough. Believe me, it was cold! And they finally decided to send 'them two boys' into it to see how it worked. Ben Johnson can tell you. It was cold!

"On a lot of Duke's movies there was a still photographer on the set. Dave Sutton was one. The other was Phil Stern. Phil had been a photographer for *Life* for many years. He and Duke were good friends, as was Dave Sutton.

"Well, Duke was a Republican, and Phil was a Democrat. And these guys would go at it. Night after night, they'd get into these political arguments, drinking tequila and having these slam-bam arguments. Of course, the next day everything was forgotten.

"Phil Stern and I were doing a picture in the Canary Islands once. We are sitting there and we are both well along. We had a nice dinner and a little wine. Phil says, 'You know Duke's birthday is coming up. We ought to send him a present.' So we put our minds together and we came up with a birthday present for Duke.

Duke, We're Glad We Knew You

We sent him a year's subscription to *Pravda* [the official Soviet newspaper].

"Duke had a lot of respect for Howard Hawks. Howard used to drink dry martinis. His idea of a martini was half vermouth and half gin—in a bucket. He was a wonderful companion and a wonderful storyteller. He claimed he once said to Duke years before, 'Look! You do two good scenes in a picture that doesn't bore anybody and you will be a star.' And when you think about it, it is true. Think about any movie you really love, and there are two particular scenes in that film that you love, and the rest of the time you are not bored.

"When we worked with Andy McLaglen, you had a full script and you did the script. With Hawks it was different. Ninety-nine percent of the time Howard would tell you what the story was. But you didn't have the script. Howard would walk around and say. 'Duke, why don't you say such and such?' And then 'Bob, you say such and such, and then you can do such and such, and then go.' That's basically it. You'd run it a few times. There was a script. But on many occasions he was rewriting it as he went along.

"So, often you hear people say that Duke just played himself. Look, the toughest thing in the world is to play yourself. If you can hide in a character, you can hide behind an accent and the makeup. In other words, you can submerge. I always felt the difference between a star and a supporting actor is that the supporting actor submerges into the character. The star submerges the character into his personality. I think that's more difficult.

"People say Duke said the same thing over and over again. Maybe he did. But you stayed there to see it. And he always said it differently. I just thought he was a wonderful actor. You don't sustain a career as long as he did unless you are striking some kind of nerve in the public.

"You never needed to [ask] where Duke stood on things. You may not have agreed with him, but you knew exactly where he stood. My experience with him was that as long as you did your job, you didn't have a problem with him. If you didn't know your job and you didn't do your job, then you had a problem with Duke.

"The last experience I had with Duke, he was down in Newport Beach. He was quite ill. I was there with Lee Majors and Lee said he was going to give Duke a call and see if we could go over and visit him. I hadn't seen Duke in several years. He said come on over, so we went over with our wives to visit him. I was the last one in the door and he took a look at me and said, 'Well, it's been a while since I kicked the crap out of you.' That was his way of saying 'Hi! How are you?' When we left Duke's house, I said goodbye, and that was it.

"And he had a laugh. When he thought something was funny, wow! He was a very good chess player. On one occasion I was watching. I don't know who he was playing, but he was chewing tobacco at the time. So he had this cup that you spit the chew into. He was so involved in the game and he turns to the side, keeps his eyes on the board, and spits. I said, 'Oh shit, Duke!' Now I have broken his concentration. He says, 'What the hell's your problem, mister?' I said, 'Goddammit, you spit on my boot, Duke!' Well he thought that was the funniest thing that ever happened. And he laughed and laughed. I don't know what he found so humorous, but he just cracked up.

"He left such a great legacy. I think off the top of my head that maybe he was the guy you always wished you had been. The qualities he stood for in his career are the qualities he really stood for: love of country, honesty, [being] a decent human being, loyalty, and fair play. He had pals that lasted a lifetime. Like I said earlier, you never needed to ask where Duke stood. He had his beliefs, and the kind of characters he played were strong characters. And on the side of right."

14. Politics and the Sixties: Duke Under Siege

> He was a wonderful American, a very decent man, a complete gentleman, and a person I was glad to know, both as a person and a friend.
>
> — Barry Goldwater, in *John Wayne: American*, 1995

> His medal [from Congress] should be made of the same stuff his heart is—solid gold.
>
> — General Omar Bradley, in *John Wayne: American*, 1995

John Wayne's politics were well known. He was a conservative Republican long before it was in vogue. He campaigned actively for Barry Goldwater for president in 1964 and for Ronald Reagan for governor of California. The protesters of the sixties reminded him of the Hollywood liberals of the thirties and forties, privileged people whose lifestyles reeked of capitalism and money.

Wayne's position on the Vietnam War was that American involvement was ill-advised, but that once American troops had been committed, the government and the country should do all they could to support the troops and win the war. He felt anything short of that was wrong.

In 1963 writer Robin Moore asked the Pentagon for assistance in writing a novel about the American special forces. Published in 1965, Moore's book, *The Green Berets*, leaped to the top of the best-seller lists. Then, taking advantage of the book's success, songwriter Barry Sadler composed "Ballad of the Green Berets," which topped the pop music charts in 1966.

Politics and the Sixties: Duke Under Siege

John Wayne was impressed with the army's Green Berets. In 1965 he bought the movie rights to Moore's novel for $50,000. He wrote President Lyndon Johnson about his plans to make a movie about the army's fighting elite. With the government behind him, in February 1966 he began recruiting a production unit. In June he went on a three-week handshaking trip to Vietnam for the USO. While signing autographs, he heard the crack of Vietcong sniper rifles. They seemed far away, but the bullets actually tore up turf within seventeen yards of him.

On May 7, 1967, Wayne turned sixty. One month later his sixtieth birthday was covered in *Time* magazine under the headline "The Duke at Sixty." He was now the greatest moneymaker in movie history, with a total film gross of nearly $400 million. Excepting 1958, he was one of the top ten box office draws for eighteen straight years. He celebrated his sixtieth birthday at the premier of his 137th picture, *War Wagon,* in Arlington, Texas. Two days later he was at Fort Benning, Georgia, staking out *The Green Berets* during a long Memorial Day weekend.

"Give or take some creases over the eyes, the huge leathery face has hardly changed. Nor have the jutting jaw, the laconic grin, the squinting eyes as blue as the big sky" *Time* reported on June 9, 1967. "The shoulders on his rangy 6'4" frame still look persuasive. . . . He still looks born to the saddle."

The *Time* piece highlighted Duke's deep commitment to Vietnam. It was his cause and he left no ambiguity as to his feelings. "Once you go over there, you won't be middle of the road. Bobby Kennedy and Arkansas senator William Fulbright and all those goddam 'let's be-sweet-to-our-dear-enemies' guys, all they're doing is helping the Reds, and hurting their own country."

But by now many had turned against the war, and the studio heads were running scared. Duke went from studio to studio with *The Green Berets* and was turned down. Eventually, Warner Brothers backed him and the film went into production. The road ahead was tough, but Wayne managed to put the picture together, and in late June the film opened in theaters across the land.

The Green Berets was lambasted by critics. Renata Adler in the *New York Times* was brutal in the extreme, calling it "unspeakable," "stupid," "rotten," and "false," even "vile" and "insane." Review-

173

ing the film for *Glamour* magazine Michael Korda called it "immoral, in the deepest sense . . . a simple-minded tract in praise of killing, brutality, and American superiority over Asians. . . ." Richard Schickel in *Life* magazine also had a field day saying, "Peaceniks may safely leave their picket signs at home, *The Green Berets* is its own worst enemy."

The film also had an international impact. On August 1, 1968, a movie theater showing *The Green Berets* was attacked in Paris by an angry group of leftists. In Stockholm, Sweden, the film was referred to as "the paid American aggression in Indochina." *The Green Berets* was pulled out of Swedish theaters after three days of demonstrations climaxed by a smoke bomb explosion.

Yet *The Green Berets* is a far better film than its reviews suggest. While not in the class of *Sands of Iwo Jima* or *Back to Bataan*, it is an exciting and action-filled war film which happened to be politically incorrect in its day.

In spite of this, *The Green Berets* was a box office hit. It generated $16 million in ticket sales during its first six months and was among the top ten box office hits of 1968. Moreover, foreign rentals later brought in millions more.

Edward Faulkner recalls the film and presents some interesting observations about *The Green Berets* and John Wayne.

Edward Faulkner

"When Duke was making *The Green Berets* in 1967, everybody in Hollywood wanted to be in that movie. I'll never forget my agent, who was a friend of Duke's, called me and said, 'Eddie, I can't even get into the office. They're not letting anyone in, no agents, no nothing. I don't know what to do!'

"I didn't know what to do either. So I wrote Duke a note. I told him something to the effect that I had worn a Stetson long enough. How about a new hat, I asked him, something like a green beret? Something real corny. I wrote a cover letter and tucked it into an envelope and sent it to Mary St. John, who was Duke's sec-

Politics and the Sixties: Duke Under Siege

With Ed Faulkner in *The Green Berets*

retary, [and] just a lovely lady. I said I knew Duke was busy, but if she had the opportunity maybe she could pass it on to him at the proper time.

"You know about four or five days after I sent the letter, my agent called and said, 'Have you seen Duke?' I told him no and asked if he had. He said no, but that I got one of the top supporting parts in *The Green Berets,* and there was a script mailed out to me. That's how I got the part. I played Captain MacDaniel. I got a lot of footage, too.

"To the best of my ability I can't remember any flack in the making of the film. Duke was involved in the whole production so he had his hands full. They brought in Mervyn LeRoy from Warner Brothers to back him up. As a point in fact, he would be

175

blocking a scene and the camera was ready to shoot it, and the cameraman or Mervyn would say, 'Duke, you're supposed to be in the scene.' He would say, 'Oh, the hell with it. Let the Deacon do it.' David Janssen gave me the nickname 'the Deacon' when we were filming. I don't remember any of the cast being concerned with any political statements the film was making. Of course, Duke was making a statement.

"I think a lot of people felt it might have been overdone. But it was a picture he totally believed in. Everybody who was in it gave their all. From my standpoint, I certainly agreed with what he was doing and what he was saying. I think most of the other actors did, too. Deep down, maybe, somebody didn't and just took it as a job.

"With *The Green Berets* Duke had a lot on his plate, being the director and having a hand in casting and everything else. He was under a terrible amount of pressure. I remember him lashing out on numerous occasions. He had a temper, and he would lash out at a crew member if he felt someone in the crew or cast wasn't giving at least 100 percent. Here was a man who gave truly that proverbial 110 or 115 percent.

"He did intimidate a lot of people, but fortunately, he never intimidated me. He didn't like 'yes people.' He'd brush them off in a kind way. People who stood up to him, even politically, he respected that. He'd get in arguments with people but he would respect what the other guy had to say. There are so many opinionated people that just say, 'Screw you, Charlie. You don't think the way I do.' But that wasn't Duke.

"We were doing a scene in *The Green Berets,* and the scene was basically on me. It was a close-up shot on the tower during a firefight. He said, 'Print it!' I turned to Duke and I said, 'Duke, I think I can do it better. Can we do it one more time?' Now that wasn't my place to do that. I wasn't the star of the movie. It was out of my province, but I just blurted it out and I felt comfortable doing it. Duke kind of looked at me and said, 'OK, let's do it again.' Well, about four or five days later when we got the print back, he came up to me and said, 'You know that scene we did in the tower the other day? Well, I've seen both prints.' He looked at me and said, 'You are right!'

"He was an absolute, complete professional. Yet he was a decent man. He was one of the most generous, big-hearted men I have ever known. When we were on *The Green Berets,* my wife and I were expecting our fourth child. Barbara delivered our three daughters by Caesarean section and our fourth child, who turned out to be a boy, was scheduled for a Caesarean delivery, too. I told Barbara I would try to call her at noon the day she was scheduled to have the baby. I knew exactly when he was going to be born. It was the 28th of August in Santa Monica. I left for Fort Benning, Georgia, on the 7th of August. Now it was two weeks later and we were at a camp they built out there in the boondocks. It was an hour and a half from where we were staying.

"Somehow it got back to Duke that I had made the arrangement with Barbara. Jimmy Hutton was a good friend of mine and Jimmy may have told Duke. We had just finished lunch and it was about 1:30 P.M. and we were getting ready to crank up again. I knew we couldn't get to our apartment so I could call Barbara. I was kind of kicking the dust when I felt this big old arm around my shoulder. I looked up and it was Duke. He said words to the effect that 'You're supposed to make a phone call.' I said, "Well, Duke, we're making a movie out here.' He said, 'Yeh, but Barb's making a baby back there.'

"Well, he just physically turned me around and there was his automobile—his limo—with the driver George Coleman. Duke said, 'George will take you back to town and we'll see you tomorrow.' He pushed me into the car and George got me back to town to make the telephone call. That's just the kind of person he was. He was very thoughtful, considerate, and he loved his profession. He absolutely adored it."

In a little more than two years, John Wayne had survived a difficult cancer operation. His picture had graced the cover of *Life* with the caption, "I licked the 'Big C'." He had made three full-length Westerns and would work on two more films in 1968, *The Green Berets* and *Hellfighters,* the first film for which he earned a million dollars.

He had been married to Pilar for thirteen years, during which they moved from a five-acre ranch in Encino to a lovely home—

simple and unpretentious—in Newport Beach, with a splendid setting at the water's edge facing Balboa Island. Aissa and John Ethan attended public school, and Marisa was still a baby.

He wouldn't hear any talk of retirement. "I'll never retire, until they just don't want me," he vowed. "I want to continue to be a worthwhile citizen till the man upstairs knocks on the door."

15. "True Grit": A Well Deserved Oscar

Wow! If I'd have put that [eye] patch on thirty-five years earlier! Ladies and gentlemen, I'm no stranger to this podium. I've come up here and picked up these beautiful golden men before, but always for friends. One night, I picked up two: one for Adm. John Ford and one for our beloved Gary Cooper. I was very clever and witty that night—the envy of even Bob Hope. But, tonight, I don't feel very clever and witty. I feel very grateful, very humble, and I owe thanks to many, many people. I want to thank the members of the academy. To all you people who are watching on television, thank you for taking such a warm interest in our glorious industry. Good night.

> — John Wayne on receiving
> the Best Actor Oscar for
> 1969

The road to *True Grit* is an interesting one. Wayne read the Charles Portis novel while it was still in galley form and instructed his son Michael to bid for the screen rights. But he was outbid by producer Hal Wallis.

He immediately went to Wallis and pleaded his case. Duke believed in the part of Rooster Cogburn and felt it fit him to a tee. Wallis, it seems, felt the same way and signed Duke for the part. He also hired Henry Hathaway to direct the picture.

There is no denying Duke's performance, and the Oscar was no fluke. He was rarely better than as the boozy marshal who helps a tough-minded young girl (Kim Darby) track her father's killers, led by Ned Pepper (Robert Duvall). The ending is more poignant than in any Wayne film, except perhaps *The Searchers*. But the film's most memorable scene begins as the "fat old man" with one good eye shouts, "Fill your hand, you son of a bitch." Then with a pistol in one hand, a rifle in the other, and his horse's reins between his teeth, Rooster rides into the gang and decimates them. It is simply a great moment in American cinema.

What is so interesting about *True Grit* is that the same critics that panned *The Green Berets* a year earlier, actively hyped Wayne for the Oscar. Although some opted for the younger Dustin Hoffman or Jon Voight for their work in *Midnight Cowboy,* when presenter Barbra Streisand announced "And the winner is . . . John Wayne," Duke received a thunderous ovation.

The Oscar was a humble and gratifying experience for Duke. To use the podium to ramble about politics as so many do today was not John Wayne's style. But he wasn't too proud to tell the world how much this long-delayed honor meant to him, particularly because he was chosen over outstanding performances by Hoffman, Voight, and British actors Richard Burton and Peter O'Toole, both also long ignored by Oscar.

After the Academy Awards, Duke and Pilar were interviewed by *Chicago Sun Times* columnist Irv Kupcinet for his TV show. Pilar, in one of her rare television appearances, admitted how nervous she had been, even though most polls had shown Duke as the winner. "I think I lost about seven pounds the last two days," she said. "Now that it's all over with I'm just so delighted." When Kupcinet asked Pilar whether Duke was difficult she said no. When he asked her if Duke was temperamental, Duke quickly interjected with, "That I am!"

The interview continued as Duke talked about his battle with cancer, not minimizing how tough it was. "But then I started thinking what I had to do and the type of thing as telling all your friends without being dramatic," he said. "It was just like somebody hit me in the body with a hard left hand. There's no other way to explain it. It's rough."

He talked about his children and grandchildren, who then numbered more than fifteen. "I even know most of their names," he chided with that sheepish grin. Then he told a story about his six-year-old son Ethan on the family boat.

"He's got a couple of friends out on the boat. Somehow or other they got around to saying, 'You know, your dad's a movie

"True Grit": A Well Deserved Oscar

star.' He said, 'Yeh.' They said, 'What are you going to be when you grow up?' He said, 'Oh, I'm going to be an actor—a movie star!' Then they said, 'When you are a movie star, will you give us your autograph?' He said, 'I'll give it to you now!'"

When Kupcinet asked whether he felt the Oscar was a little late coming after forty years in the industry, Duke paused a second or two, shook the glass of ice water he was holding, and said no.

"No, I never really went into that field of endeavor [trying to win an Oscar]. I think that in order to get the critics and the vocal group in our organization interested in you for an Oscar, you have to be in a certain type of picture. It was an accident that I was in this picture. It was just a natural for me."

He went on to say *True Grit*'s author didn't want him because Portis thought Rooster Cogburn should have a mustache and Duke refused. "Now I have a hat down to here," Duke points. "I got an eye cover," he points to his eye. "Now he wants to put a mustache on me. I wouldn't have been in the picture. That was his constructive criticism."

Duke indicated he would like to make three pictures every two years. He mentioned Batjac and how son Michael had earned a nice reputation in the business and how proud he was of both his boys, Michael and Patrick. He confirmed it was not director Raoul Walsh but Winfield Sheehan who was responsible for the name John Wayne. "It took me quite a little while to get used to it," he told Kupcinet. "But now I am very happy with it."

True Grit had the critics eating out of Duke's hand. "The richest performance of his long career" crowed the *New York Times*. In the *Atlantic Monthly,* Don Wakefield commented, "Whether or not John Wayne ever joins the ACLU, he is a hell of a good actor who obviously took great relish in the opportunity to play a meaty role." *Time* ran a cover story on him as an American institution. *Life* had a field day with its cover story, amusingly contrasting the polarization of the year's most celebrated actors—John Wayne and Dustin Hoffman—under the banner "Dusty and the Duke." The article featured photos of Duke in color and Hoffman in black-and-white.

When Wayne mentioned the eye patch in accepting his Oscar, the words were music to the ears of Luster Bayless, who designed the patch. Born in Ruleville, Mississippi, in 1937, Bayless is the owner of United-American Costume Company in North Holly-wood, California. Following his success in designing Wayne's eye patch for *True Grit,* he served as Wayne's costume supervisor in a dozen films, including his final film, *The Shootist.*

Since Duke's death in 1979, Batjac CEO Michael Wayne has been one of Bayless's most valued advisors. In fact, when Bayless founded American Costume Company in 1978, it was Michael Wayne who encouraged the venture and loaned Bayless the costumes from Batjac Productions to get him started. Today, United-American Costume Company covers more than forty thousand square feet of showrooms, workrooms, tailor shops, and offices. It has become one of the largest costume houses in North America.

Bayless remained a close friend of Wayne until his death in 1979. His stories about the John Wayne he knew and loved are engaging and his acknowledgment of his debt to the great screen star who took him under his wing is sincere and touching.

Luster Bayless

"The first time I met Duke Wayne was in 1961 when I was with Western Costume Company and he was making *The Comancheros,* a nice Western he made for Michael Curtiz which also starred Lee Marvin and Stuart Whitman. Of course, my first impression came when I had to fit him. He was a powerfully built man and instinctively knew what was right for him. But the first time I actually saw him on location was when we were making *McLintock,* and he came walking down the street.

"Immediately you knew he was on top of every area of film-making. I recall he was always close to the camera and had some very definite opinions on how things should be done. Years later I asked him why he didn't direct more. 'I can't afford to,' he told me. He said as a director you have to take about six months for preparation. There was so much involved, he insisted—editing and the works—that he just couldn't afford the time. But let me assure you he would have made a hell of a director; he knew how to stage a scene. He knew instinctively what would work. I would

"True Grit": A Well Deserved Oscar

Bayless today displays Duke's hat and jacket

really find out just how much he knew when I worked closely with him in *True Grit* and *The Shootist*.

"It was after making *In Harm's Way* for Otto Preminger that Duke first discovered he had cancer. The next project was *The Sons of Katie Elder* directed by Henry Hathaway. Henry was one of the great directors. He had directed Duke in *North to Alaska* in 1960, then later in his Oscar-winning role for *True Grit*. I know he had the greatest respect for Henry both as a director and as a man. Duke was the kind of person who had a lot of respect for his director until the director proved otherwise.

"John Ford was another story. Duke was almost meek in his presence, and Ford could get away with things that no one else could. I recall after winning the Oscar he was shooting *Rio Lobo* for

Howard Hawks. Ford visited the set and we sat together watching the shooting. After the take Ford said to me, 'They printed that, didn't they?' I said, 'Yes, sir.' He made off he didn't hear me so I said, 'Yes, sir!' again, this time louder.

"He turns to me and says, 'Get Duke over here!' So I walked over to Duke and said, 'Duke, Mr. Ford wants to see you.' Duke walks over just like he's a bashful kid and says, 'Yes, sir.' Ford says to him, 'They printed that first take on you?' 'Yes, sir,' Duke replies. Then Ford shoots back, 'Just cause you've won that damn Oscar, you're no actor. It usually takes eighteen takes to get a performance out of you!' Duke just kicks and says, 'Yes, sir.'

"Another time I heard Duke tell how he went on a hunting trip to a place called Monument Valley and thought it would be a good place to shoot Westerns. He came back and told John Ford. Later they were at a party, and right in front of everyone and right in front of Wayne, Ford told the gathering that he had found the greatest place in the world to make Westerns, a place called Monument Valley. That's the real story behind Monument Valley and let's just say I heard it right from the horse's mouth. But Duke didn't say a word to contradict Ford. Like I mentioned, I never saw Hathaway, Hawks or anyone else get away with something like that. But I can relate to this. Here was Wayne working as a young prop man at Fox and struggling when Ford discovered him.

"Duke liked Howard Hawks a lot. It was Hawks you recall who directed Duke twenty years earlier in *Red River,* Hawks's first Western film. I heard Duke say how much he needed *Red River* at the time. We were coming out of World War II and there was no more need for all the military things Duke had done. Duke was saying how they were down there in Arizona, and Hawks was talking about putting something on Duke's leg to show the age of the man he was playing in the film, to make him a little like Walter Brennan. Duke pointed to an older man out there in a saddle and reminded Hawks how erect the guy looked. Well, after that Hawks never mentioned anything more about such a gadget. Again, Duke just had a natural feeling for what would work.

"Although I met Duke in 1961 and got to know him some in 1962, I didn't really see him again until the filming of *True Grit.* Henry Hathaway was directing and he really liked the way my boss, Frank Beetson Jr., worked and took him in as an assistant director. Frank, in turn, told Duke he was going to get Luster Bayless for wardrobe. So I was on the set through the entire shooting of *True Grit*. It was here that I really got to know Duke well.

"I'm often asked if I knew right along that Duke had an Oscar winner with *True Grit*. The answer is no. I thought this character was great, and of course, he wasn't playing the usual flamboyant John Wayne, he was playing a great character. While he won the Oscar for *True Grit*, he had given other Academy Award–caliber performances. *Sands of Iwo Jima* comes to mind immediately. But Republic Pictures didn't know how to handle Duke's nomination for *Iwo Jima*—I'm talking about advertising or the concept of it. It was the first time the studio ever had a nomination for Best Actor. Then in *She Wore a Yellow Ribbon* he played a much older man than he really was, just as he had done in *Red River*. I think it was one of his best roles.

"Remember, too, that Duke was a hell of a good actor. They always said he was just a reactor. In fact, Duke would say that himself at times. But he knew he was a good actor. He'd talk to you, and he listened to you. He would look at the script and read through it. But he never wanted to memorize too much because he believed things could get so planted in your head you couldn't erase them. At times I'd do some dialogue with him. He'd pull out the script and I'd play the other part.

"His work habits were remarkable. He was always on the set on time. You never had to yell for Duke. I remember situations when he'd ask what time it was. I'd say it was seven o'clock and he's just say something like 'Hell, I got up too early.' That was a lot of bull. He was out there because he wanted to see where the damn camera was, where the director was going to set up the camera before the first scene. He wanted to get the feel. So he never walked in a little late or just in time. He was there early so he could feel he was on top of things.

"In fact, he never had a motor home until *True Grit*. He'd say that a home was nice but it doesn't help you a bit with your performance. We were doing *Rio Lobo* and somebody asked him where his dressing room was. 'See that nail on the wall,' he answered. But even when he had that motor home he was always on the set.

He would go in and get made up in the morning, maybe have his lunch there and lie down for a few minutes, but he was always on the set, not like some others in the business, I might add.

"We were having a fitting at Western Costume and discussing the character Rooster Cogburn. Of course, the writer had written him to have a mustache and an eye patch. Duke was concerned that no one would know it was John Wayne, so we decided to take off the mustache and go with the eye patch. I might also add that his hat was the same one he used in *The Comancheros* and *The Alamo*. We just changed the block around.

"I was very much involved with that famous eye patch routine. See, I had made some eye patches which were solid, others with a small hole, and more with big holes. When we got on location Duke said, 'I want a damn eye patch I can see through on every shot!' He said he could fake it but when you have only one eye it's impossible to know everything that's going on out there. He needed a fresh patch every day and didn't want anything which would irritate his eye.

"Well, we were out in the desert and Duke needed an eye patch he could see through and [I was] all out of leather. So I worked all night and came up with an idea. I cut the eye patch out, put a screen inside, then took the gauze and sprayed it. So now you could see through it and with no light behind you, you never saw the hole. Duke used several of those through the course of the day. Each morning he'd check the thing to see if there was any makeup inside it.

"I have already mentioned that at the time he won the Oscar we were doing *Rio Lobo* for Howard Hawks, and Duke came back to Tucson the next day. I came up with an idea to put an eye patch on everyone—the crew, the actors, even the horse. Now we see Duke coming down the street, and we have everybody turn around. When he arrived, we all had our backs turned and he wondered just what the hell everyone was doing. He was probably a little tipsy from all the celebration the night before. When he gets up close, all of a sudden everyone turns around, all those eye patches staring him down. He was really amused.

"I recall, too, that he got a telephone call from President Nixon at the hotel where we were staying. All that Duke could say was

"True Grit": A Well Deserved Oscar

'Isn't that nice. The president of the United States called.' John Ford came down to visit, as I indicated, and Henry Hathaway came down to talk about a future project.

"After his first cancer and the successful operation, Duke never let the thing bother him much. He was a little short of wind at times, but he had quit smoking and I never saw much of a problem even when we worked high in the mountains.

"The heart problem came up toward the end of *Rooster Cogburn*, which Duke made with Katharine Hepburn in 1975. We were in the valley [in Bend, Oregon] and he said to me one day that he felt the hills and mountains were closing in on him. He just couldn't breathe and was quite concerned. Well, we got him out of there. He went home, and I had heard he was having some problems, but that was it. However, by the time he started to film *The Shootist*, he was hurting. I didn't know too much about the problem at the time. He was a little touchy during the fitting. Soon I realized he was having trouble walking twenty feet. The problem then was his heart. Contrary to stories we hear, he did not have cancer then. The tale that he knew he was dying from cancer during *The Shootist* is a bunch of bull.

"The first day, we did three days' shooting in one day. Duke was hurting, though. He got pneumonia and we had to shut down for a week. Duke was very irritable, and I think Don Siegel, the director, was aware Duke was having some health problems. But Duke didn't advertise anything.

"There was some friction with Siegel, too, which had to do with the ending. We had shot something Duke hadn't seen and he wanted to see it.

"It had to do with the last scene, when Ronnie Howard shoots the bartender who killed Duke. Duke insisted that Ron look at him when he was dying, look back at the gun he had lived by with blood on the tip, then take the gun and throw it out of his life. Duke would not compromise on that scene. 'I will not compromise!' I remember those exact words. And that is how the scene was finally shot. Duke was also instrumental in writing that scene. Don Siegel, a very nice guy, would go to Newport Beach to see Duke [and work on the script].

"In the original script, Ron Howard was supposed to take the

187

gun at Duke's request, and knowing he was badly wounded, he would shoot Duke. Duke said, 'If the kid kills me, he will never work again in the business. He's not going to kill me, he is going to kill the other guy.' He insisted. And boy did that scene work! His instincts were right on target again.

"In *The Cowboys,* which he made four years earlier, Duke ran into similar differences with director Mark Rydell. Duke liked Mark but the two had a different opinion on how the ending should be. Duke didn't believe the boys should take the law into their own hands. He thought they should lasso bad guy Bruce Dern and bring him in. He didn't think there should be all that violence. I agreed with Duke on that. Duke left an option. Since he didn't think he should die at the end when he was shot in the back, he made a bit of a movement in the final scene just in case they decided he shouldn't die. He left them an option, but Rydell did it his way.

"It was clear now that Duke had to have an operation on his heart. It was that bad. He went to a specialist in Boston for the surgery. I understand they couldn't find anybody on the West Coast to operate on him, because who wants to have the reputation of losing Duke on the operating table? Think about it. It makes sense. He had one lung and he had difficulty with this microvalve in his heart. I went down there because Duke wanted his clothes altered for a Great Western Savings commercial he was doing. He also needed a horse and couldn't find his saddle, so Ben Johnson went, too. Ben went separately and I brought two tailors with me. When we got there I was stunned. Duke looked like a champion, fit and ready to work.

"He told us he had been laid up in this damn hospital room and after thirty days it had gotten real small. He said back on the West Coast they didn't want to operate because they felt they could control it by medicine. Duke said, 'I told them to either operate or open up that window. It was the eighth floor and I meant it. I had no quality of life like that. It worked. They brought me here and I'm glad they did.' I left and he looked great. I didn't talk with him again until Christmastime.

"Duke really loved Christmas and always sent a Christmas card. He'd shop for you personally. He'd send gifts to my family, for my children. He would pick out little jackets. On Christmas Eve I called to thank him for the gifts. He sounded bad. I asked him if he was in bed. He said he was feeling bad, that those sons of bitches were telling him it's his gallbladder, but that he thought it was something else. I told him not to talk like that and left well enough alone. I wished him Merry Christmas.

"That last year Pat Stacy was with him a lot, and his new driver would see him. He'd bring the mail. I was doing *Tom Horn* with Steve McQueen and the next thing I see in the news was that John Wayne was going into the hospital for an operation.

"When he was in for a long time, I knew it was serious. They cut him all the way, but he came through OK. I called him at home and I could hear a lot of clinking going on. I said I was sorry if he was eating. 'Look,' he said, 'I have to eat every couple of hours. They took out half my stomach.' He asked how things were going in my life, my family, on the set and such. We talked about a lot of things. It was like he didn't want to hang up. We must have talked for thirty minutes on the phone before we hung up.

"I didn't see him again until he was in UCLA hospital. Michael said I could go see him. I think he was on the fourth floor. I recall how nervous I was and how I didn't know if I could handle it, that maybe I'd break up. When I got there I saw his daughter Melinda and some others. They took me into this room. Duke was in another room separated by glass. We could see the doctor doing things. I just couldn't stay around, I was that grieved. So I went back to work.

"I heard later that when they went in they said 'Duke, Luster was here.' He asked why they didn't let me in. He was worried that maybe they had turned me away. Anyway when I got home I wrote him a note. 'Duke, you got a tough poker hand dealt to you.' I took it over to his driver, Barney, and he gave it to Pat Stacy. When she read it to Duke, I understand he just smiled. About two weeks before he died he called Pat into his room and had her send out a couple of mailgrams that day. One was to me. It read, 'Dear Lus, that's the best way to get them, Lus. From the folks you love.' It was signed 'Duke.'

"I didn't go to the funeral, it was a family thing. Funeral services were held at five A.M. in a nearby Catholic church, and his burial was completed two hours later behind locked cemetery gates. If it had been an open funeral, the world would have been there. This I understood, and this I respected.

"If there was one thing I really admired about John Wayne, it was his candor and his honesty. He was direct, but never believed in insulting a person. He loved his country and had his feelings about politicians just like everyone else, and he most certainly wasn't a bigot in any way. He was a conservative Republican and I was a registered Democrat. We could have our beefs about this and that, but he never let his politics get in the way of friendship. I recall once he said to me, 'Shit, Nixon didn't do anything other presidents didn't do!' I said, 'Yes, he did. He got caught!' Duke thought for a few seconds, then he laughed and said, 'You're right!'

"And talk about loyalty. I think he invented the word. I go back to *True Grit* with Hathaway. The insert man wasn't filming Duke the way he thought was right, and the way he was being photographed made Duke feel funny. Well, he got angry at the guy and said some things he probably shouldn't have. That night they fired the guy.

"I was over at Duke's hotel and I said to him, 'Duke, you won't have to worry about that still man.' He asked me why. I told him he had been fired. Duke said, 'What? You tell them if he isn't there tomorrow morning then Duke won't be there either.' When I got on the set in the morning I said, 'Gentlemen, I guess we won't have to work today, 'cause Duke won't be here.' They asked why and I proceeded to tell them what Duke had said, that he told me last night that if the cameraman they fired [wasn't there], then neither would he [be]. I reminded them again I was just repeating what Duke told me.

"Well, let me tell you, they just rushed to get that man back. When you worked with Duke and you tried, nobody had to fear getting fired. He might chew you out, but you didn't have to worry about losing your job. When Duke showed up, he explained certain things and how he wanted to be photographed. But he put his arm around the guy and made him feel assured. That was Duke Wayne for you.

"There's another incident that also comes to mind. I remember we were playing poker down in Mexico during the filming of *Rio Lobo*. He just loved those poker games. He liked to be with the guys. He was what you'd call a 'man's man.' Duke was no womanizer either. He was a one-woman man. When he was married, he was married. He took that very seriously. Well, one night we played and I got busted. I owed Duke some money when I quit. The next morning I'm at work and I see Duke in the elevator. He [had] just gotten out of the poker game and told me to join him. So we went to his room where he dumped all this money on the bed. He said, 'Well, it took me all night, but I finally cleaned 'em all out.' He asked me to straighten out the money so he could get dressed. I said, 'Duke, I owe you five hundred!' 'Forget it,' he said. 'I already made enough.' The main thing he liked was that I never told Duke anything but the straight and honest truth. He appreciated that.

"It's hard to believe it's been more than fifteen years that he's gone. I think about him a lot still. John Wayne was a one of a kind. He was magnetic, you could feel him and his presence. He had real greatness. Yes, there was real greatness in the man."

16. Maturity, Mirth, and Mentor

From head to toe, he is all of a piece. Big head. Wide blue eyes. Sandy hair. Rugged skin—lined by living and fun and character. A nose not too big, not too small. Good teeth. A face alive with humor. . . . When I leaned against him, thrilling. . . . As an actor he has an extraordinary gift. A unique naturalness. An unself-consciousness. . . . He's a very very good actor in the most highbrow sense of the word. You don't catch him at it.

— Katharine Hepburn, *TV
Guide* (September 17, 1977)

Duke and Pilar found the proper place for the Oscar on a shelf below what Wayne called the "Fifty Years of Hard Work" wall. There he recorded memories of a lifetime, such as pictures of his children and a faded photograph of himself, John Ford, Henry Fonda, and Ward Bond, proudly displaying a sailfish caught near Cabo San Lucas in the early thirties.

Duke was an avid collector of furniture, art, and other objects he picked up over many years of travel. Other displays included a small collection of guns, many fine examples of Western American art, and Native American artifacts. His collection of Kachina dolls was begun in the days when Wayne rode into Monument Valley to make films.

"Look," he was quoted in *Architectural Digest* in 1977, "I find things that appeal to me and I try to blend them in here. I don't give a damn if anyone else likes them or not. But I think I've done a pretty fair job." According to the magazine, "A close look [evokes] a particularly human image—the image of a man of taste and sensitivity, deeply interested in his family and his home . . . the clearest image of the man himself . . . warm, generous and comfortable."

Because of the unanimous praise accorded both the film and his performance, Duke believed *True Grit* was the kind of movie he would never see again. But he had yet to anticipate *The Shootist* which would come a few years later. Between his Oscar-winning role in *True Grit* and his brilliant final performance in *The Shootist*, his best piece of work may well have been *Chisum* in 1970.

Directed by Andy McLaglen and with a cast that included Forrest Tucker, Ben Johnson, and Bruce Cabot, it is a gem of a Western picture. Based loosely on the life of cattle baron John Simpson Chisum, the film became the favorite of then President Richard Nixon. It was also during the filming of *Chisum* that Wayne learned his pal John Mitchum was not just a fine character actor, but a talented poet as well. It was Mitchum's "America, Why I love Her," which Duke narrated for an RCA record album. The album was nominated for a Grammy Award and sold well enough to inspire a paperback version of its poems.

Mitchum has appeared in more than sixty movies, including *Dirty Harry* and *The Enforcer,* where he was Clint Eastwood's sidekick, Frank DiGeorgio. An actor, songwriter, singer, storyteller, and poet, he is also the author of *Them Ornery Mitchum Boys,* an anecdotal account of one of the movie business's most remarkable families.

In addition to writing "America, Why I Love Her," he wrote stories the late Dan Blocker of *Bonanza* fame recited on the RCA album, "Our Land, Our Heritage." Having worked with John Wayne on a number of projects, Mitchum offers insight into Wayne as an actor, and friend.

John Mitchum

"The first time I met John Wayne was on a picture called *The Flying Leathernecks* in the early nineteen fifties. We shot it down at Camp Pendleton, California, which is a marine base. You were awed by Duke when you first met him, because he is 6'4" and a big, big man, very direct, and very forward. The kind of man who means what he says.

Duke, We're Glad We Knew You

"So we had quite a time down there and he fit in with almost everybody. We had a marine fighter pilot unit from Georgia, which had also been in Korea. In fact, the Korean [War] was going on at the time and these guys from Georgia were the wildest bunch of fliers I have ever seen. They would be drinking until five in the morning, then suck straight oxygen out of tubes, and go straight in the air.

"Wayne, of course, was simulating one of those, so he took on the mannerisms of some of the pilots and was a little brash on occasion. It was a very interesting experience. I was in the war but in a very different thing entirely. I was in a boat company and had no idea what those pilots were like until I got close to them. They were a fearless bunch, and we had a lot of experiences with these pilots off the set when we were through for the day. And none of them was reticent about being very macho.

"But Wayne held up very well. He just did a beautiful job and he was very convincing as a marine pilot. He had all those pilots around him, and you couldn't tell one from the other, he was that good. Before I worked with him on the set, I wasn't that well acquainted with Duke. Now here I am, this neophyte facing this giant. It was very impressive. As the years went by, I found he never wavered. He was exactly off the screen as he was on the screen.

"Duke had enormous presence both on and off the screen. Someone once asked me if Duke really was the way he was personified. I told him something about Duke. 'If he says he's going to knock you on your ass, you better find a place to fall.' He said what he meant.

"He matured beautifully as an actor, too. Some people said he couldn't act. Like hell, he couldn't. His reacting was the best acting you ever saw. He was a very subtle actor. On the screen large movements are ridiculous. Wayne was a master of the small movement. It's very hard to realize that this big man was making small gestures.

"For example, if he knew a gunfight was coming up, it wasn't a huge reaction with lots of noise and bravado. It was a more subtle response. That's how Wayne would do it. And he would do it so effectively. He and Bob [Mitchum] are both masters of underplaying. And that's what people don't understand. Keep watching more and more and you'll see looks he gives. There is nothing boisterous about his demeanor. There is nothing portentous about him.

"I worked on a picture called *El Dorado* with Duke and brother Robert. And to see the two of them together was really marvelous, because they are both legends of the screen. It came across that the two really respected each other. At the end of the picture when the two of them walk down the street together, each one being wounded in the opposite leg, these two on one leg are better than most people on two legs. It was a good picture. They did a beautiful job.

"John Ford knew how to handle Duke. So did Howard Hawks. Duke had a lot of respect for Hawks, too, [and for] anybody who knew the business. He and Andy McLaglen got along beautifully together. Ford was very strong and resilient. Howard Hawks was very knowledgeable, and Andy is a charming man, a very charming man. Each of them knew the movie business inside out.

"But while John Ford certainly influenced Duke as an actor, I wouldn't say that was at the root of his ability. Wayne was a very bright man and a very alert man, and he absorbed things wisely. He absorbed and, of course, he worked with a lot of very good people. He watched them, too. He learned to observe and react, which is largely what acting is. I worked with Clint Eastwood many times, and Clint is the same way.

"Duke was professional to a tee and loyal, absolutely. He was definitely a 'man's man.' He knew the film game from the ground up. When he was working on a picture he would listen and pay attention to what the cameraman was saying, or what the electrician was saying. So Wayne knew every angle, and I mean every angle, of the picture business. He was also an outstanding horseman. He was a Western rider. He learned through the Fats Jones stables. (Fats Jones was Ben Johnson's father-in-law.) That's how he got as good as he was. He was a beautiful rider. He had that natural aptitude.

"Among the proudest moments of my life was writing the album 'America, Why I Love Her,' which John Wayne recorded for RCA. We were doing *Chisum* down in Durango, Mexico. Forrest Tucker was the villain in the show. Tuck was the bad guy.

Well, he happened to come up to me because he wanted me to hear a tape somebody sent him from Chicago. Tuck was a song-and-dance man, too. He was from Chicago and he was tired of singing that same, 'Chicago, Chicago, that toddling town. . . .' I listened to the new tape and it wasn't a very good song. He was disappointed, I could see. So I told him I would write a Chicago song for him. Well, I went back to my room with my guitar and composed a song for him. He loved it, and he used it everywhere he went.

"He wanted to hear some more of my stuff. So I recited something I wrote called, 'Why Are You Marching, Son?' The next morning he grabbed me by the arm and said to John Wayne, 'Duke, I want you to hear what Mitch has written.' And so I recited it and Wayne was very moved. Tuck said to him that if it meant so much, 'Why don't you record it?' Duke said, 'I will!' And that was it. He did. There was no lawyer. No business representative. He just said, 'I will!' His word was bond.

"The poem is in my book, *Them Ornery Mitchum Boys.* There is an interesting story behind it. My son, who was fourteen at the time, put the newspaper down on the kitchen table and said, 'Dad, look at this. You got to do something about this. There are people burning the flag in Central Park in New York.' So I wrote this poem as a result of this. When Wayne heard it, there were tears in his eyes. He was really that touched. So in time we did the album.

"It was quite a chore, too. Because at the time Duke's throat was sore. I would go down and get him a little bottle of Jack Daniels. He said, 'Just for my throat.' He'd sit there and sip it. But every now and then, he'd say with a laugh, 'Oh that one slipped!' He'd take a drink of it.

"Duke was a genuine patriot, for God's sake, yes he was. It was real, honest patriotism, no phony stuff. He loved the country. That's why he liked 'America, Why I Love Her' so much. It had nothing to do with politics, you see, nothing to do with power or prestige. It was the country.

"The industry per se never really understood John Wayne. The media have always been left-wing. And Wayne certainly was not. As far as I am concerned, somebody has to keep the straight and narrow. Somebody has to say, 'Hey, hold on! Enough of this.' With

Maturity, Mirth, and Mentor

With Ben Johnson in *Chisum*

Wayne, if he had his mind made up, that was it. He didn't care what you thought. Oh, he might have cared, but he wasn't going to alter his thinking.

"At lunchtime we'd go across to the Brown Derby Restaurant which was located on Vine Street. One time we were coming back, and here's Duke doing this very patriotic album. These three hippies stopped him. I mean, these were real ponytail guys. Then one of them says, 'Hey, man, there's the Duke. Look at that, man!' And he went up to Wayne and said, 'Hey, man. I saw you in *The Undefeated*. You were great, man! Lay a dime on me!' Well, Wayne went through the roof. We had to restrain him from giving them something else. What an insult. Not a dollar or five, but 'give me a dime.' Well [Duke] just shook his head and walked off, and we went back to the studio.

"When we were down at his place in Balboa working on the album, his secretary Pat [Stacy] brought all his mail. He opened one letter and became livid. He said, 'One thing I can't stand is a liar!' And bam, he hit his closed fist on the table! I didn't know what was in the letter, but I remember thinking, 'Dear God! Who was it?' I think the person would have been headed right toward the bay.

"Another story comes to mind concerning *Chisum*. In the movie, Gregg Palmer, who is 6'4" and weighs 285, was one of the cattle rustlers. He's sitting in jail and Wayne is talking to him. Gregg says, 'I wasn't wrestling,' pronouncing it like the sport rather than 'rustling,' the term associated with stealing cattle. So Andy [McLaglen] says 'Cut!' Gregg says, 'What's the matter?' Andy tells him you don't 'wrestle' steers, you 'rustle' steers. They did it four times and for some reason Gregg couldn't get it right. So finally Wayne comes over and says, 'Grizzly (that's what he called him), 'if you say I wasn't "wrestling" one more time, I'm going to knock you on your ass. You were "rustling," not "wrestling!" Action: 'I wasn't rustling,' Gregg says clear as can be. He got the message.

"When Wayne was working, it was no-nonsense. A case in point is when Forrest Tucker had a chance to fly back to Chicago and make an enormous amount of money over the weekend on a personal appearance thing. Again it was during *Chisum,* and if he had gone back it would have delayed shooting for one day. So Wayne said no. Tucker suggested they could shoot around him. Wayne wouldn't have it. 'Are you a professional, or are you not? You signed on to do this show. We're shooting Saturday. You're shooting on Saturday. I'm shooting on Saturday. We as a company are shooting on Saturday. Because that's what we all signed up to do.'

"Now Wayne and Tucker went back a long time. All the way back to *Sands of Iwo Jima* in the late nineteen forties. But Wayne talked to him straight out. It was to the effect that 'you're a pro, I'm a pro. We're here to work. I don't care how much money you could have made. It's none of my business, but you signed on to do the show, and that's what you are going to do.' There was nothing wishy-washy about Duke. Any job was a job to be done right.

"I recall when Geoffrey Deuel, a nice guy but small—[he] came about up to Duke's abdomen—was arguing with director Andy McLaglen, who is 6'7". He was wondering about his 'motivation,' and told Andy he couldn't get the right feeling for a particular scene. He tried everything but he couldn't get motivated for the scene.

"Well, Duke was sitting about five feet away and he had heard enough. He walked over to Geoffrey, spread his wings, all 6'4" of him, and said, 'Motivation! Motivation! You're getting paid. That's your goddamn motivation!' He swung on his heels and walked away.

"*Chisum* was the last film I did with Wayne. I didn't see much of him after that. I was having my own personal problems. My wife died at that point. We were married for nearly twenty-five years.

"When you think of what to say about John Wayne, you have to remember that close up he was a very big man. Not only physically, but spiritually and morally, too—a big, strong man who epitomized America.

"He was a kind man and a thoughtful man. He was very, very careful about animals. He didn't want to see an animal ever misused. That, to me, is a good sign. Talk about loyalty. If he was your friend, he was your friend. That's as simple as that. There was no other man, other than my dear brother, that I would like to have with me if I got into a brawl with a whole bunch of people.

"But the warmth of the man was real, very, very real. I introduced him to my son-in-law. My son-in-law is a man who is only about 5'5". I'll never forget that when Wayne met him, Duke, who is 6'4", reached over and said, 'I'm John Wayne!' Well, who else could it have been! My son-in-law looked up at him and his mouth seemed to drop down about four feet. Duke introduced himself just as anyone might have, if they weren't a big celebrity. He could be very humble.

"He worked well with most of his leading ladies, all of whom seemed to respect and admire the man. But of all his leading ladies, the best chemistry, I feel, was with Maureen O'Hara. There may not been anything going on between them in an emotional way, but there was a chemistry. My brother Bob never had anything going with Deborah Kerr. But the two of them literally loved each other, the same way as Duke and Maureen. They had a real caring for each other.

"We have talked about seven or eight pictures which might have warranted Academy Award consideration for Duke. The major point here, I think, is that with twenty-five or twenty-six

199

Duke lands a haymaker on Forrest Tucker in *Chisum*.

pictures in that category how can anyone possibly say the man really wasn't a fine talent. Some people get one picture and they crow about it for thirty years. He did thirty and never crowed about any of them. I think the man is to be patted on the back no matter where he is because he did a wonderful job.

"John Wayne always understood that if the United States of America fails, the world fails. Wayne instinctively knew that. And he used the line as a true patriot. I have nothing but respect and honor for that man.

"We were doing a recording of 'Taps.' The story of 'Taps' is a beautiful story. It is how [during the Civil War] the armies were so close together that when they had a burial party the Union soldiers would fire the first volley over the dead. The rebels would answer it with mortar fire and kill the burial party. So Col. Dan Butterfield, who was a man of music as well as being a good soldier, wrote some notes for his bugler to be

200

played at the next funeral. On July 2nd, a canoneer was killed and as they buried him [they played] the strains of 'Taps' for the first time.

"Well, John Wayne comes in and it's been almost a hundred years since that sound was born. He turns to me with tears in his eyes and says, 'Mitch, aren't people going to be mad at me for talking while they are playing that?' Now that's real humility.

"It was a wonderful experience knowing him. There was nothing small about John Wayne."

17. The Waning of the Western

It's true that too many people either endorse or
deplore Wayne because of his political views. Wayne
will be remembered, I guess, as an extra-effective
character actor whose unique qualities and talents have
been explored by two great directors, and have
enriched a host of others of varying degrees of ability.

> — Peter Bogdanovich, in
> *Esquire* (May 1972)

In his post-Oscar interview with Irv Kupcinet, Duke said he would like to make three pictures in the next two years. He was true to his word. *Chisum* was released in 1970. Then in 1971 Duke did *Rio Lobo* and *Big Jake*. The Western genre was alive and well. Since 1967 when *War Wagon* and *El Dorado* were released, through the premier of *Cahill, United States Marshal* in 1973, Duke made twelve movies, ten of which were Westerns. And nine of the eleven films Wayne made in the nineteen seventies were Westerns.

Nevertheless, the seventies was the decade when the Western slowly faded from the screen, and in the nineteen eighties only a handful appeared. The times were changing as were movie audiences. But John Wayne continued to defy the changing times. He was as big or bigger than ever. He was still one of the most popular movie stars in the world, and the awards and honors never seemed to cease.

He was master of ceremonies at California Governor Ronald Reagan's second inaugural. *Photoplay* magazine awarded him its Gold Medal Award for 1971, the fourth *Photoplay* award he received. That same year he was presented with the Veterans of Foreign Wars National Americanism Gold Medal Award. Duke's record "America, Why I Love Her" was released on March 1, 1973. In the first two weeks, the record sold more than one hundred thousand copies. Then on August 13, Wayne received the U.S. Marine Corps Iron Mike Award.

When John Wayne and Robert Mitchum worked together so well in *El Dorado* in 1967, Mitchum's son Christopher was hardly thinking of a movie career for himself. "When I was twenty or twenty-one years old, if someone would [ask] what in the world was the last thing I'd like to do, I would say to be an actor," says Mitchum. Yet by 1970 he had appeared with John Wayne in *Chisum*. Then in 1971 and 1972, he landed major roles in *Rio Lobo* and *Big Jake*. In 1972 *Photoplay* magazine named Mitchum the Most Promising Male Actor of the Year. A graduate of the University of Arizona, Mitchum holds a Bachelor's degree in literature. He has been involved in the picture business as an actor and writer or in production for more than twenty-five years. He also rodeos and has done his own stunts.

Christopher Mitchum

"From the time I was a young boy I had seen the downside of being an actor. My father was hardly able to go out for dinner. When we would go out as a family, he was constantly bothered by people grabbing his hand to get an autograph when he was trying to eat dinner. It was something I never wanted to have as a part of my life.

"When I was in college in Tucson, I worked on a short-lived TV series. Sam Manners, the production manager, said if I got to Los Angeles I should look him up. He would get me a job as an actor if I wanted one. So when I graduated and moved back to Los Angeles, I looked him up. I was able to get a few small acting credits and that led to my becoming a production assistant. I was doing a thing called *Big Foot*, a motorcycle monster movie in 1969. When actor Jody McRae wanted $10,000 for the picture, they turned to me.

"I did a couple of [different] things before an agent asked if I'd like to be an actor. Because he said I could act and stay in production too, I agreed. In time I read for the role of Billy the Kid in *Chisum*. I remember I was waiting to hear back if I was going to

With Chris Mitchum and Dean Smith in *Rio Lobo*

get to work with John Wayne. Well, I got to play a character who was Billy the Kid's sidekick. It was pure fun.

"There was one scene where we were bringing back the wagons to get supplies into the other store in competition against the bad guys. We were attacked by the bad guys in the middle of the river. We roll up the [canvas] sides [of the wagon which] have riflemen [inside] and there is a big shoot-out.

"They gave me about six pistols to stick in my belt. They said, 'Don't drop them, we're shooting one-thousand-foot mags. We had three cameras going. So I was to keep shooting. Empty one gun, tuck it in your belt, and go for another. Well, I saw where all the stunt guys were going to be falling. So every time a guy would ride up on a hill to do his horse fall, I would shoot and he'd fall down. It was great. Ten weeks of being a kid and I only had two or three lines in it. So to me it was nothing but fun.

The Waning of the Western

"I was sitting on a horse in the third row. They were doing a shot, and Duke walks up and has a chaw [of tobacco] in his mouth. He slaps my thigh and says, 'You know, you should have played Billy the Kid.' After the shot he pulled me aside and said, 'I'm gonna be doing a film with Howard Hawks. When he comes down, I'd like you to meet him.' So Duke introduced me to Howard. He said, 'Chris, here's my card. When you come to Los Angeles, come see me and we'll talk.' So I did.

"In those days you got to talk to the producers and the directors. I went in there and I talked with Howard for about two hours. He told me the whole story of *Rio Lobo*. Actually, I never really had a script for that story. After the meeting on Tuesday he asked me to come to the screen testing on Thursday. I actually tested for the part Jorge Rivera had, and he screen tested for mine. Then we switched. I played Tuscarora Phillips. Jorge played the Confederate captain, Pierre Cardona. So I went from three lines with Duke in *Chisum*, to costarring with him in *Rio Lobo*.

"We were shooting in Tucson. Duke came back from winning his Academy Award. We were having the big celebration on the main street that day. Duke pulled me aside and said while he was in Los Angeles he made a deal to do a picture called *Big Jake*. He asked me if I would mind playing his son in the picture. I said, 'Jeeze, Duke, I'd be honored.' So I went off and did *Big Jake* with him. It is the most frequently played John Wayne movie on TV.

"At first I was fairly intimidated by him. For me, he was one of the two big stars as I was growing up. One was Elvis Presley in 1956, the other was Duke, who when I worked with him was kind of the backbone of America. He was the fifth face on Mount Rushmore. When I met him the guy was bigger than life. He had a presence that even his whisper carried across the street. My father has that kind of presence. He walks into a room and suddenly everybody knows he's there. His voice carried. His stance, an attitude, a position. It's a presence. It leaps at you. Plus the fact that Duke was close to 6'5" with large hands. He was a big guy.

"He was very easy-going. I remember the first couple of days on the set, he asked me if I played chess. I had been a pretty avid chess player all my life. I said, 'Sure, Duke! I love to play chess.' We sat down, and he was cheating. He'd reach over with one hand to move a bishop and with his thumb he'd slide a rook over. I didn't know what to say. Here I am playing chess with a god. He's also kind of my boss on the show, and I didn't know quite what to say.

"I told Eddie Faulkner that Duke was cheating in chess. Ed replied, 'Of course he is! You tell him to knock that crap off. He's just trying to intimidate you!' So the next time we're playing, he kind of starts to do something. I say, 'Excuse me, Duke, you're moving two pieces.' He says, 'I was wondering when you were going to say something.' So after that we got along fine, and I started beating him.

"I remember Eddie [Faulkner] was playing Duke. Out of one hundred games, Eddie might possibly win one. Because he seldom beat Duke, to even come close was a big thrill. Well, this time he was just trouncing Duke. Eddie had eight or nine pieces on the board and he was down to three pieces. He was murdering Duke. Then they get a call to go on the set. Duke reaches over and picks up one of Ed's own pieces and checkmates him with his own piece. And Ed was so conditioned to losing, he looks up and says, 'Jesus, Duke, I didn't even see that.' Well, I started to say something, and Duke looks up and nudges me with his elbow and gives me a wink and says, 'Yeah, well let's just set them up again.' We walk off to work, and Eddie is just shaking his head. I don't think to this day he realizes what happened. Duke was quite a character.

"I'll say this for Duke. He had a great sense of fairness. If he made a mistake he would stand up and apologize for it as loudly as he would stand up and criticize something. I recall one time we were on *Chisum* and an actor was standing there. Duke asked him why he didn't sit down in the shade. The guy said, 'I don't have a chair, Duke.' Well, Duke called the prop guy out and lambasted him in front of everybody. Part of his job was to get chairs for the actors. Remember, Duke started out in props.

"The very next day that same actor was walking down to lunch, and we were supposed to check our guns before we sat down to eat. They wanted to keep all the guns on the set. The prop guy ran down the street, caught up with him, and took the gun back. Now Duke waited until everybody was at lunch and he lambasted the actor. He said the prop guy had his job to do and asked you to check your gun. You had no business making the guy run down the street after you. He really lit into the guy. For Duke, everyone was there to do a job and to help everybody else do theirs. He was an absolute professional.

"There was one time that Forrest Tucker had gotten permission to fly from Durango to LA because he wanted to surprise his wife on her birthday as a present. When he got to the airport, they realized they needed him for one shot. They fetched him at the airport and brought him back.

"Well, it was about 9:30 in the morning and Tuck was sitting out in the middle of the street drinking straight scotch with a beer chaser. He was a pretty hard hitter. He [was sitting in] one of those high director's chairs. Meanwhile, I was behind one of the trucks talking with Duke. One of the guys comes up and gives Michael [Wayne] half an ear of complaints [from Tucker]. Duke looks over and says to Michael, 'What's the problem?' Michael says, 'Nothing, Pop, everything's fine.' Duke looks over again and there is Michael listening to complaints. This time he says it a little louder. 'Michael, what's the problem?' So he tells Duke about Tucker's complaints, that Tucker was unhappy that he didn't get home.

"Duke's response is right out of a movie. He says, 'I'm not going to get mad! The hell I'm not!' He came around the corner of that truck and his voice was carrying across the street before he ever rounded the corner. Man, if you ever wanted to see some guy become an island in the middle of the street in a hurry! People scattered. It was great.

"Something else about Duke. When we did *Big Jake*, [in one scene] he goes into the bar and hits the toughest guy in town and the guy beat him. He always wanted guys who were bigger than him. If he had an adversary who was small it made him look like a bully. So he liked it when you could get somebody like Tucker with whom he could square off. He really enjoyed doing that scene in *Big Jake*.

"Duke was very human, and he did have his share of frailties. But one thing for sure is that he was very loyal. When we did *Rio Lobo*, Jim Davis's child had just died in a automobile accident. Duke had heard that Jim was hitting the bottle a lot. So he brought him on to *Rio Lobo* and gave him a part that wasn't even in the script.

Duke, We're Glad We Knew You

With son Patrick Wayne and Chris Mitchum in *Big Jake*

He knew that if [Jim] went to work and had to stay sober, it would do more for him than sitting home drinking.

"*Big Jake* was a great time. Even at that time I was aware of the fact that I was working in the vestiges of Old Hollywood. I could see the business changing. The motorcycle scene was all scripted. When they hired me I just had finished my first year racing, so I could handle a bike pretty well.

"Duke worked well with his son Ethan in the film. But let me tell you, Ethan was a real pain in the ass. Oh, he was, and Duke knew it, too. Here is his dad, who's the star, and here is this kid everybody's treating a little special because he's a kid and Duke's kid. Any time Duke heard him mouth off to anybody or be disrespectful, he'd grab him by the back of his coat and pull him aside and say, 'Now Ethan, You can't do that!' He'd straighten him out, but as soon as [Duke] turned his back, he'd get cocky again. Oh, he was a brat. People didn't know what to do, he was

Duke's kid. You wanted to grab him but you couldn't. You'd have to deal with Duke.

"But Duke was real good with kids. My son Bentley and daughter Carrie are both actors. Carrie in fact worked on *The Bold and the Beautiful* for four years. Anyhow, I'll never forget this. Bentley was about four and Carrie was six the first time they met him. I said, 'Duke, I'd like you to meet my children.' He hunkered down so he would be at eye level with them and said, 'Hi, my name is John!' And he held out this huge hand to shake hands with them. It really impressed me. He knew how to talk to kids. Despite the fact that he did have that incredible presence, he was humble as can be. It was all so natural. You get some of these actors that try to dress up like stars. He was just 'The Duke.'

"It was Howard Hawks who made me want to be an actor. Hawks was the one who instilled in me the love of acting. Before, I would act for the money. I really still wanted to work production. Howard showed me aspects I hadn't seen before. The cumulative effect of having worked with him and Duke ignited a passion for the art.

"Howard was the only one who had a script. We'd walk on the set to work that morning, and the secretary would hand us something like ten pages of new dialogue. I learned very quickly to just crumble it up and throw it away. It meant absolutely nothing. But we'd get the pages as we came on. We'd set up the scene and block it out. Howard was really easy to work with. He was so comfortable with actors. We'd block out the scene together until we found where it was moving really nicely.

"I would have a line like, 'They have forty men out there.' Duke would be leaning on the desk and say, 'You know, Howard, I think I should say that.' Howard would say, 'You're right, Duke. You say that!' The poor secretary is sitting writing shorthand as we're writing the script. We didn't have a script until Howard said print. That was the script. So while we did have a script, Howard was rewriting it constantly. Howard cut the film in the camera. He knew the movie he wanted to shoot.

"Duke told me he did some of his best work with Howard Hawks, because Hawks wasn't afraid to direct him. When we did *Big Jake,* George Sherman—an old director from Republic who

With his son Ethan in *Big Jake*

might have been 5'4"—was directing. You should have seen those two step off to the side and argue about a scene. There's George with his head back looking straight up, and there's Duke with his hands on his hips looking straight down. Duke pretty much directed that film himself through Georgie.

The Waning of the Western

"Hawks was not argumentative, but this is how he would work it with Duke. Duke would be sitting on a desk and say 'You know, Howard, this is good. I think it would be better if I was standing over there by the door.' Hawks would say, 'That's a good idea, Duke.' Then he'd just stand there and continue what he was doing and totally ignore what Duke said. Other directors would feel totally intimidated by him. Howard would take the input, but he directed the movie the way he wanted.

"I did three pictures in a row with Duke. Then I never worked with him again. This resulted from an appearance on the *Johnny Carson show*. Somebody recently sent me the transcript so I could try to see where I made a major mistake. I was on the Carson show because, among other things, I had been awarded the Most Promising Male Actor by *Photoplay* magazine. When we did the show, I came out and Johnny asked me what I had been doing. I told him I had been working on the first people's environmental initiative to get on the California ballot.

"Back then the lines were drawn that if you wanted clean air and clean water, it meant in some people's minds that you were against all big business and you were a liberal. Today people realize having clean air is something that concerns all of us. Even though I have always been fairly conservative in my politics, to me, clean air and clean water were something we all should have. So I was working on that initiative.

"Duke was on the show, too, and he piped up and said, 'What are you working on something like that for?' Duke said, 'If I had known you were a pinko Commie . . .' We got into it a little bit and things got a bit feisty. I said, 'Duke, well, you can't teach an old dog new tricks.' And he said, 'Well, son, you can't teach some pups anything.' It went back and forth, right on the show.

"During the next week, I probably received a hundred or so letters from people who had written to Duke and sent me a copy of the letter. Basically, the attitude towards Duke was two-thrust: 'I did not realize you were against cleaning the air.' And two, 'I thought you were very rude when Chris came on. You dominated his time on the show. You already had your time.' Duke never spoke to me again. Duke had just signed me to a five-year contract with Batjac, and I never heard from them, either. I just vanished from his life.

With Maureen O'Hara, circa 1972

The Waning of the Western

"I wrote him a couple of letters. I was living in New England when he was in Boston having his heart valve operation. I wrote him a letter and said, 'Duke, I'm only an hour away and if you'd like to have a game of chess, I'd be happy to come down. Here's my phone number, give me a call! I'd like to come visit you.'

"Nothing! About two months later the PR department at Batjac said Duke responded personally to every card, letter, and telegram he received. I never heard from him. The man was my mentor. He was like a father to me. He took me from three lines to costarring with him. He basically gave me my career. It hurt a great deal. I could not understand why we couldn't have a difference of opinion and still respect one another.

"In my case, politics interfered with friendship. Personally, I thought our government was doing some major screwups during Vietnam, especially search-and-destroy missions. You let boys die taking land and you give it back to the enemy. So I had some gripes with the government. At the same time, my wife and I took all the money we were going to use to buy Christmas presents for friends, and we contacted the local marine station and asked what our guys needed over there.

"We went out and bought things and made care packages for our soldiers over there. Our feeling was whether the government was right or wrong, we still have American boys over there fighting and we have to support them. I appreciate John Wayne speaking up and supporting our troops. He did it with dignity.

"I went out for a film audition, and this was right after I had gotten the *Photoplay* Gold Medal Award. I was in *Box Office* magazine as one of NATO's [North American Theatre Organization] top five stars of the future, along with Ryan O'Neal, Stacy Keach and a couple of others. The audition interview was for a film called *Steel Yard Blues* with Jane Fonda and Donald Sutherland. I walked in and sat down and they looked at my credits and said, 'Oh, you've been in three movies with John Wayne.' I said yes. They said, 'Thank you for coming in.' I told them, 'Don't you want me to read or something?' They said, 'No, you worked with John Wayne.' I said, 'So?' They said, 'This is a movie with Jane Fonda and Donald Sutherland.' I said, 'Yes, I know that.' They told me they may be talking politics on the set. I said, 'I'm halfway through my master's degree. I'm capable of talking politics.' They answered, 'You worked with John Wayne. It's not going to work.'

"The aura of working with him put me on the side of being what they perceived as an arch-conservative. It basically black-balled me from some of the formidable producers. When I was first vice president of the Screen Actors Guild, we had a meeting with [Charlton] Heston. I said, 'Chuck, what the liberals do is hire each other and get each other into the public view and show each other around so they can promote each other.'

"Conservatives are so damned individualistic. We don't do that for each other. We go out and hire an actor because he is a good actor. They go out and hire the same actor because he's liberal. If the reverse had happened, if Batjac Productions hadn't hired Bridget Fonda because she is a Fonda, you would have seen a lawsuit. They do it all the time. They lock you out. So I definitely feel my association with John Wayne was used against me. I have tangible proof because I was told so when they wouldn't interview me.

"I think Wayne was very much a traditional conservative Republican in that he put big business over the environment. I think if he was alive today he would have mellowed a lot and have gone for a more moderate approach toward the environment. If he came out with an incorrect statement and felt he was wrong, he would come out and admit it loudly.

"Vietnam and politics didn't affect our work on the set. We'd hear about a demonstration at a college, a flag burning or a draft card burning. Duke would just shake his head and say, 'What's wrong with those kids? Don't they know what they're doing to this country?' Duke was basically tolerant of the views of others. In my case, I think if our conversation had happened in private, things would have been fine. I think he would have been persuasive in trying to get me to change to his point of view. I think the fact that it happened in public caused a lot of embarrassment to him because of the negative reaction. I think he felt it was because of me that it happened.

"He absolutely adored Maureen O'Hara. I think there was a tremendous amount of professional respect. He had a warm spot in his heart for her. He admired her as a person. My father had that same kind of relationship with Deborah Kerr. Professionally and

The Waning of the Western

Honored by the Shriners in 1970 (Courtesy Jeanette Mazurki Lindner)

personally, they held each other in the highest regard. It's amazing, when [O'Hara] was around, [Duke] became even more of a gentleman. He'd become more professional and defer to her in the conversation. His attitude would definitely change when she walked on. This doesn't pertain to Maureen, but on the set of *Rio Lobo* a reporter asked him, 'Duke, did you ever sleep with your leading ladies?' Without blinking an eye, he said with that special grin, 'Well until I met Pilar, I thought it was obligatory!'

"I've always admired Duke's work. I know that one of his favorites was *The Searchers*. *Red River* I loved. *Stagecoach* I loved. Of course I'm kind of fond of *Big Jake*. As a kid, I recall that I loved *Sands of Iwo Jima, The Flying Tigers,* and *The Flying Leathernecks*. I believe there are several qualities which explain why he has [endured]. I think the fact that he was honest in his acting is very important. Basically, what you saw on-screen was the guy who was doing it. There is something else, too. This is the essence of the Western. A Western is an American soap opera. You have a good guy. You have a bad guy. Good triumphs over bad. There are very definite battle zones. You do not have victims of society. The worst villain in town is ready to draw a line in the sand and die for what he is doing. They take responsibility for their own actions. That's it.

"I think this ended with two films: *The Wild Bunch* and *Butch Cassidy and the Sundance Kid*. I think these two Westerns single-handedly destroyed the Western genre. All of a sudden the bad guys were our heroes. I've been riding since I [was] a teenager. I go all over the country and meet the real cowboys in America. They are constantly asking when are they going to start making good Westerns, when are they going to stop using vulgar language, and when are they going to start keeping their clothes on? Why do we have to see so much blood?

"Westerns are very simple. Everybody knows there is going to be a little bit of love interest, and sooner or later a time will come when they have to strap on their guns. John Wayne gave us those kinds of Westerns."

18. Still Sexy at Sixty

> John Wayne was bigger than life. In an age of few
> heroes, he was the genuine article. But he was more
> than a hero; he was a symbol of many of the qualities
> that made America great—the ruggedness, the tough
> independence, the sense of personal conviction and
> courage—on and off the screen—that reflected the best
> of our national character.
>
> — President Jimmy Carter, in
> *John Wayne: American* (1996)

Few film critics display as keen an insight into movies as Molly
Haskell. And perhaps none have explored the role of women in
film quite as perceptively. An Eastern movie critic with admitted
feminist leanings, her admiration, even adulation for John Wayne
has tended to surprise some of her liberal cohorts.

We have seen how Duke's leading ladies generally had deep
respect for him personally and professionally, even when they
turned off to his conservative politics. He was mostly considered a
man's man during his long career. What is interesting is how
women, especially many younger women today, find something
very special about him. Molly Haskell saw this early on.

"In that role as the Ringo Kid . . . Wayne hasn't the narcissistic
beauty of Cooper, nor the glib, easy charm of Gable. Awkward with
women, he becomes a character lead rather than a romantic one. He
is closer to Fonda and Stewart in type and the movie terrain he will
come to occupy," Molly Haskell wrote in the *Ladies' Home Journal.*

Haskell concludes that women, less demanding of physical per-
fection than men when it comes to the opposite sex, can see that
"youth has nothing to do with virility" and respond to Wayne
more passionately than ever, and on many levels.

"Unlike . . . Paul Newman in *The Drowning Pool,* [Wayne] does-
n't require an endless supply of nubile nymphets whom he can
take pleasure in rejecting! That . . . is what *macho* is all about:

With business partner Rollie Harper and son Pat (Courtesy Jeannette Mazurki Lindner)

sexual arrogance and preening, excesses of masculinity that come at a time when the real thing—the functional masculinity that Wayne represents—is disappearing."

In the light of women's struggles for independence, Haskell contends, father figures have gotten a bad name. "Father figures were not just authority figures and watchdogs and mentors, they were people with whom we identified, whom we molded ourselves upon, as much as we did our mothers.

"Wayne is all of a piece; at any given moment, he is the sum of his past performances and experiences. He resonates and grows richer with each performance, while modern actors slip in and out of theirs without a trace."

What John Wayne did better than anyone else was to stand for something: "self reliance, generosity, largeness of soul and moral consistency." Unlike modern actors who invent themselves with each role, John Wayne came from a classical tradition of Hollywood

acting which was built on type—they used their faces and personalities as basic texts to build their characterizations. This aspect of
Duke's artistry is gender neutral. It appeals to both women and men.

And during the nineteen sixties and seventies John Wayne
managed to defy the prevailing ethos of youth. He matured well.
He showed audiences he could have rich, sensual relationships
with mature women such as Patricia Neal in *In Harm's Way*, Colleen
Dewhurst in *McQ*, and Katharine Hepburn in *Rooster Cogburn*.

To understand this concept is to understand the lasting appeal
of John Wayne. In his later films he was able to employ this trait
to the highest degree. We see it as Wil Andersen in *The Cowboys*,
then ultimately as John Bernard Books in *The Shootist*. We see it in
Rio Lobo, when Jennifer O'Neill prefers to snuggle up to Duke on a
cold night rather than the younger and more dashing Jorge Rivera,
because Duke is "comfortable." When the beguiling and sensuous
Ann-Margret starts to sweet talk him in *The Train Robbers*, Duke
tells her, "I have a saddle older than you are, Mrs. Lowe."

Marie Windsor is one the few female stars to have worked with
John Wayne during three different decades, making *The Fighting
Kentuckian* in 1949, *Trouble Along the Way* in 1953, and *Cahill, United
States Marshal* in 1973. Dubbed the "Queen of the B's," by the *New
York Times*, her career spans seventy-six feature films, 130 televi-
sion shows, and dozens of stage productions. Twenty-two of her
films were Westerns. She is very much aware of John Wayne's
appeal and the respect he accorded others.

Marie Windsor

"I made three films with John Wayne. The first was *The Fighting
Kentuckian* with Duke and Oliver Hardy for Republic Pictures.
Hardy was a sweet gentleman. He liked to chitchat a lot on the set.
Duke was a lot of fun on the set, too. It seemed everyone on the
Republic set was a friend of his. I mean the actors, the crew, all the
working people, in fact. He had a lot of stories to tell and was full
of practical jokes. But at all times he was a serious professional.
When it was time to work, he worked. We all worked.

Duke, We're Glad We Knew You

Duke's widow, Pilar, in 1993

"By time I did *Cahill, United States Marshal* in the early nineteen seventies he had slowed down some. He was in his mid-sixties, had been ill and had survived cancer. Yet at all times he still maintained that same strong sense of professionalism and that endearing personality he carried all his life. When on occasions I saw him suddenly lose his temper, he'd usually have good reason to do so. But even then he would cool off quickly, and I never knew him to hold a grudge.

"He was still fun and charming. He was always very nice to me. In the early days at Republic he was sure full of the devil. He and the guys were always playing jokes on each other and there was lots of laughter. I did one non-Western with him in 1953. It was called *Trouble Along the Way,* and it was directed by Michael Curtiz at Warners. It was a nice sentimental picture with John as a disillusioned and divorced ex-football coach who tries to come back by coaching a ragtag team at a Catholic college. Over these many years, I continue to remember John Wayne as a very nice man and a true gentleman."

In 1973 Duke and Pilar announced they were separating after nineteen years of marriage. Duke had always found women difficult to fathom. This he freely admitted.

When May Mann, a reporter for *Photoplay,* asked him in 1973 if Pilar was his best friend, he said with conviction, "My wife is not my best friend." Nor was she supposed to be. In John Wayne's world, men and women were not made to be best friends. Men were supposed to have other men as best friends, and women were supposed to have other women as best friends. A bit simplistic perhaps, but that's the way it was for him. Women were to be wives, mothers, lovers, even associates, companions, and employees, but not best friends. "I still don't understand women," he said. "And I don't think there is any man who does."

If there was anyone who doubted Wayne's capacity to act, these doubts should have vanished in 1972 with *The Cowboys.* Duke is superb once more as Wil Andersen, who is forced to hire eleven young boys to help him get twelve hundred head of cattle from his Double-O Ranch to the railhead four hundred miles away. And once the trail drive starts, the boys slowly become men under Wil's fatherly guidance. Directed by Mark Rydell, it is one of Duke's strongest and sometimes less-appreciated roles.

Rex Reed was impressed and wrote in his *New York Daily News* review that ". . . in *The Cowboys* all the forces that have made [John Wayne] a dominant personality as well as a major screen presence seem to combine in an unusual way, providing him with the best role of his career. Old Dusty Britches can act. . . ."

Duke was winning over some new foes as well. In 1974, in exchange for publicity for one of his new films, Wayne agreed to a roasting by the *Harvard Lampoon.* He arrived in Cambridge, Massachusetts, on an armored personnel carrier for a press conference. The kids that jeered him as the Godzilla of American imperialism cheered him later. One student listening to his speech in the Harvard Square Theater asked him, "Do you look at yourself as an American legend?" "Well," Duke drawled, "not being a Harvard man, I don't look at myself any more than necessary."

As for cheering him, Duke told Molly Haskell with a laugh, "Yeah, they went from one extreme to the other. They thought I was a horse's ass, but when they saw I was as honest about what I thought as they were about their beliefs, they came around. Then they went too far the other way. We stayed up all night drinking. I guess I was the father they never had."

The media and the cultural elite may have portrayed Duke as a right-wing fanatic, but the rest of the country loved him. By the seventies John Wayne had become one of the most highly recognized and respected men in the world.

Awards came in steadily: the George Washington Award from the Freedom Foundation, the Scopus Award from the Friends of Hebrew University, and the American Patriot Award from the American Educational League. In 1976, he was again chosen America's favorite movie star, this time over Jack Nicholson and Robert Redford.

Much of Wayne's opposition to the liberal establishment of the sixties and seventies mirrored his feeling for Hollywood communists of the nineteen thirties and forties. He felt these liberals reeked of guilt. By finding themselves a cause—a downtrodden individual or group—and throwing money at it, they could live with the fact that they were the most privileged people in the world.

"They're Beverly Hills, Bel Air liberals, feeling guilty about living in million-dollar homes, driving Rolls Royces and Mercedes and making obscene amounts of money. . . . I am, too. The difference between me and them is that I don't feel the least bit guilty about having worked my ass off and having made a good living."

No actor has ever had as poignant a screen epitaph as John Wayne in *The Shootist*. However, there is no indication Duke considered this his last film or that he showed signs of recurring cancer at that time. Yet *The Shootist* paralleled Duke's life in so many ways that many fans continue to think it was written especially for him.

The opening credits relive a nostalgic journey with clips from four Wayne films—*Red River, Hondo, Rio Bravo*, and *El Dorado*—to show John Bernard Books, a well-known gunfighter, in action. Books arrives in Carson City, Nevada, in 1901, where the doctor (Jimmy Stewart) confirms an earlier diagnosis of cancer. Focusing on character rather than a spate of action scenes, *The Shootist* becomes a testament to the life of John Bernard Books. At its completion, it marked the end of John Wayne's fiftieth year in motion pictures.

In a climactic showdown, Books sets up a fight in the saloon with three shady characters played by Hugh O'Brian, Richard Boone, and Bill McKinney. The three gunmen represent Books's past. The present is represented by young Gillom Rogers, played by Ron Howard, and his mother, played by Lauren Bacall. It is through their eyes that we see the full tapestry of John Bernard Books, the man called "The Shootist."

Bill McKinney well remembers working with John Wayne in his final film. McKinney, who played villains in such films as *Deliverance* and *The Outlaw Josie Wales*, has worked six times with Clint Eastwood and credits Eastwood with suggesting him to director Don Siegel for *The Shootist*.

Bill McKinney

"[When I was] a kid growing up in Chattanooga, Tennessee, John Wayne was pretty special. He stood out. The first John Wayne film that caught my fancy was *Reap the Wild Wind*. It came out in 1942 when I was just a young boy. It really knocked me out and to this day remains vivid in my mind. He was a sea captain, but I could see early on that he was a leader. A leader is a leader whether he is a sea captain or a trail boss. It takes the kind of responsibility I admire. He was a versatile actor as well. He could be a marine, cowboy, naval officer, or whatever. His imposing presence was always there.

"He was so natural I didn't even realize just how good he was when I worked with him in *The Shootist*. I had just worked with Clint on *The Outlaw Josie Wales*. He pitched me to his friend Don Siegel. It worked out real nice. I liked Don Siegel and I liked John Wayne. I don't think Wayne and Siegel liked each other very much. There were subtle signs.

"But Duke could get salty. I played Jake Cobb and was driving that milk truck with Ron Howard when Duke rides into town. In the movie I say 'You old son of a bitch, get that clack out of the way!' He would say 'I want you to say these lines like this. Are you going to say that goddamn line or not!' That kind of hackled me some. I think he did it on purpose. He knew what he was doing. A couple of days later he called me over and said, 'You finally got those lines right. I like the way you read those lines.'

"He was very instructive. He perfected so many of his moves—the way he drew a gun, the way he fired a gun. When I was expecting to shoot him in the bar, or to shoot at him, I watched him prepare for all that stuff. He was a heck of a technician. He had the craft covered. He learned his trade from the ground up.

"He was the personification of a hero. He was big, he was strong, and he was a man of his word. He was a man of conviction, he was so much of what we feel a man should be, and people responded to that. There is something very deep inside all of us which responds to that. That deep core inside everybody that says, 'Here is a guy I can trust. I can lean on him. He will lead and will stand by his word.

"One of the reasons he still is an American hero is because he had opinions, and by God, he would speak his mind. I respect a guy who will do that. His views during the sixties were not the prevailing views in the industry. In fact, conservative views today still are not. He was a good conversationalist. He would sit right down and talk with you. There are others we thought would last forever: Humphrey Bogart, Clark Gable, Jimmy Cagney, Gary Cooper. All these people were terrific, but we don't remember them like we remember John Wayne. There was just something there.

"Somehow I had a hunch this would be his last movie. I really did. He had the flu when I was working on the show, and they had to pound him on the back in the morning to get his lungs clear. I was taking some vitamins on the set. We were standing there and Wayne asked me what I was doing. I told him I was taking vitamins. He told me he wished he had done that when he was my age. I could hear the melancholy in that.

"The picture looked like it was going to turn out well. They spent a lot of money on the set. I knew we had something good with *The Shootist*. It's like hitting a baseball or a golf ball. You get a feeling of elation. But it takes more than just that to put a movie together. A lot of things go into it. When I was working with Duke, I never thought of him as John Wayne in particular, because I really had to think of the character I was playing.

"But he had an affect on me. You know, I had a dream close to when he died. It was a strange dream. It seemed that he was out on a stage at UCLA making a big speech with a tuxedo and a bow [tie]. In the dream, I was behind him on the stage just observing. He had a star over the top of his head that started getting wider as it came down, and then the ears were gone. People cheered and he left the spotlight. He started to sob and then he crumbled. It was probably my [vision] of a person's mortality, because he was such a strong, vibrant guy.

"If you look at his work, there is really very little which isn't good. He could knock off some booze, too, but it didn't affect his work. He didn't muff lines. He was a pro. He was basically a man's man. I don't think he communicated with women like he did with men.

"Sure he did a great job in *True Grit,* but really he did have that Oscar coming more than once. Like with Clint [Eastwood]—although the two are very different kinds of guys—these people for some reason don't get popular with the voting crowd in the academy. The conservative factor had a lot to do with it. I think Tom Selleck is a good example of that today. Consequently, he doesn't have a great movie career. It seems to follow a pattern.

"Over the years, I have seen and worked with lots of people and have seen his movies over and over again. Duke was a hell of an actor. He was so natural. He played different characters. You can lay the picture out. This guy was subtle. He was not subtle in anything but his work, but with his work he was an absolute master.

"John Wayne was unique. He did the best with what he had and made a big impression on people's hearts, their souls, and their minds. He just left a big, indelible impression on people."

19. A Hero for All Seasons

> Our country thrives on change. . . . No guns or bombs
> or Army coups. Just the biggest and best weapon of all,
> our right to vote. X's on paper. The ballot box, a good
> thing.
>
> — John Wayne, in the *Saturday
> Evening Post* (September
> 1979)

When John Wayne was born in 1907, the Western was a mere
five years old. Before that there had been hand-cranked stories
with Western themes for peep-show use. But it was director Edwin
S. Porter who put the West on the screen in a ten-minute movie
called *The Great Train Robbery*, filmed, ironically, in New Jersey.

Soon the new art form was tried by a fellow named Bronco Bill
Anderson in a story called *Bronco Billy and the Baby.* For our purposes, the most notable thing about Bronco was that he was the
cowboy who began the tradition of the hero fumbling his hat in
the presence of a lady or in other situations calling for gentleness
or mild embarrassment. In later years John Wayne was able to
parlay that hat trick into an image which endeared him to ladies
both on and off the screen.

When Duke was a teenager in the nineteen twenties, the most
famous movie Westerners were William S. Hart and Tom Mix.
There were some similarities between Hart and Wayne. Hart was
the first of the strong, silent Western heroes, a form Duke perfected. Occasionally Hart was allowed to become roaring drunk in
his characterizations. We see this, too, in Duke's characterization
of Rooster Cogburn. Wayne, like Hart, did his own riding.

John Wayne would spend ten years making B Westerns. Ironically, *Stagecoach*, which Duke did for John Ford in 1939, started a
string of A Westerns that soon did in the Bs. Ford followed *Stagecoach* with *My Darling Clementine*, then used Duke in three more

A Hero for All Seasons

Westerns in the nineteen forties: *Fort Apache, She Wore a Yellow Ribbon,* and *Three Godfathers.*

By the time he received his Oscar for *True Grit* in 1969, John Wayne was past sixty. His litany of Western films spanned five decades. Duke's feelings about Westerns were unqualified and definite. "Don't ever," he insisted, "make the mistake of looking down your nose at Westerns. They're art—the good ones, I mean. Sure, they're simple, but simplicity is art."

He was the Duke, but he was also mortal. He was sixty-nine years old when *The Shootist* was released in August 1976. It was his seventy-sixth Western and his 153rd film. It was to be his final ride across the silver screen.

Appearing with Merv Griffin on a taped ninety-minute show, Duke explained his feelings on how he wanted to appear on the screen. They were walking around Duke's vast Arizona ranch when Griffin asked if every part he played had to be built to fit John Wayne.

"Well, I don't know," Wayne answered. "I have certain feelings about what I do. I like to play a character that a large number of people can identify with, whether it's that they can say he's [their] father, uncle, brother, or whatever. It's human dignity . . . nothing mean or petty, cruel or rough. Tough, that's all right . . . but nothing petty or mean."

Over the years almost everyone had a private and personal image of Duke. He projected a degree of human dignity and strength bordering on the absolute. His range of character was positive, deep, yet emotional. His very presence had undeniable impact. "John Wayne is the only movie star I've ever met that was not only exactly what I thought he'd be, but more," said Burt Reynolds.

During one talk show, Gene Kelly was discussing such words as *beauty* and *grace*. When asked by the interviewer to name a man he thought of as graceful, Kelly immediately replied, "John Wayne." He went on to describe the way Duke moved with the grace of an athlete and the poise of a man who, knowing his strength, can also show himself to be tender and gentle.

In 1975 when Emperor Hirohito of Japan visited the United States, he asked to visit John Wayne, as if he wanted to see the personification of the power and determination which beat his country in World War II.

Artist Henry Jackson had admired John Wayne for many years, both on and off the screen. They first met in 1969 when *Time* magazine commissioned him to do a figure of Wayne as Rooster Cogburn in *True Grit* for the cover of the magazine.

"When I got to know him a little better," Jackson said, "I had real respect for him because he was like so many of the people I grew up with as a cowboy in Wyoming. There wasn't anything phony about them. Duke was the same way.

"He was much more basic and real than most people realized. His code of living was a thousand years old, and that firm foundation of honest love for mankind seemed complicated because of its simplicity."

At first Jackson had been skeptical about doing Duke as Rooster Cogburn and leaned toward working on a piece from *She Wore a Yellow Ribbon, The Alamo,* or *Red River*—three Wayne films he admired.

All that changed once he saw *True Grit*. "I almost cried," Jackson said, "because I was so relieved to see Duke playing himself— an over middle-aged man who drinks a bit. I knew I could do him. I selected the scene where all the odds were against him, and he just shouted, 'Fill your hand, you son of a bitch!' and rode across the meadow to whip the bad guys."

In time Henry Jackson would create a seven-ton, twenty-one-foot bronze sculpture of John Wayne on horseback. The project, which was started in 1982, was unveiled in Camaiore, Italy, on August 30, 1983. The beautiful work titled "The Horseman" appeared in conjunction with the 1984 Olympics in Los Angeles.

The Shootist had taken a big toll on Duke's health. Not since *The Sons of Katie Elder* in 1965 had he felt so bad on the set, and then he had just had a lung removed. Nevertheless he performed many of his stunts and wrapped up the film on schedule.

Throughout 1977 and early 1978 Duke's health started to deteriorate perceptibly. On April 3, 1978, he underwent heart surgery at Massachusetts General Hospital. According to Pat Stacy, Duke's secretary and steady companion the last seven years of his life, Wayne got more than one hundred thousand get well wishes. At the Academy Awards that same night, Bob Hope wished Duke well after his open-heart surgery. His recovery was hindered by a case of hepatitis following his return home.

In January 1979 John Wayne was interviewed by Barbara Walters for ABC News. He had already won over Walters who recently had made a long, hard climb up the ABC ladder. Now, he won over her crew.

"When I went with my staff to Newport Beach to interview [him], there were some on the staff who felt rather lukewarm about the assignment. They didn't agree with John Wayne's politics, and it colored their feelings about him," according to Walters.

"But by the end of the two days we spent with him, there wasn't one of us who didn't feel affection and respect for the man. He was straightforward, honest, and tough, in the best sense of the word. He never once tried to force his views upon us and was enormously considerate. At the end of our taping, like kids for a high school graduation, we asked 'Duke' to pose with us for a class picture. Each of us today treasures his snapshot."

What Walters did not know about until she arrived at Bayshore Drive was Duke's impending stomach surgery. The interview was set at his house and aboard his yacht, the Wild Goose, the day before he went into UCLA Medical Center. The conversation took a philosophical turn when Walters asked Duke about the meaning of life. As usual, Duke was direct:

"I have deep faith that there is a Supreme Being. There has to be. The fact that he's let me stick around a little longer, or she's let me stick around a little longer, certainly goes great with me. I want to hang around as long as I'm healthy and not in anybody's way. Has it been a good life? Great for me. . . ."

When asked if he feared death, he replied, "I don't look forward to it because maybe he won't be as nice to me as I think he will, but I think he will. . . ."

John Wayne checked into UCLA Medical Center on January 10, 1979. To protect his father's privacy, Michael Wayne took charge of handling the press. Duke had put him in charge, and only Michael and Pat Stacy had unrestricted access to him. The physicians spoke only to Michael, then he relayed news to the other six children, who then passed on whatever they heard to

Duke's ex-wives Josie and Pilar. The early story was that John Wayne was in excellent health but needed routine gallbladder surgery.

The terrible truth was that John Wayne had stomach cancer. "Dying's my own business," John Bernard Books said in *The Shootist,* and Wayne insisted on absolute secrecy. He would undergo radiation treatment, but the ordeal would not be food for public consumption. This he made clear.

On April 9, 1979, John Wayne made his final public appearance at the Academy Awards ceremony at the Dorothy Chandler Pavilion, presenting the award for Best Picture to *The Deer Hunter.* It was true grit all the way, but this time for real. The ovation from the crowd was thunderous.

The late Ron Talsky helped costume the Academy Awards show that year. He never forgot that night—the sweet, the bittersweet, and the sad.

Ron Talsky

"I called Michael [Wayne] before the awards to ask if Duke would need any alterations, meaning that his tuxedo was probably too big on him because he was losing weight. He said no, they were handling it. I asked if there was anything I could do. Michael said they would be at the Bonaventure Hotel, and I said they should call if they needed me.

"When Duke arrived, he recognized me immediately. I'm sure he couldn't help but read my face. At Western Costume Company, he was the star of my first big movie, *The Alamo.* And we had worked together on *How The West Was Won* and *Liberty Valance.* When he saw me at the awards, he grabbed my forearm and said, 'Take care of yourself, kid!' Because we were all hard drinkers, hard smokers. That's just what he was saying. He did not want to go."

Duke's health was failing fast. Shortly after his stomach surgery in early 1979, there was a feeling in film circles that something should be done to acknowledge John Wayne's contributions to America.

A Hero for All Seasons

Two of filmland's most glamorous stars, Elizabeth Taylor and Maureen O'Hara, pleaded before a Congressional subcommittee that a special Gold Medal be issued on Duke's behalf. "John Wayne is not just an actor. John Wayne is the United States of America," a tearful O'Hara told the committee. "Please let us show him our appreciation and love. He is a hero and we have so few left."

An official proposal was made by Senator Barry Goldwater. The Arizona senator and 1964 Republican presidential candidate revealed that he and Duke were members of the same college fraternity—Wayne at USC and Goldwater at the University of Arizona. Goldwater then said, in part: "He has dedicated his entire life to America and I am safe in saying that the American people have an affection for John Wayne such as they have had for very few people in the history of America."

Congress approved the measure and President Jimmy Carter signed it. On Duke's seventy-second birthday the White House sent him a special letter to explain the medal. The Congressional medal was no small honor for Duke Wayne. Since the first such medal was struck in honor of George Washington, only a select few individuals, including Winston Churchill, Gen. Douglas MacArthur, Dr. Jonas Salk, singer Marian Anderson, and poet Robert Frost have been considered by Congress worthy of being immortalized by the nation.

On June 9, 1979, at Duke's request, Patrick Wayne called Father Robert Curtis, the Roman Catholic chaplain at the UCLA Medical Center. Father Curtis came to the room, baptized Duke, then delivered the last rites. John Wayne died at 5:23 P.M. on June 11, 1979.

John Wayne is buried in an unmarked grave in a Newport Beach, California, cemetery. "It seems to be a special bit of irony that this most visible of men in his lifetime is anonymous in death," says Joseph Bell, a Newport Beach neighbor. In an article in the January/February 1992 issue of *American Film,* Bell relates how this is what the Wayne family wanted, and that "Draconian measures" have been taken to prevent public knowledge of his burial place. "The last thing either Duke or his family wanted was the expectation that the public would turn Pacific View into a posthumous Disneyland."

For several months, security guards explained to hordes of visitors that the grave was unmarked and flowers in Wayne's memory could be left under a cemetery flagpole. The number of visitors has fallen steadily with the passing years. John Wayne remains in the hearts of millions, but today just a half dozen inquiries a month is the norm at Pacific View Memorial Park.

Epilogue:
The Unbroken Legacy

"He had been through so much and beaten it all. We couldn't believe he couldn't beat the last one too."

— Pat Stacy in *Duke: A Love Story,* 1983

"He gave the whole world the image of what an American should be."

— Elizabeth Taylor in *Reader's Digest,* October 1979

News of John Wayne's death spread quickly around the world. KEWB Radio in Los Angeles began playing the theme song from *The High and the Mighty,* and it played continuously that day and night. In a figurative sense, the music still plays. On Tuesday, June 12, 1979, the headline "John Wayne Dies at 72" was emblazoned in bold print across the *Los Angeles Times.* The *Los Angeles Herald Examiner* simple read "The Duke Is Dead."

Moreover, the awards and testimonials have never stopped. Duke's congressional medal was approved: Public Law 96–15 was enacted May 26, 1979. The Orange County airport was renamed John Wayne Airport on June 20, 1979.

John Wayne remains an American hero at a time sadly bereft of heroes. Sure, cynics might say heroes are fodder for kids and dreamers. But as life goes, so does that little kid which lurks inside us all. We felt safe with the Duke. We knew he could protect us. We knew he'd be there. And he was there, if only for a couple of hours on a Saturday afternoon. It wasn't a short ride. It lasted more than half a century.

John Wayne's legacy surfaced again in Cannes, France, at the 1995 Cannes Film Festival. The occasion was to honor John Ford's

233

one hundredth birthday. Among the honored guests were Harry Carey Jr., Ben Johnson, Claire Trevor, Carroll Baker, and Duke's children, Patrick and Melissa. Upon his return from the Cannes Film Festival, Harry Carey Jr., who appeared in ten films with Duke, gave the author an extended interview.

Harry Carey Jr.

"The Cannes Film Festival [event] was on account of the legacy of John Ford and John Wayne. It was an incredible experience. John Ford and John Wayne's legacy to Ben and me, Claire, Carroll, Pat, and Marisa, is tremendous. Whatever success I had in films is due to movies of John Ford and John Wayne. I believe I have gotten a lot of work because of that, as well as a lot of other successes.

"When we arrived at the Cannes Film Festival, I was convinced that the homage to John Ford would be off in a more remote theater—certainly not the main theater—and that Ben and I, Pat, and Carroll would just be engaged in that part of it. It turned out to be just the opposite.

"They picked us up about 4:30 or 5:00 in the afternoon. We each had a [car] with Cannes Film Festival flags. Marilyn [my wife] was just thrilled. I figured we were going to go to some theater to see one of John Ford's films. Well, they pulled up at the Palace de Festival, the biggest theater there. You see all the red carpet coming down from the entrance. You have to walk up these steps on this red carpet. I had seen the biggest stars in the world walk up that red carpet. Every time they use it, they take it down and put another one up. This is where Ben and I, Marilyn and Carroll Baker got out of the car.

"Well, there must have been a hundred photographers, fifty on each side. As we went up the red carpet, we had to keep stopping for pictures. I kept looking around, thinking that someone like Martin Scorsese or Steven Spielberg must be behind me. When we finally got in, we got an ovation which lasted five minutes. It went on and on. This was because of John Ford and John Wayne. It was one of the rewards. They showed *Wagonmaster* at the Palace de Festival. Twenty-five hundred people just applauded and applauded. I was absolutely stunned. And when the movie was over they applauded like that all over again. In France they really appreciate history, certainly movie history.

"They showed twenty-five of John Ford's pictures at the festival, but we only saw *Wagonmaster*. They had *Stagecoach* the night before when Claire Trevor was there. We didn't go because it was Claire's show, and we decided she should be there alone. Then it was *Wagonmaster* and the following day it was *Yellow Ribbon*.

"There were lots of questions at the press conference, lots and lots of questions. We had earphones, and the questions were translated from French to English. It was just great being with Claire Trevor. She looks wonderful. She's eighty-five years old and looks about seventy. She still smokes and drinks and is lots of fun. I danced with her and we had a hell of a time.

"The entire Cannes Film Festival lasted two weeks. We were there for four days. It was tremendous. I'll never have a moment like that in my life again, I know that. And John Ford and Duke Wayne made that all possible."

Bibliography

Books

Bogdanovich, Peter. *John Ford.* Berkeley: University of California Press, 1968.

Carey, Harry, Jr. *Company of Heroes.* New Jersey: The Scarecrow Press, 1994.

Clark, Donald and Christopher Anderson. *John Wayne's The Alamo: The Making of the Epic Film.* New York: Citadel Press, 1995.

Ford, Dan. *Pappy: The Life of John Ford.* New Jersey: Prentice Hall, 1979.

Kieskalt, Charles John. *The Official John Wayne Reference Book.* New York: Citadel Press, 1993.

Liebert, Billy and John Mitchum. *John Wayne's America, Why I Love Her.* New York: Simon and Schuster, 1977.

Parkinson, Michael and Clyde Jeavans. *A Pictorial History of the Western.* London: Hamilin Publishing Group, 1972.

Pfeiffer, Lee. *The John Wayne Scrapbook.* New York: Citadel Press, 1994.

Ricci, Mark, et al. *The Complete Films of John Wayne.* New York: Citadel Press, 1995.

Roberts, Randy and James Olson. *John Wayne American.* New York: The Free Press, 1995.

Stacy, Pat. *Duke: A Love Story.* New York: Atheneum, 1983.

Wiley, Mason and Damien Bona. *Inside Oscar.* New York: Ballantine Books, 1996.

Zolotov, Maurice. *Shooting Star.* New York: Simon and Schuster, 1974.

Articles

Barzman, Ben. "The Duke and Me." *Los Angeles Magazine,* January 1989.

Bell, Joseph "True Wayne." *American Film.* January/February 1992.

Bogdanovich, Peter. "Hollywood." *Esquire.* May 1972.

Bibliography

Burchell, Sam and Fritz Taggart. "John Wayne, Best Actor for True Grit," *Architectural Digest,* April 1990.

Cavander, Fred (editor). "A Tribute to John Wayne," *The Saturday Evening Post,* July, August 1979, September, October 1979.

Didion, Joan. *"John Wayne: A Love Song."* Saturday Evening Post, August 14, 1965.

Haskell, Molly. "Wayne, Westerns and Women." *Ladies Home Journal,* July 1976.

"John Wayne: The Iron Duke." *Saturday Evening Post.* Spring 1972.

"Let the Bad'uns Beware." *Time.* March 3, 1952.

Lewis, Richard Warren. "*Playboy* interview: John Wayne." (excerpted 35th anniversary retrospective issue). *Playboy,* January 1989.

Marks, John. "Riding Out of the Sunset." *U.S. News and World Report,* November 20, 1995.

Sarris, Andrew. "John Wayne's Strange Legacy." *New Republic,* August, 1979.

Schickel, Richard. "Duke: Images from a Lifetime." *Time,* May 28, 1979.

Sutton, David. "John Wayne: Image vs. Man. *Post* Interview." *Saturday Evening Post,* March 1976.

Thomas, Mark, "Iranians Find Duke to be a Revelation." *Variety,* February 7, 1990.

Videos

John Wayne: Bigger Than Life. Burbank Video. 1970.

The Kup Show. "Interview with John Wayne." Irv Kupcinet. 1970.

The Quiet Man: The Fortieth Anniversary Edition. Republic Home Video. 1992.

Standing Tall. PBS television special, 1989.

Young Duke. Leonard Maltin Productions. A&E *Biography* series, 1995.

Notes

Introduction

"Like William Faulkner's," A. Sarris. *New Republic,* August 4, 1979, pp. 33–36.

Chapter One

1. "I don't think it's possible," Randy Roberts, Olson, James S. *John Wayne American.,* p. 44.
2. "Duke could not abide." *Ibid,* p. 44.
3. "He was a great guy." *Ibid.*
4. "John and all of us." Lindsley Parsons. *Young Duke. A & E Biography* (series).

Chapter Two

Personal interviews were conducted with Nancy Morrison Marshall and Jeanette Mazurki Lindner.

Chapter Three

1. "You one of Howard Jones boys," Dan Ford, *Pappy: The Life of John Ford,* p. 40.
2. "His problem was that." Lindsley Parsons, *Young Duke. A & E Biography* (series).
3. "It was laughable to imagine." Cecilia Parker. *Ibid.*
   "I was under contract." Gene Autry. *Ibid.*
   Personal interview of this chapter with Tom Corrigan.

Notes

Chapter Four

1. "As a newcomer." Dan Ford. *Pappy: The Life of John Ford*, p. 127–28.
2. "In the summer of 1938." *Ibid*, p. 125
3. "I was working with John Ford." *Ibid*, p. 129.
   Personal interview for this chapter with Harry Carey Jr.

Chapter Five

1. "Bob Fellows." Ben Barzman. "The Duke and Me." *Los Angeles Magazine*, p. 36 plus.
   "I'm not going to apologize." Lindsay Anderson. "Interview with Robert Montgomery." *About John Ford*, pp. 226–228.
   Personal interviews for this chapter with Harry Carey Jr., Jeanette Mazurki Lindner, and Andrew McLaglen.

Chapter Six

Personal interviews for this chapter with Harry Carey Jr., Pierce Lynden, John Agar, and Ben Johnson.

Chapter Seven

Personal interviews conducted with Budd Boetticher and Walter Reed.

Chapter Eight

"We lived in California." Toni Wayne. *The Quiet Man* Fortieth Anniversary (video).
"My father was a movie star." Michael Wayne. *Ibid*.
Personal interviews with Harry Carey Jr., Lee Aaker, Leo Gordon, and Robert Totten.

Notes

Chapter Nine

Personal interviews with Harry Carey Jr. and Yvonne Wood.

Chapter Ten

Personal interviews with Harry Carey Jr. and Dean Smith.

Chapter Eleven

Personal interviews with Ron Talsky and Michelle Mazurki.

Chapter Twelve

Personal interviews with Peri Alcaide, Leo Gordon, and Edward Faulkner.

Chapter Thirteen

Personal interviews with Burt Kennedy and Robert Donner.

Chapter Fourteen

Personal interview with Edward Faulkner.

Chapter Fifteen

Interview with John and Pilar Wayne by Irv Kupcinet. *The Show,* April 1970.
Personal interview with Luster Bayless.

Notes

Chapter Sixteen

"A close look." Sam Burchell. *Architectural Digest,* April 1990, p. 240 plus.
Personal interview with John Mitchum.

Chapter Seventeen

Personal interview with Christopher Mitchum.

Chapter Eighteen

1. "In the role of The Ringo Kid." Molly Haskell. "Wayne, Westerns and Women." *Ladies Home Journal,* July 1976. p. 88.
2. "Unlike . . . Paul Newman." *Ibid,* p. 94.
3. "Wayne is all of a piece." *Ibid,* p. 90.
   Personal interviews with Marie Windsor and Bill McKinney.

Chapter Nineteen

1. "John Wayne: Everybody's Hero: Tribute to John Wayne." Gene Kelly. *Saturday Evening Post,* September 1979.
2. "John Wayne is the only movie star." Burt Reynolds. *Ibid.*
3. "The Bronze Duke." Jerry McGuire. *Saturday Evening Post,* July, September, and October 1979.
4. "Well, I don't know." John Wayne. *Ibid.*
5. "When I went there with my staff." Barbara Walters. *Ibid.*
6. "I have deep faith." John Wayne (Barbara Walters interview). Robert, Randy, and James Olson. *John Wayne American,* p. 629.
7. "It seems a special bit of irony." Joseph Bell. *American Film,* January-February 1992, p. 64.

Epilogue

"Cowboys at Cannes." Herb Fagen. *Classic Images,* August 1995, pp. 46–48.

Index

Aaker, Lee, xi, 108, 109
Agar, John, xi, 73–76, 77, 79, 84–85, 118
Agee, James, 62
Alamo, The (1960), xxv, 100–45, 153
Alcaide, Peri, xi, 153, 155–56
Allegheny Uprising (1939), 47
Allen, Elizabeth, 149
"America, Why I Love Her," 193, 195–96, 202–3
Anderson, Bronco Bill, 226
Anderson, Lindsay, 61–62
Angel and the Badman (1947), 21, 66–68
Ann-Margret, 219
Armendariz, Pedro, 118, 120
Arness, James, 109, 114–15, 127
Autry, Gene, 29, 31
Avalon, Frankie, 124

Back to Bataan (1945), xxii, 51–54, 58
Bacon, James, 160, 161
Barnes, Harold, 76
Barzman, Ben, 52, 54–55
Bayless, Luster, xi, 161, 181–91
Beetson, Frank Jr., 185
Big Jake (1971), 205, 207, 208–11
Big Jim McLain (1952), 88
Big Trail, The (1930), 13, 22, 23, 25–27
Boetticher, Budd, xi, 88–97, 163, 164
Bogdanovich, Peter, 126, 202
Bond, Ward, 10, 16, 19–20, 43, 105, 109, 141–42
Bradbury, Robert, 29
Bradley, General Omar, 172
Brennan, Walter, 72
Bronco Billy and the Baby, 226
Brown of Harvard, The, 10
Brown, Mary Alberta. See Morrison, Molly
Buck, Florence, 11–12, 13–14
Bullfighter and the Lady (1950), 88–90

Butch Cassidy and the Sundance Kid (1969), 216

Cahill, United States Marshal (1973), 220
Canutt, Yakima, 29–30, 32, 37, 66, 142
Carey, Harry, 39, 40, 47, 48, 123,
Carey, Harry, Jr., xi–xii, xvii, 39–45, 47–48, 63,66–67, 77, 78, 79,104, 122–23, 131, 234–35
Carey, Marilyn, 39, 40, 42–43
Carey, Olive, 39, 47–48, 123
Carr, Trem, 28
Carter, Jimmy, 217, 231
Cast a Giant Shadow (1966), 161–62
Chandler, George, 113
Chisum (1970), 60, 80, 168, 193, 197, 198–99, 200, 203–5, 206–7
Churchill, Marguerite, 23, 25
Clarke, Col. George S., 52–54
Clemente, Steve, 25–26
Clift, Montgomery, 69, 70, 72
Clothier, Bill, 157
Cole, Nat "King," 160
Comancheros, The (1961), 182
Conqueror, The (1956), 111, 112, 116–21
Conrad, Paul, xix
Cooper, Gary, 114, 125
Corrigan, Ray "Crash," 30, 31–33
Corrigan, Tom, xii, 30–33
Cowboys, The (1972), 188, 219, 221
Crista, Linda, 128, 129
Crowther, Bosley, 70, 76, 77
Curtis, Father Robert, 231

Dakota (1945), 55–56, 59
Dark Command (1940), 46
Davis, Jim, 207–8
DeMille, Cecil B., 50–51,
Deuel, Geoffrey, 198–99
Devine, Andy, 145

Dewhurst, Colleen, 219
Didion, Joan, xvii, 159
Dietrich, Marlene, 21, 49, 52, 64, 151
Dmytryk, Edward, 51–54
Donner, Robert, xii, 167–71
Donovan's Reef (1963), 141, 148–51
Douglas, Kirk, 161–62, 164

Eastwood, Clint, 167, 195, 223, 225
Ekberg, Anita, 58
El Dorado (1967), 165, 166–67, 168–69, 195
Elam, Jack, 139

Fabian, 124
Farnsworth, Richard, 70
Farrow, John, 107, 109, 112
Faulkner, Edward, xii, 174–77, 206
Fellows, Bob, 117, 163
Fighting Kentuckian, The (1949), 88, 219
Fitzgerald, Barry, 105
Fix, Paul, 39, 40, 43, 109, 142
Flying Leathernecks, The (1951), 193–94
Flying Seabees, The, xxii
Flying Tigers, The (1942), 64
Fonda, Jane, 213
Ford, Dan, 22–24, 34, 36
Ford, Glenn, 109
Ford, John, xviii, xxi, 22–25, 34–38, 40,
    41, 44, 48, 49, 61–64, 71–72, 76–78,
    82, 102, 104–6, 121, 123–25, 133, 138,
    142, 145–46, 148–51, 163–64, 183–84,
    233–25
Fort Apache (1948), 71–73, 74, 76

Gaze, Gwen, 32
Gibson, Hoot, 126
Girls Demand Excitement, 27
Goddard, Jean-Luc, xvii–xviii
Goldwater, Barry, 172, 231
Gone With the Wind (1939), 37
Gordon, Leo, xii, 109–14, 157–58
Grainger, Edmund, 82
Grant, James Edward, 66, 92
Grapes of Wrath, The (1940), 49
Great Train Robbery, The, 226
Green Berets, The (1968), xxiii, 60, 93,
    127,172–77
Griffin, Merv, 227
Gunsmoke, 114–15

Hairston, Jester, 132

Hardy, Oliver, 219
Harper, Rollie, 218
Hart, William S., 226
Harvey, Laurence, 129
Haskell, Molly, 141, 217–19, 222
Hatari (1962), 153, 154–56
Hathaway, Henry, 47, 138–39, 141, 161, 183,
    184–85
Hawks, Howard, 69, 124–26, 153, 156,
    166–67, 170,184, 209–11
Hayward, Susan, 118–21
Hepburn, Katharine, 187, 192
High and the Mighty, The (1956), 87, 98, 99,
    113, 165
High Noon (1952), 125
Hondo (1953), 88, 107–12
Hopper, Hedda, 20
Horse Soldiers, The (1959), 99, 126, 130
"Horseman, The," 228
Howard, Ron, 187–88
Hughes, Howard, 78–79, 117–18
Hunter, Jeffrey, 121–22, 124
Hutchins, Will, xviii

I Cover the War (1937), 32, 38
I Married a Woman (1958), 136
In Harm's Way (1965), 219
In Old Arizona (1929), 25
Island in the Sky (1953), 87, 88

Jackson, Henry, 228
Jarman, Claude, Jr, 77–78, 87
John Wayne: American, (video) 217
Johnson, Ben, xii, 76–77, 78–82, 169, 197
Jones, Dr. John E., 159
Jones, Howard, 10, 23

Kelly, Gene, 227
Kennedy, Burt, xii, 162–66
Kennedy, John F., 127
Kerr, Deborah, 199

La Cava, Antonia Maria Wayne, 65, 106
Ladd, Alan, 108
Lady Takes a Chance, A (1943), xxi
Last Picture Show, The (1971), 80, 81
LeRoy, Mervyn, 93
Levine, Nat, 28
Lindner, Jeannette Mazurki, xii, 16–21,
    55–56, 148–51
Long Voyage Home, The (1940), xxi, 48, 50
Long, Audrey, 47

Longest Day, The (1962), 152–54
Lyden, Pierce, 69–70

Majors, Lee, 170–71
Maker of Men (1931), 27–28
Maltin, Leonard, 3
Man Who Shot Liberty Valance, The (1962), 141,142–43, 145–48
Marshall, Nancy Morrison, xiv, 12, 13–17, 19
Martin, Dean, 125–26, 161, 165
Marvin, Lee, 145, 150, 151, 165
Marx, Groucho, 133
Massen, Ossa, 48
Mathias, Bob, 136
Mazurski, Mike, 16, 17–20, 55, 148–51
McKinney, Bill, xii, 223–25
McLaglen, Andrew, xii, xvi, 56–61, 156–57, 169
McLaglen, Victor, 56, 57, 59, 61, 105, 106
McLintock! (1963), 58, 60, 156–58, 182
McQ (1974), 219
Men Like That (1931), 27
Milland, Ray, 50
Mitchell, Thomas, 34, 37–38, 39, 48, 49
Mitchum, Bentley, 209
Mitchum, Carrie, 209
Mitchum, Christopher, xii, 203–16
Mitchum, John, xii, 193–201
Mitchum, Robert, 163, 165, 166–67, 195, 199
Mix, Tom, 226
Montgomery, Robert, 63–64
Moore, Robin, 172
Morrison, Clyde Leonard, 4–7, 11–12, 13–14, 15
Morrison, Marion Michael. See Wayne, John
Morrison, Molly, 4–7, 11–12, 15, 20
Morrison, Robert, 5, 15
Motion Picture Alliance for the Preservation of American Ideals, xxii–xxiii, 54
Murphy, Al, 166

Neal, Patricia, 219
Neel, Archie, 9
Nelson, Norm, 9
Nelson, Rick, 124
Nixon, Richard, 133, 186, 193
North to Alaska (1960), 124

O'Brien, George, 72, 79
O'Donnell, Bob, 162
O'Hara, Maureen, 16, 61, 77, 87, 95, 102–6, 157, 158, 199, 212, 214–15, 231

O'Neill, Jennifer, 219

Padgin, Jack, 26
Page, Geraldine, 108, 109, 111
Palmer, Gregg, 198
Pappy: The Life of John Ford, 22–24, 34, 36
Parker, Cecilia, 29
Parks, Larry, xxiii
Parsons, Lindsley, 28
Pittsburgh (1942), 49, 52
Porter, Edwin S., 226
Portis, Charles, 179, 181
Powell, Dick, 112, 118

Quiet Man, The (1952), xviii, 16, 61, 77, 87, 102–6
Quinn, Anthony, 51, 58

Raines, Ella, 47, 53
Ralston, Vera Hruba, 55–56, 59
Range Feud (1931), 27
Reagan, Nancy, xx
Reagan, Ronald, xx–xxv
Reap the Wild Wind (1942), xxi, 50–51, 223
Red River (1948), xviii, 33, 69–71, 72, 184
Reed, Donna, 63, 111
Reed, Rex, 221
Reed, Walter, xiv, 92, 96–101, 130
Reynolds, Burt, 227
Richardson, Ralph, xvii
Rio Bravo (1959), 124, 125–26, 165, 168
Rio Grande (1950), 69, 71–72, 77–78, 81, 87, 105
Rio Lobo (1970), 183–84, 186–87, 204, 205, 207–8, 219
Rivera, Jorge, 205
Roberson, Chuck, 142, 157
Rogers, Roy, 137
Rooster Cogburn (1975), 187, 219
Royko, Mike, xxv
Russell, Gail, 21, 66–68, 71, 95
Rydell, Mark, 188

Van Cleef, Lee, 111

Wagonmaster (1950), 71–72, 234–25
Wake of the Red Witch (1948), 46, 68, 71
Wallis, Hal, 181
Walsh, Raoul, 25, 26, 46, 181
Walters, Barbara, xv, 229
War Wagon (1967), 162, 163, 164, 165
Wayne, Aissa, 124, 157, 178

Wayne, Esperanza Baur (Chata), 19, 20, 42, 65, 66, 92, 93, 104, 106–7
Wayne, John
  birthplace of, xviii, 3
  childhood of, xxi, 5–10
  children of, xxiv, 14, 21, 89, 177. *See also* La Cava, Antonia Maria Wayne; Wayne, Aissa, John Ethan, Marisa, Melinda, Melissa, Michael Patrick.
  death of, xv, 231–33
  as director, 127–34, 172–77, 182–83
  drinking habits of, 19–20, 42–44, 90–92, 97, 99–100
  football and, xxi, 5, 8, 9–10, 11, 23–24
  illnesses of, xxv, 14, 61, 159–61, 166, 187, 188–89, 228–31
  nickname of, xxi, 7
  parents of, 4–7, 11–12, 13–14, 15, 20
  political views of, xxii–xxiii, 44–45, 52–54, 60, 76, 100, 133, 211–14, 222
  as producer, 65–66, 87–90, 98–99, 109, 153, 172–77
  stage name of, 26, 181
  stepsister of, xiv, 12, 13–17, 19
  and Vietnam, xxiii, 172–74, 214
  and World War II, xxi–xxii, 63–64, 76
  wives of, 100, 113. *See also* Wayne, Esperanza Baur (Chata); Wayne, Josephine Saenz; Wayne, Pilar Pallete.
Wayne, John Ethan, 117, 124, 178, 180–81, 208, 210
Wayne, Josephine Saenz, 11, 35, 65, 93
Wayne, Marisa, 178
Wayne, Melinda, 65, 106
Wayne, Melissa, 43
Wayne, Michael, 65, 93, 104, 106, 117, 120, 134, 157, 181, 229
Wayne, Patrick, 21, 65, 100, 106, 120, 157, 181, 208, 218
Wayne, Pilar Pallete, 58–59, 93, 117, 118, 124, 154, 157, 177–78, 180, 220, 221
Webster, Paul Francis, 132
Wellman, William, 98
Westward Ho (1956), 29
"Why Are You Marching, Son?," 196
Widmark, Richard, 130–31, 144–45
Wild Bunch, The (1969), 216
Wills, Chill, 132–33
Windsor, Marie, xiv, 219–21
Withers, Grant, 19–20, 102, 141–42
Wood, Natalie, 121, 123
Wood, Yvonne, xiv, 118–21
Worden, Hank, 86

Yates, Herbert, 55–56, 104–5, 128
Ybarra, Al, 129

Zanuck, Darryl, 152–54